The Feng Shui of
Abundance

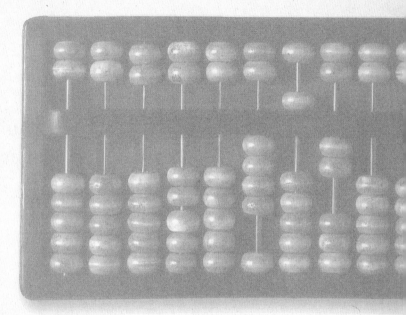

Suzan Hilton, CPA

The Feng Shui of Abundance

A Practical and Spiritual Guide to Attracting Wealth into Your Life

BROADWAY BOOKS   *New York*

PRINTED IN THE UNITED STATES OF AMERICA

Broadway Books titles may be purchased for business or promotional use or for special sales. For information, please write to: Special Markets Department, Random House, Inc., 1540 Broadway, New York, NY 10036.

The excerpt in Appendix C: Red Envelopes is extracted from Part One of Lynn Ho Tu's response in the "Questions and Answers" section of the *Yun Lin Temple Newsletter,* Issue 11, Volume 3, September 1996. Reprinted with permission of *Yun Lin Temple News.*

Watercolor paintings on pp. 175, 179, 202, 218, 226, 244, and 274, courtesy of the artist, Master I-Hong Chou.
"Fancy Ba-gua" on p. 282 created by Frances Li.

This book is designed to provide accurate and authoritative information on the subject of personal finances. While all of the stories and anecdotes described in the book are based on true experiences, most of the names are pseudonyms, and some situations have been changed slightly to protect each individual's privacy. It is sold with the understanding that neither the Authors nor the Publisher are engaged in rendering legal, accounting, or other professional services by publishing this book. As each individual situation is unique, questions relevant to personal finances and specific to the individual should be addressed to an appropriate professional to ensure that the situation has been evaluated carefully and appropriately. The Authors and Publisher specifically disclaim any liability, loss, or risk, which is incurred as a consequence, directly or indirectly, of the use and application of any of the contents of this work.

Visit our website at www.broadwaybooks.com

Library of Congress Cataloging-in-Publication Data
Hilton, Suzan, 1949–
    The feng shui of abundance : a practical and spiritual guide to attracting wealth into your life / Suzan Hilton.—1st ed.
        p. cm.
    Includes bibliographical references.
    1. Finance, Personal. 2. Wealth. 3. Feng shui. I. Title.
HG179. H514 2001
332.024'01—dc21   2001035913

Book design and diagrams by Lee Fukui
Illustrated by Diana Selene

ISBN 0-7679-0750-7

10 9 8 7 6 5 4 3

May the Divine Spirit

breathe through,

move, and inspire all

Contents

Acknowledgments

any of the ideas presented here were first experienced at workshops with Drs. Gay and Kathlyn Hendricks of The Hendricks Institute, some from seminars by Context Associated, Inc., and books and lectures by Wayne Dyer and Gary Zukav. Thank you for going before me and lighting the path.

My life has been immeasurably enhanced by wonderful teachers, and like all students, I stand on the shoulders of those who walked before me:

Feng Shui Grand Master His Holiness Professor Thomas Lin Yun Rinpoche and his students, Crystal Chu, Sarah Rossbach, and Ann-Marie C. Holmes, all keepers of the sacredness of the earth and the ancient wisdom.

Norman Vincent Peale, Earl Nightingale, and Napolean Hill.

Sogetsu School of Ikebana: my own teacher, Master Keiko Kodachi, her teacher Master Takashi Suzuki, the late Headmaster Hiroshi Teshigahara, and founder Sofu Teshigahara.

Kathleen Weymouth Skinner, who pointed out a new path. Julia Cameron and *The Artist's Way* for opening the door to creating possibilities, Jim Navé for heartfelt creativity, and Mark Bryan for his undivided attention when I was ready to take a major detour.

Drs. Gay and Kathlyn Hendricks and The Hendricks Institute, who shared their hearts, minds, and wisdom—in workshops and way beyond.

Reverend Mary Manin Morrissey, who still dreams of a world filled with love.

Special thanks to my agent, Craig Nelson, and to my editor, Suzanne Oaks, her assistant Claire Johnson, and the staff of Broadway Books.

Kung-Be Master I-Hong Chou for his beautiful Chinese landscape watercolors.

Hats off to Steve Sisgold, who, like the great coach and friend that he is, believed in me even when I did not.

To Mom, who was there at the beginning, and my sister, Jacqueline, who remembers so many things and has loved me all along the way.

Thanks to special friends for believing in and journeying with me: Diana Selene, Jody Houghton, Tricia Rock, Susan Christine and Colin Hay, Marilyn McFarlane, and Shane and Debbie Beck.

Abundant thanks to many more friends whose hearts and lives have touched mine. May many blessings rain down upon you, filling your crystal lake and inspiring you to continue on your sacred journey to open-hearted abundance.

Any errors are mine. May compassion enfold all hearts and minds so they flow with abundance.

Preface

by His Holiness Grandmaster Professor
Thomas Lin Yun Rinpoche

the world's chi—heaven chi, earth chi, human chi—are constantly interacting, regardless of whether "East winds gradually blow to the West," or vice versa. Eastern and Western cultures have always been interchanging at various levels within different cultural contexts. In fact, everything that we have seen from the time of science's flourish and transformation to current developments in advanced technologies, are testimonies to "West winds gradually blowing to the East."

Within the realms of consciousness, spiritualism, esotericism, and folk culture, the East has transmitted a great deal of knowledge to the West. Geomancy [divination through lines and figures] is a case in point. Since the publication of four feng shui masterpieces by the multi-talented feng shui expert and scholar, Sarah Rossbach (*Feng Shui: The Chinese Art of Placement; Interior Design with Feng Shui; Living Color: Master Lin Yun's Guide to Feng Shui and the Art of Color;* and *Feng Shui Design: The Art of Creating Harmony for Interiors, Landscape and Architecture*), feng shui's immense popularity has risen steadily over the past twenty years in the Americas and Europe, where feng shui lectures, workshops, publications, new schools of thought, consultations, and certifications emerge like bamboo shoots springing up after the new rain.

Having seen Suzan Hilton's *The Feng Shui of Abundance*, I feel that it too is a new force in feng shui suddenly come to the fore. Basing her initial observations and analysis on logic and incorporating many transcendental ideas, and through her systematic analysis of the linkage between body and mind of the East and the West, the author shows the reader how to increase wealth and create abundance. She teaches us to combine the essence of eastern and western cultures based on the principle of harmonizing *ru-shi*—the mundane/rational/reasonable/logical, and *chu-shi*—the transcendental.

Supplemented with wonderful illustrations, *The Feng Shui of Abundance* emphasizes the West's practical methods, including minimizing waste and extravagance, knowing when one is spending beyond one's means, stimulating wealth generation with your money, and saving. Using the River of Gold as a metaphor, Ms. Hilton, with her excellent background as a certified public accountant, teaches the reader how to stimulate new creativity by paying attention to body sensations, emotional responses, and rational analysis, and emphasizes the importance and influence of feng shui. Through these methods, the reader will learn how to stabilize unsuccessful and unstable financial situations amidst financial turbulence, and how to navigate to "safety" amid the torrents of financial crisis. As such, even an ordinary person will learn how to overcome difficulties and obstacles in personal and professional lives, and how, as if creating an oasis in the desert, to build up wealth from nothing. Finally, the author teaches us how to hold on to financial stability once we have made money and become wealthy and how to solidify the wonderful state of steady wealth accumulation.

The choice of illustrations and the book cover's artwork are original and novel. In particular, the rare opportunity to include the exquisite Chinese brush paintings by the renowned artist, Master I-Hong Chou, adds to this wonderful book. This book offers detailed explications on feng shui, yin yang, the five elements, circulation of chi, energy, the cyclicity of renewal and rebuilding, and includes other topics such as the "Three Entrance Trigrams," the importance of transcendental aspects of omens relating to wealth positions, and how to increase income, reduce expense, and prevent depletion of wealth by decorating the wealth position with color and other objects.

If, after studying this book, you are inspired to thoroughly understand and practice the book's methods of wealth creation and accumulation spanning the East and the West, the mundane and the transcendental, and if, as a result, you rise from poverty to riches, and your wealth grows from nothing and multiplies, you should remember two important points:

First, the "Red Envelope Question." In her book, Suzan raises this issue. Primarily, the transmission of transcendental solutions relating to wealth (and other matters) is considered to be revealing sacred heavenly secrets, which, according to traditional Chinese beliefs, is harmful to the teacher, and offers no particular benefits to the recipients of this knowledge. Therefore, you must accept red envelopes to acknowledge the "sacredly precious" and "mysterious" natures as well as "utmost cautions" associated with the transmission of these transcendental solutions. For details regarding red envelopes, please refer to Appendix D, which includes discussions on the topic by Lynn Ho Tu and Dr. Chang Chiu, both of whom are experts and scholars of the Black Sect Tantric Buddhist School of feng shui, and the I-Ching as well.

Second, how should you handle your wealth once it has grown from nothing to abundant, from small to big? I once wrote a poem, which I will share with you now:

Regarding Wealth

"Do not associate seeking wealth with greed,
For one could bring relief to the needy in difficult times if one has money;
If not properly acquired or spent,
Money will do harm instead of good, like water capsizing a boat rather
than carrying it afloat."

LIN YUN
July 2001
translated by Jonathan W. Y. Chau

The Feng Shui of
Abundance

Introduction: Money, Feng Shui, and the River of Gold

There are plenty of books about creating abundance from a seemingly rational step-by-step approach, yet they leave out your imagination, your dreams, and your heart. My purpose here is to communicate directly with you—with all of you—both the modern and recently rediscovered ancient ways of creating abundance.

Feng shui (pronounced *fung shway*) literally means free-flowing wind and water. It is the ancient Chinese Art of Placement to create harmony for people within an environment. The patterns of energy that flow, stagnate, experience a cross current or undertow, or totally stop are felt, seen, sometimes heard, and acknowledged by feng shui practitioners.

Westerners associate feng shui with physical space, especially in the home or place of business, and many people use feng shui to improve their careers and relationships. It can, in fact, be applied much more extensively. As this book will show you, I use feng shui as both a metaphor and an actual experience, a template that will affect your finances, your creativity, and your values.

The Feng Shui of Abundance is a different approach to creating wealth. Most books in this area focus attention only on the Western, logical, goal-oriented actions we can take to decrease our expenses and increase our assets. Since my days as an accountant, I have learned that many other things are also important in creating abundance. In this book we will delve into various Eastern and Western belief systems, the hidden messages we send to ourselves and others, and the growing awareness of the body and mind working in relation to each other. We will see how harmonizing breath, spirit, intentions, mind, emotions, and physical objects in a new pattern can lead to the ocean of abundance.

To get an overall perspective when you are down in the trenches of your everyday life, looking at a map, a pattern to follow, gives you a larger view of the journey. In this book, I have included a metaphorical map of the journey to abundance along the River of Gold that will help you understand the patterns of the various challenges and detours you experience from day to day.

Also woven throughout the book are the standard Western principles of wealth accumulation. Having a spending plan, living below your income, buying products of good quality, saving and investing regularly, buying low and selling high for investment success, diversification, and having enough liquid assets to meet a six- to twelve-month challenge are all important elements of creating abundance. This is solid, wise advice, but people don't implement these actions when they are overwhelmed by fear or emotions they don't understand or blinded by a history of shame and unworthiness around creating abundance. *The Feng Shui of Abundance* shows you a new, engaging way to address these issues.

My Journey

My family was poor—*really* poor. As in cardboard-in-the-soles-of-one-pair-of-shoes poor and never-throw-away-a-sliver-of-soap poor. The summer I was eight years old, I helped my dad mow the lawns of wealthy people. My job was to run the smaller gasoline mower. I can still picture the grass clippings flowing, into the barrel—small green rectangles of newly mown grass. Thousands of cuttings, hundreds of trips to dump the clippings, hours of dragging metal cans and winding garden hoses. One day I set the trash can on the edge of a long, U-shaped driveway, looked at the large beautiful house, the vehicles parked in the driveway, the manicured yard, and I thought to myself, These people must know something about money that my parents don't know. I decided then and there to learn everything I could about money; then I returned to racing after the gasoline mower and dumping the clippings. I couldn't stop my classmates from calling me "Amazon" (at the age of eight, I was five foot nine), but I could make my life better in other ways. I had a secret plan.

Ever since I watched the grass clippings pouring into the trash can, I have been studying flow, how we stop it and how we enhance it. In college I first studied air and blood flow in humans as a respiratory therapist. Then I watched money flow as an accountant. My studies of the Japanese art of flower arranging, *ikebana,* were about the illusion of flow with static but living materials and how they change the energy in a room. In 1992 I began to study feng shui and its focus on one's environment and the patterns of the flow of energy there. Later I learned to meditate, and when my marriage ended, I began to study, with the Hendrickses, the flow of energy and love between people. I was also studying how the pattern of our mental flow, our thoughts and intentions, affects the flow of actions by other people and the opportunities that life brings us.

Always, I have been focusing on understanding the flow of life's abundance and how to enliven it. Wind symbolizes breath, inspiration, movement, intuition, new thoughts, intangible things, and the Divine Spirit. Water represents money, emotions, body sensations, and tangible physical objects. Water can also represent profound silence and depth. Flowing waters are symbolic of the flow of money, currency, and energy, while gold is both the coins and ingots you can own and a symbol of wisdom.

As a child I slipped my small vessel into the river, beginning with my first money: a meager allowance. In the years that followed I have capsized and righted my vessel in larger rivers, experienced floods where there was more money than wisdom, swamps where money and life seemed to stand still, and droughts where I ran aground and money dried up. I have visited the headwaters of my life to understand my beginnings and trudged through the shallows, seemingly alone, on my journey to become a master river guide. I know how the River of Gold flows to the ocean of abundance. I can guide you there.

Who Can Benefit from This Book?

Do any of the following apply to you?

- You work hard, put in long hours, experience some struggle with your money, and wonder if there is an easier way to live life and create abundance.

- Your life is a constant struggle, there is very little money, and you wonder if there is something you don't know and could learn.

- Your family never "made it," and you wonder what else besides working hard, scrimping, and saving would make a difference in your accumulation of money.

- You make good money yet you wonder where it all goes.

- Your income is huge yet you do not feel abundant, let alone wealthy. You wonder what you are missing.

- You are a feng shui junkie and want to know my angle.

- You're doing great and are always interested in learning more.

You may be any one of these people—someone who wants greater abundance and is open to the ideas and exercises in *The Feng Shui of Abundance.*

Welcome aboard!

Money and Feng Shui

Money is about *more*: more freedom, more challenges, opportunities, and energy. How you handle more energy in any way it shows up is the key that unlocks the flow to having and enjoying more money. Feng Shui is a key to using this energy in the most harmonious way.

So, you may be wondering, what does *abundance* mean? Let's begin with *Webster's* definition: great plenty; an overflowing quantity; ample sufficiency; fullness, overflowing; fully sufficient; exuberance; riches; copiousness; wealth. My own definition includes: more than enough for you, your heart's desires, and beneficial to and for your family, friends, the earth, and all your relations. Wealth with open-hearted wisdom. Balance, harmony, and abundance.

My approach to creating abundance is very different from the usual CPA approach. A quantum difference, one that takes into consideration and plays with the changes of the last two centuries. Remember this common saying: "East is East and West is West and never the twain shall meet"? That belief is long gone. Now we know that East meets West and the two are forever changed. Here I combine the two into a thought-provoking, comprehensive approach to personal finance that integrates feng shui, intention, movement, and emotion.

An executive in a major corporation recently said to me, "I had kept my meditation practice very private and separate from my business life, until I realized I was in upper management and could set the tone. I considered changing when a consultant shared how she meditated and moved her body creatively when she faced a challenge. She had us try some new activities and share our experiences. Much to my surprise, several of my colleagues also meditated. I threw caution to the wind and we began to meditate as a team on our business challenges." Thirty years ago in the West, this would have been unthinkable.

Meeting and integrating the differences and the similarities of Eastern and Western thoughts and approaches about money is the essence of my approach. I want to get down to where your cells vibrate and where they don't. I want to go to the outer reaches of the space where your possibilities reside. I want you to see how you flow with money in your day-to-day life and how you respond to uprising energy, the "more" of life and abundance. I will teach you to enliven your breath and your life, embrace your emotions, and notice where you harbor the things you really treasure and the money you have growing for your future. My job is to help you navigate on the River of Gold and set you sailing to a lifetime of harmony, realized dreams, peace of mind, wisdom, and abundance.

Creative Energy

Personal finances rarely seem fun or creative, yet trust me when I tell you that money is one of the most creative energies we have! Unfortunately, many of us equate money with cruel and unfriendly experiences, and we unconsciously resist abundance. However, if you take a step back and look at money as creative energy that will flow easily toward you, it's much more interesting, and a lot less intimidating. We all have fundamental response mechanisms when faced with sudden influxes of money—what I call uprising energy. The key is to recognize these responses and learn how to keep the flow of money coming.

When you come up against a challenge, how do you react? Do you fight back? Do you flee the scene? Perhaps you freeze in place, or maybe even faint. The four fundamental responses to uprising energy—fight, flee, freeze, and faint—are your Four F Preference and are reflected in the way we each react to the creative energy of money. For example, if you're a fighter, you're probably the first to take action, to buy, save, and invest your money. Sometimes you might move so quickly that you miss out on information that indicates this action may not be in your best long-term interest. If you tend to flee from financial situations, you could move so fast in the opposite direction that you don't even realize you already pulled out your wallet and handed over some cash or your credit card.

Perhaps you freeze in these situations and take no outward action at all, neither engaging or disengaging. Freezers find it difficult to let go of money, unable to pay their expenses or put their money where it can increase. The last type of response, fainting, actually eliminates one's ability to participate in a financial situation in any capacity; fainters check out so fast that they never even notice there may have been a deposit slip in their checkbook and money flowing in from their automatic deposits. For fainters, even receiving a little money may be a crisis.

Everyone has a fundamental response to uprising energy, especially when it's money. It's important to recognize your Four F Preference and use it to slow yourself down when caution is necessary and to move you forward when there is clear sailing. Think about this as you go through the book. The creative energy of money can be enormously fun when you learn how to embrace it! Ready for more?

THE RIVER OF GOLD

Five currents create the River of Gold. Each one is like a series of frequencies that you can tune in to through your thoughts, body sensations and actions and experience as a current of flowing energy in a deep river.

Revealed in this book are the secrets, the tools and techniques to navigate on all five currents in the midst of life's challenges. These are the skills that place you in the River of Gold and lead you to the ocean of abundance with heart, where your most cherished longings and values are honored.

The five currents that create the River of Gold are:

1. Feng Shui Current

2. Body Sensations Current

3. Emotional Current

4. Creative Current

5. Rational Current

These five currents are always flowing through your life, and when they all flow freely and smoothly, they create the River of Gold. Each of the five is like a series of frequencies that you can tune in to, a current or bandwidth of flowing energy. Picture dialing in a station on your radio. You actually tune in to the frequency that is broadcast, the bandwidth of sound waves, on the radio, and you can hear the difference when you are slightly off the mark. In the same way, you also can tune in to each of the currents and sense when you are out of the flow.

Each of the currents can change its position relative to the others, surfacing or going to the bottom of the River of Gold depending on whether it is honored or not. Most people focus exclusively on one current while ignoring the rest. Picture yourself trying to live with a hand that has only one finger. You could do it, but life is so much easier and richer if all five fingers are engaged and move freely. Revealed in this book are the secrets to enhancing harmony and flow among the Five Currents and how you can navigate back to deep waters, and a full bandwidth, in the midst of the challenges of life.

The *Feng Shui Current* leads the way. A 3,500-year-old system, the Chinese Art of Placement honors both the tangible and intangible aspects of a physical place, the pattern of the flow of "wind and water" in your environment. The wind, which represents the intangible things, the cognitive thoughts, intentions, and emotions, is just as important as the water, or the things we can see, touch, taste, smell, and hear, and our own body movements. Feng shui focuses on the art and science of creating harmony, peace, flow, and abundance with and for people and their physical environment. Feng shui is important in its own right for indicating where you have placed your physical belongings, the layout of your environment, and where your Wealth Area is located. It also represents the energy of the other four currents that have congealed into physical form. Your physical belongings and their place-ment are the outward manifestation of your mental, emotional, and creative energies. What you think and feel about each of the objects in your space and their meaning in your life literally shows up in your physical environment.

Feng shui also reveals where you have placed the belongings that give you access to your Creative Current, the right brain, and how much focus your Rational Current, your left brain, is allowed. Feng shui indicates the aliveness of your Body Sensations Current and the flow of your Emotional Current. How does feng shui reveal these things? you may wonder. By indicating where the energy in your en-vironment can flow freely and where it is blocked, dissipates, floods, or flows like a whirlpool down a drain. With feng shui, physical objects and their placement also symbolize the patterns of your life and what is happening in and with it.

Your *Body Sensations Current* is like having your finger on your own pulse, noticing all of your juicy body sensations: the tension in your shoulders, the tickle in your throat, the itch you are not scratch-ing, your fingers playing with your hair, your upset stomach, and the knot in your chest. This current focuses on all of the tactile sensations and actions of some part of your body connecting with yourself or with someone else.

Noticing when your breathing has changed or initiating some movement tunes you into this current. Breathing exercises are included in Chapter 4. Paying attention to your body sensations requires the use of your Rational Current and is an excellent way to become calm and slow down the racing thoughts of your rational analytical mind. Tuning in to this current so you keep moving and breathing, even a little, pre-vents many of the common aches and pains we experience, especially tension headaches and stiff muscles.

Bob, a hardworking lawyer, was glad he discovered the connec-tion between emotions and body sensations. He said, "The knot and ache in my chest had gone on for weeks. I ignored it. One day I admitted to my therapist that I missed my daughter, who had moved out to go to college. And when I told her about the knot in my chest and allowed myself to feel my sadness and longing, the knot, its ache and emotions, all subsided. My own body sensations were emotional, not medical."

The *Emotional Current* freely flows from one emotion to another, running to extremes or stopping dead in its tracks depending on the amount of play you allow yourself. This energetic current is like the ocean with a new wave coming in every few minutes, even if you are not finished with the prior wave. It is very responsive and freely associates with the other four currents and with visual and tactile stimuli if you allow it some room.

A common belief in the West is that stopping one emotion has no impact on any of the others. This is one place where common sense is missing. All your emotions are connected to the same source, you. As everything is connected, constricting the nozzle in one area constricts it for the others, eventually creating a backlog that someday must be released, or eventually the stagnation will foul everything. Emotions, like waves, have a beginning, a crest, and an ending. Stopping the flow means you are incomplete with that cycle. Completion of the cycle is as simple as allowing yourself to *experience* the full wave of an emotion. Ever wonder why one person looks so much older than another, even though the two are the same age? Notice whether they contain and stop or experience the full cycle of their emotions.

"I had been feeling sad," Dan reflected, sitting in his office. "This had gone on at a low level for a while. My marriage had ended a year earlier, and I was facing the inevitable filing for divorce process. One day I realized I was angry. Being angry was not acceptable in my family of origin. My mom had claimed that emotion. I realized that I had never been allowed to acknowledge or experience my anger. Expressing my anger, in a friendly way, to anyone, myself included, was a totally foreign concept. Here I was fifty and furious, and admitting it for the first time. I wondered if that was connected to my reduced energy level. Hmmm? Interesting thought. Over the next month I allowed myself to experience several waves of anger—and my energy level increased."

The Emotional Current is the place where the "open-hearted response" to money and life dwells and where you experience the sense of abundance in your life.

The *Creative Current* is the imaginative, visionary mind considering what is truly possible in a nonlinear, sky-full-of-moving-clouds dream-world. With this current we think with our hearts, hear with our eyes, and see with our sense of touch. This is the imaginative place of poets, artists, writers, and dreamers, and it's where intuitive businesspeople find their vision. The Internet exists because the Creative Current was paired with the Rational Current to imagine and create more flow. Saying "Hmmm? I wonder . . ." or visiting an art gallery or nature scene opens the locks that dam this flow of energy. This is the current that is encouraged when you relax. It is a mental current that can partner with the Rational Current, giving it a well-deserved rest. Picture two oxen, equally paired, plowing a field. Much more gets done with two heads and four strong shoulders than one.

The *Rational Current* is the classic mental cognitive approach that uses intellectual logic. It asks how and why, analyzes, makes to-do lists, sets step-by-step goals, thinks, and judges, deciding if something or someone is good or bad. People who consider themselves "cerebral" often heavily favor this current. The Rational Current created most of the logical aspects and the follow-through focus of accounting, business, economics, law, and science. The I-think or Let's-be-rational comments signal the flow of this current. Saying "I can't think" indicates this current has stopped or gone underground.

Your Rational Current can flow in circles faster than any of the others, creating what is called "analysis paralysis." When someone says he can't sleep or is driving herself crazy, this is often a sign that the Rational Current is overactive. Tuning in to the other four currents helps this one to become more peaceful. This indirect approach works wonders to quiet your mind. We'll cover it in Chapter 7.

Now let's put all the currents together. The Body Sensations and Emotional currents can create an incredible dance with the Creative Current. Picture the people who bungee-jump, paint, sail, windsurf, write, or sing at the top of their lungs, and you get a sense of what is possible with these currents. The Rational Current may fight and overpower any or all of the other currents, insisting they are illogical, dangerous, and trite. Sometimes they are. Yet when your life is balanced, you can distinguish one from another and appreciate the richness each of them offers. For example, a midlife crisis is often a signal that the other currents are demanding some attention and validation. You know your Emotional and Body Sensations Currents are flowing when you well up with tears, laugh, sing, sigh, tingle all over, or ache in your chest area when someone sings the blues.

A highly successful business owner once talked to me about "enough" and values. He said, "I had everything: money, head of my company, first class all the way, a big house, Lamborghini, five-carat diamond. And I felt like I had been cheated. With each step up the ladder of success I felt less happy and peaceful. All of the stuff of success meant nothing. A sense of abundance was totally missing from my life, and my wife's. We had only focused on more money and prestige, until one day I shifted direction and began to follow my heart. I sold the company and the big house and moved to a slower-paced seaside community. My wife was reluctant at first, then she began to write. She is now very happy. I'm involved in a local program for at-risk kids, and that empty feeling is gone. This is abundance."

Now that we've been introduced to the River of Gold, it's time to get ready for our journey.

Where to Begin?

Right where you are standing or sitting, pause and take a deep breath in and release it, then ask your whole self, your mind, body, heart, and spirit:

Am I willing to embark on a new adventure?

Take a second breath, then tune in to your body sensations, and sense any hesitancy or tension. Perhaps there are fluttery feelings in your stomach or . . . tingling sensations on your skin. What emotion are you experiencing? Now . . . allow your answer to resonate with the totality of yourself and the universe. Take several deep breaths and relax. Experience your own breath and come into harmony with the subtle energy of the wind as it flows through your body. You are present and centered, aware of what is happening here and now.

Your breath is the key that unlocks the door to more ease, more energy, and abundance. Many people have no idea how much struggle they experience in their lives, nor how shallowly they breathe. The two are connected. Breathing is also called inspiration. It is the first thing you do as you begin this life, and it is your grand finale. It is the Divine Spirit flowing through us, literally enlivening us, or it can be thought of as the wind flowing through human form. It's an intangible aspect, like new ideas and inspiring thoughts flowing to you and through you.

Building a Safe Vessel to Navigate the River

Feng shui is about creating a sacred container, and since your protection in a rapidly moving river is of utmost importance, it's important to build a strong vessel for your journey—one that is rock solid and watertight. Your space is limited, in your vessel, home, work space, and life so taking along the most important things is the next focus. Integrity, intention, honesty, and commitment are the keys to getting you safely down the river.

INTEGRITY. Integrity is like the double hull of your vessel, where your internal thoughts, emotions, and body sensations harmonize with your outer actions and behaviors. For example, you create integrity when what you say and how you think and feel about another person are the same. You step out of integrity when you think and feel something different from what you express. The challenge is how to be both truthful and friendly in your expression when you are facing a challenge. Having this double hull means you can weather the rocks and storms that seem to suddenly collide with your vessel.

INTENTION. Simply put, you navigate the river toward abundance successfully only if you intend to do so. Your intention is the rudder that guides your vessel, hidden below the waterline, silent and very important. Speaking your intentions out loud, even if you are alone, will bring them to the surface so they can create more harmony and results in your life, including more abundance.

Setting an intention is both simple and profound. Here you tune in to your body sensations and your emotions. You become quiet, tune in to yourself and imagine, for a minute, the kind of sensations, experience, and outcome you want during and after your projects and your day. Consider what would be uplifting, expansive, creative . . . the positive things and experiences you would like to result from your interactions.

Intentions are the subtle energy that guides your life. Speaking your intentions out loud, even if you are alone, will alert and send those vibrations out into the universe so they can be matched, create resonance, and bring more harmony and results into your life. Once you begin to set clear intentions you will come to realize how many below-the-surface intentions float around in your life and the lives of other people. Taking these steps to set an intention will enhance your experience on the River of Gold and the flow of abundance into your life.

Action Step

Tune in at the beginning of your day and set an intention for the day. If you are beginning a project, set an intention for it before you begin. If you are in the midst of a project, especially if there is some conflict with people or some challenges, then set an intention for how you would like the process to proceed, and what outcome you desire.

You may now be wondering about your underwater intentions. Yes, you have made them—and they will begin to surface. What to do? The short answer is to love yourself, laugh, and set a new, clear intention. The long answer requires a larger framework, so just allow yourself to travel along, enjoying the view, reading and participating in the exercises. Later in this book, we'll revisit your intentions.

HONESTY. We gloss over so many things that add up—things that seem small and yet create leaks in our vessel—and then wonder why we "suddenly" have a pile of things to address. Being honest with yourself enhances your rock-solid and watertight vessel. Being truthful with yourself—about what you are sensing, thinking, and experiencing—is the focus here. *Nothing* is ignored. You also give up disagreeing and arguing with yourself and experience whatever seems true for you. You become honest to the penny, because the smallest item of value does in fact have value.

COMMITMENT. Are you committed to this journey? Commitment itself comes from Latin; *com* means "together" and *mittere* means "to send," so *committere* is to bring together and send off. You literally gather yourself, all of your energy, and focus so that you can take the first step and move forward toward some destination. It is a subtle action, yet it signals a huge shift in your ability to move forward and to create abundance. You are either ready to embark, or you are not. Not being ready has nothing to do with the kind of person you are, it's just your commitment level for this moment. Ask yourself: "Am I ready? Have I gathered up my energy, am I focused and ready to embark on this adventure?" Feeling some hesitation or an emotional experience is actually a "no" response. In reality, you are not committed to the journey right now. Commitment is the glue that holds your vessel together, so when you are ready, we'll embark.

Travel Log

We're almost ready to go! However you can't get started without something in which to jot things down. Heading off on a journey calls for a Travel Log so you can record notes, thoughts, exercises, key words, and your own insights. You get to decide whether the cover is fancy or plain. Your preference may be for a ringed binder with tabs, or maybe a simple sketch book. The only requirement is that it be big enough; I recommend the 8 1/2-by-11-inch size. Include some unlined pages to give you the most options. Deciding on the type of Travel Log is the first challenge you face and now integrate if you have favored "nice and orderly" all of your life.

So let's begin this journey. We'll start with a deeper look at feng shui and how it enhances your wealth and abundance. I'll guide you as if we are talking one on one.

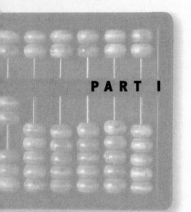

PART I

FENG SHUI

This current focuses on your physical environment and establishes a pattern for analyzing the other currents and the flow of the River of Gold.

1

Feng Shui and Energy Flow

everything—everything in the universe—vibrates at its own frequency. Colors, chairs, tables, people, dreams, and longings—all are in continuous motion, though it may not be visible to the naked eye. How can I say that? Well, scientists have recorded the vibrational frequency of many if not most things: light and sound frequencies in ranges we can see and hear, visible and infrared light, radio frequencies, X rays, chemicals using spectroscopy, tuning forks . . . the list goes on. Perhaps you remember the recording of the vibrations made during the earthquake in the Seattle area in 2001—a pendulum suspended in sand drew a rose pattern, and beauty emerged from the shifting of the earth itself.

Feng shui recognizes that everything vibrates and focuses on encouraging harmony among the various vibrations by creating alignment. Creating harmony is about singing the same tune as the things surrounding you and as your dreams and heart longings. That like attracts like, vibrating at similar frequencies, creating resonance between the objects, is a basic scientific statement and a major step toward manifesting your heart's desires. Picture people singing "Auld Lang Syne" on the Fourth of July with the fireworks in full display. Seems a bit off to me! There is no harmony between the holiday and the music; they are out of alignment. Yet when you're in harmony and alignment, your River of Gold flows peacefully, you move with ease and comfort, and wealth and abundance flows to you.

Abundance has a particular vibration, a signature energy field. Learning to resonate in harmony with anything leads to both more flow and more energy between you and your focus. Coming into resonance with the vibration of abundance opens the flow in your life so your heart's desires flow to you.

Resonance, in electronics, is the condition of adjusting a circuit to allow the greatest flow of current of a certain frequency. In physics, it is the reinforced vibration of a body exposed to the vibration at about the same frequency as another body. Used here, resonance is allowing the vibration of a certain frequency to match the frequency in your body, your space, and your life. Resonating in harmony with the frequency of abundance leads to more money and a greater sense of financial freedom. My goal is to enhance your abundance as open-hearted energy. Now what does that mean? Open-hearted means being in tune with your values, in alignment with your deep inner guidance, knowing what you value with your most positive emotions and thoughts, and knowing what brings you joy as you create abundance.

Feng shui is based on noticing where energy is felt on the land and in a building or a room—your physical environment. Wealth and abundance have a different vibration from relationships, career, or family. You'll come to know this in your body and your environment as we continue on this journey. There is a natural order and flow in life that includes a sense of abundance. Consider how many leaves are on one tree. Now think about how many trees you see in a week's time. In the middle of winter you can still remember the leaves that were there last summer. Acknowledging the cycles of the seasons reminds us that patterns and changes are a natural part of life. Feng shui connects you to the harmonious patterns and gives you reminders before you go too far in any one direction. Remembering and experiencing abundance in one area of your life creates a pattern, an energy field, that you can use to experience abundance in other areas of your physical environment and your life.

FENG SHUI

More money is about more flow—economic flow. Wealth and abundance are about accumulating part of that flow. Let's cut to the chase: Does feng shui really work for enhancing money flow and accumulation? There is only one way to know: results. In the end, it is the final outcome, the results, that determine whether it's thumb's up or not. The bottom line: Everything gets reduced to one simple answer: more money or not; yes or no.

Surprised that an accountant would use the term "bottom line" and focus on results? I hope not. I love the warm, sensitive aspects of life, and I also appreciate having real money to spend and invest. Balancing both leads to floating with ease on the River of Gold and enjoying the abundance I desire.

Why would an accountant approach money from a feng shui focus? Because it actually works! Feng shui reveals what and how you think about money, and the flow of economic energy in your life, themes that are covered in detail in Chapters 2 and 3 and woven throughout the book. There are suggested changes, called "cures" in classical feng shui, to enhance your life and to produce results. Changing your environment eases the path to changing your thoughts and actions and experiencing more abundance in your life. What and how you think about money, the thoughts you hear yourself say and those that just flow out of your stream of consciousness show up in your physical environment. What you truly believe about yourself and your relationship to abundance is reflected in the setup of your physical environment. Strange as it may seem, where you choose to physically place your possessions reveals your relationship with money. Things are symbols and give a message each time you look at them. You also issued a message when you placed the physical objects and when you agreed to occupy the spaces you live and work in. We literally mirror our environments. Like attracts like and vibrates in harmony. The mystical actually influences the practical.

Feng shui can be a rich and somewhat complicated philosophy taking years to master, yet the basics can be understood in a few minutes. The first concept to be aware of is the nine areas in both your physical environment and your life.

Your **Wealth and Abundance** area is one of the nine. Chapter 2 covers this in detail.

The other areas are

- **Fame and Reputation**
- **Marriage and Relationships**
- **Creativity, Children, and Projects**
- **Helpful People, Travel, and Angels (Benefactors)**
- **Career and Life Path**
- **Self-Knowledge and Wisdom**
- **Ancestors and Family**
- **Health and Unity**

We will also discuss the concepts of ch'i (*chee*), breath or energy and its flow, yin and yang, and the Five Elements. All of these forces affect the nine areas.

A basic idea that permeates feng shui is that your home and work space represent your life and mirror what you think and experience. Changing your physical environment will change your life. This will become much clearer as we proceed. Understanding the message comes through the language of symbols. The words we use, orally or on paper, are symbols of something real, some object, mark, or experience. Rather than carrying around these physical things and showing them to one another, we use symbols to communicate. We also use symbols to communicate what is abstract and intangible. Metaphors and poetic language are especially useful here, and they are used throughout this book. Physical things have a double meaning, that of the thing itself and then a message that depends on its placement in your space. Sometimes the message is right in front of us and we misinterpret it, until we check our results. For now, just notice the results.

Here's an example: My Wealth Area in a former home was 90 percent windows. Too many windows allow energy to leak out. I had hung crystals in the windows when I first moved in, a classic feng shui cure, assuming that that was enough to contain the energy flowing out. I also have always shared my time and abundance very easily and freely. I was the person you could always count on to volunteer to help, from decorating Christmas trees for a charity to dropping everything to meet an unexpected friend at the airport. The year I was bitten by a poisonous spider and nearly died, I began to reexamine my life. One day I realized that I literally gave myself away, expecting nothing in return. Energy and money just flowed out of my life. It was then that I truly saw the significance of the wall of windows. I immediately closed the lower shades and rehung the window coverings on the corner windows in my Wealth Area to hold more energy inside. Within a week I received four checks. My new motto? "How can I honor my self and share my time and energy, so that I also benefit from the flow?" Quite a radical shift!

The goal of feng shui is to create alignment and flow in all areas of your life. If your home office is in your Relationships Area, or if you have romantic pictures and flowers in your Wealth or Ancestors areas, those parts of your life will not be as harmonious as they could be until you realign some things and create more harmony. Even more revealing is where your Wealth Area is located in your living environment. It may be your bedroom, bathroom, kitchen, or another room; each holds a different energy and a different message about what you think, feel, and experience about abundance.

One businesswoman shared with me that a good relationship with her clients was more important to her than making a lot of money. I wasn't surprised to see a bathroom in the Wealth Area of her business space. The lidless toilet and open floor drain both allowed water, a symbol of the flow of money, to go down the drain, indicating its lack of importance in her business life. True to form, she made very little money with her business. I'll address cures and enhancements in Chapter 3.

To produce the best results, my focus is on what is efficient and effective. Many times the most effective method, that which results in the most positive outcome, starts with an indirect approach. The ability to see more than what is in front of your nose, more than the obvious, is the gift of the indirect approach, of metaphors and poetic language.

Three questions that lead to results you can count on are:

1. Am I breathing (full, deep breaths)?

2. Is my body moving and flexible, even in a subtle manner?

3. Am I emotionally and mentally ready to take the next step?

Creating abundance requires "yes" answers. Realizing that you are frozen or stuck in some way begins to release the blockages you are experiencing.

Feng shui may seem indirect as we begin this journey. It is a language of symbols and energy flow. These two things are not commonly associated with our Western education and experiences with money—unless you watch the stock markets. There the stock quotes are noted by symbols, in various combinations. The fluctuations in stock prices and number of shares changing ownership represent huge amounts of energy being added to or withdrawn from that moneymaking activity.

Rivers are currents of moving energy. Feng shui is a current of moving energy. Living in harmony with abundance requires that you move with the flow of all aspects of the current, mentally and physically, and stay flexible and alert so you can accept what you truly want when it comes into view.

Here is another indirect approach: Top salespeople are using their Creative Current when they post pictures of their career goals in plain view—vacation destinations, a new home or vehicle, whatever their heart desires. When they have placed that picture in the correct feng shui area, their Career Area of their work space, they can literally see the abundance that lies ahead. Salespeople who use this technique have consistently better results than those who don't use it. Try it out for yourself.

Robert, a computer programming consultant, found an old goal list one Saturday, while cleaning out his files. "I had been wondering when I would meet my current income goal when I came across this list. I realized that I now had twice the number of clients and more than twice the income I had when I created the list only two years earlier. I had to laugh as I noticed that I had passed that 'finish line' without any acknowledgment on my part. I then wrote in my calendar a semiannual goal of check-ins and a week's vacation with my wife as well." Goals have both due dates and celebrations. The journey can be fun!

Some Fundamentals

Here are some concepts that are fundamental to understanding both feng shui and flow. They are immediately useful and essential to your understanding of metaphors as the book progresses. Feng shui is the language of symbols. Think "symbols" and see pictures in your mind. The symbols are not the thing itself, but they are how we communicate with written and spoken words.

CH'I. Ch'i is energy and breath to the Chinese. It is the life force, the cosmic energy that is around and in everything, the energy that moves water and creates waves, that causes things to grow, the sun to shine, and the earth to turn. To the Western mind, it is often attributed to God or the Creative energy of the Divine Spirit. I use it in both ways, combining the Eastern feng shui with the Western approach to creativity and movement. For both traditions, ch'i is what is unseen and yet causes movement and growth in all areas, humans, plants, animals, businesses . . . wealth and abundance.

Ch'i circulates and pulsates on the earth and in humans, plants, and animals. Healthy ch'i flows harmoniously and is in dynamic balance. Too much ch'i, too much energy and movement, and you can have a tornado, hurricane, earthquake, or flood. Too little ch'i, too little breath and flow, and things stagnate and die, as in a desert or swamp. Focusing on your own breath and on the movement of air in your environment are ways of tuning in and sensing the flow of ch'i.

YIN AND YANG. The Chinese concept of yin and yang (*yin* and *yawng*) represents the two energies that govern the movement of energy, the ch'i. From the circle, the oneness, they emerge as opposites that compliment each other and are held in dynamic balance. These energies flow from one to the other to create movement and the beginning of patterns. In the West we call them polar opposites. Yet nothing is truly totally the opposite. The Eastern approach recognizes this with the dot of the opposite within the main body of each. Each is found within the other, interdependent and interrelated. And when they are balanced they easily create flow.

While yin and yang originated in Asia, there are Western counterparts. In a text that is esteemed by many people in the West, we have "the Spirit, breath or wind, moving upon surface of the deep waters,"

(Genesis 1:1 and 2), and from that movement an enormous creativity flowed. So the symbol also works for a very basic Western concept of something intangible, Spirit or breath, moving or touching something tangible, water. Again, "wind and water" interact in a Western context. In the West we are beginning to recognize that nothing is ever truly black and white. There is always something else to consider when things appear to be cut and dried. Both the Eastern and the Western approaches include the mystical and transcendental, that which cannot be totally explained by the rational, the logical.

Creating balance is the focus. So if someone or something is very yang, then enhancing the space with some yin energy will create a dynamic balance. Over time and with the movement of ch'i, it will become more balanced as yin characteristics are added.

Yin and yang are flowing energies. Yet when they slow down enough to become physical, they align with the following characteristics:

YIN	YANG
Dark	Light
Moon	Sun
Interior	Exterior
Negative	Positive
Earth	Heaven
Rivers	Mountains
People	Offices
Places of the dead	Places of the living
Feminine	Masculine
Shadow	Bright
Yielding	Firm
Quiet or silence	Loud music/sounds
Relaxed	Active

From the flow of yin into yang and back again comes all of the other flow of the basic elements of life. Please note that I omitted good versus bad or the right versus wrong that often appears when considering polar opposites. The focus is on discernment, rather than judgment and condemnation.

Five Elements

The Five Elements are the foundation and basic building blocks of the frequencies of energy on this earth. When you live and work in a city surrounded by concrete, asphalt, and tall buildings, you can easily become ungrounded and disconnected from the earth's basic cycles and abundance. You also can become ungrounded and out of balance with your money when the Five Elements in your environment are not flowing harmoniously. Feng shui and the Five Elements are connected to the flow of energy from the earth. So paying attention to and including the Five Elements in your environment helps to ground you and maintain your connection to the earth, the cycles of seasons, and the flow of the larger patterns of life.

Recognizing the flow of the Five Basic Elements is also one way of sensing the flow of ch'i in an environment. This is a section to read through, set aside, then come back to and read again. While it is a basic building block of feng shui and abundance, you may not feel you understand much of it with your first encounter. When you need the information it will be here waiting for you.

The Five Basic Elements, the essence of matter and ch'i, are symbolized by metal, wood, water, fire, and earth. Each element is associated with moods, colors, tastes, a season, space, and organs of the body. Harmonizing the feng shui aspect of your environment and the Five Elements can assist you in reaching your deepest desires and creating abundance when they flow in harmony; otherwise these elements can work against you without your knowledge. In the West we tend to ignore these elements until they flare up in our faces or when a cycle comes to a grinding halt, and we wonder why. Knowing a few simple tools to correct these challenges can make a huge difference when we take a deeper look at our environments and our money flow. You'll use the cycles of the Five Elements later when you look at your environment, when you make corrections to bring things back into balance, and when you want to enhance an area.

In the financial world, money can appear to "go up in flames" when we are ungrounded and there is too much raging fire energy in our environments and lives. Think about the most recent huge drop in the stock market. Stocks had been selling—for a long time—at price/earning ratios that were not supported by the companies' real worth, earnings, and cash flow. And of course lots of people got excited and bought more stock as the prices continued to go up. While underneath there was no foundation for the stocks' sale price, the talk raged on that things could only go higher. Then the stock prices dropped, people became frightened, prices dropped even more, and things swung in the other direction. Suddenly the talk in many quarters shifted to a recession . . . or worse, again, an imbalance. With feng shui and the Five Elements you can shift your own pattern in response to re-create balance in your environment and life, regardless of what is happening anywhere else.

Here are just a few of the many aspects of the Five Elements:

Element	Metal	Wood	Water	Fire	Earth
Color	white	green blue	blue black	red	yellow, orange brown
Shape	round, arched, oval	rectangular, tall	wavy, curved, irregular	triangular, spiky	low, flat, square
Season	autumn	spring	winter	summer	all year
Objects	hard stone	bamboo, paper	glass, ponds	plastic (use sparingly)	clay, cotton, soft stone
Energy	→← ↑	→← ↑	↓	↑	↻
Location	west	east	north	south	center

Like yin and yang, the Five Elements are two cycles of moving energy, with a building or Creative cycle and a destroying or Regeneration cycle. When one element is out of balance, looking at the appropriate cycle can indicate a cure for the imbalance, enhancing the movement toward growth and abundance. You will use this information as you begin to enhance your environment and again when you have looked at the obvious aspects of an area and still cannot understand why you are not experiencing a positive change.

CREATIVE CYCLE The Creative Cycle flows in a supportive circle where fire creates earth (producing ash), earth produces metal (which is mined from the earth), metal creates water (water forms on the outside of a metal cup holding cold water), water cultivates trees and plants (trees need water to grow), and wood feeds fire. And then the cycle begins again.

Each element enhances and supports the ch'i energy of the element that follows it in the cycle, hence the name Creative Cycle. First use

Creative Cycle

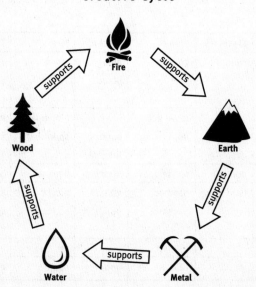

colors to quickly "get things rolling" with this cycle, beginning at the bottom of a room and progressing upwards. What do you want to enhance? Start with that element's color; for example, some black for money and water, then green for wood, red for fire, yellow for earth, and end with white for metal.

REGENERATIVE (DESTRUCTIVE) CYCLE Too little or none of an element leads to a cycle of destruction where you have the pattern of a five-star shape that flops over and stops moving, instead of a supportive circle that rolls and moves you forward. The Regenerative (or Destructive) Cycle points out that fire melts metal (producing ash), metal breaks wood (think of an ax head), wood penetrates earth (the roots of plants), earth absorbs water (thereby negating its effect), and water puts out fire. With this cycle, something is out of balance and things slow down or totally stop moving in a harmonious way.

Stated another way, fire requires fuel, the wood element, which requires water to grow. No fuel means no fire, so there may be too lit-

Regenerative (Destructive) Cycle

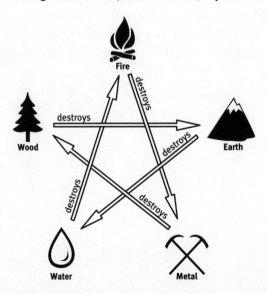

tle action or passion in your work or life. Too much of the element that is one step away also leads to destruction. For example, too much water puts out a fire. Suddenly receiving a lot of money may douse your passions for work and creativity; you may now just want to spend money and play. Just the right amount of water, contained in a teapot, leads to a nice beverage and maybe a pleasant afternoon interlude while you consider some new ideas for creating abundance.

Your financial abundance is also influenced by many events, and there are multiple causes for your current challenge. Each of the Five Currents contributes to the causes and the solutions. Each has some aspect that is out of balance. Throughout this book you will discover your own particular pattern and series of events—and how to "cure" them to create alignment, harmony, and flow.

In the West we rarely focus on a daily rebalancing of our energies and our lives, yet due to the fast pace of events and the demands of our days, maintaining a positive balance requires that we take some time out and add practices to create this balance. And as you incorporate the various action steps into your life, you will be creating a positive balance, like more money in your account and a sense of inner peace.

Let's begin to use feng shui to enhance your Wealth Area.

2

Your Wealth Area

how many times have you seen this octagonal sign? Do you remember the first time someone explained it to you?

You probably have seen it thousands of times and take it for granted. Actually, it conveys an array of messages. It says Stop. Cease moving in your everyday activities. Pay attention to right where you are. Look around you. See who and what are here in this place, and take note of the various signals people and equipment are giving. Ask yourself whose turn it is to move next. Who or what is coming toward you? Will they be able to stop before you start to move forward? Does anything not make sense? Is anything out of alignment? Those are all questions a Westerner might ask a young driver. The Eastern approach might say: Be fully here before you move forward. There can be harmony and flow wherever the stop sign is displayed. Or there can be injurious crashes, symbols of painful disharmony among drivers, vehicles, and pedestrians. Your journey can be one of flow and harmony, getting you to your destination and enjoying the process, or near misses and injurious events. Which do you want? What is your intention?

Recently I watched someone drive through a stop sign. I held my breath and tensed my body waiting for a crash. Luckily everyone else had hesitated before moving forward, giving the intersection and the errant driver some extra time and space. Clearly, the one driver was not paying attention or not present or aware of the situation at hand. Avoiding a crash required everyone else to be more aware, more able to respond to the situation. Being unaware while driving, even for a moment, can lead to a major challenge that involves many people.

The practice of feng shui makes use of this very familiar shape, one that already gives the message to stop, look around, pay attention to your surroundings, then proceed with awareness to create more harmony in your life.

The Ba-gua

The stop sign is similar to an important feng shui symbol, the Ba-gua (pronounced *bah gwa*) of the Black Sect Tantric Buddhist School of feng shui. The Ba-gua octagon provides a quick and easy way to map out the energies of an area, indicating the nine sections: Wealth and Abundance; Fame and Reputation; Marriage and Relationships;, Creativity, Children, and Projects; Helpful People, Travel, and Angels (Benefactors); Career and Life Path; Self-Knowledge and Wisdom; Ancestor and Family; and Health and Unity. Like the stop sign, the Ba-gua is a symbol that tells us to step on the brakes, stop, look, and listen. Its shape is the design that will guide you into the feng shui of your personal environment. (Relax; you don't have to understand the parts of the symbol. Just be aware of the shape.)

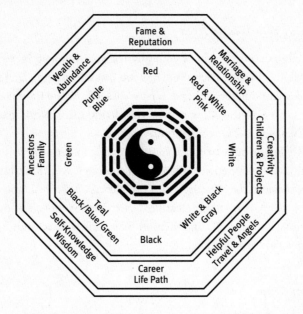

The Ba-gua, after 3,500 years of study

Each side represents a particular energy in your life and some mental and visual concepts. The center area is the ninth focus. I will explain some of these focuses step by step in later sections. Notice the yin-yang symbol in the center. Each side flows into the other, containing a small amount of its opposite, and the two are in balance, a key element in this system. The Ba-gua comes from centuries of the analysis of flow and polarity by fung shui masters. It includes wisdom from India, Tibet, and China, and indicates patterns of flow from the trigrams of the ancient book the *I Ching.* See Appendix B for more information.

This Ba-gua is a simplified version of the more complex octagon used by feng shui practitioners. To start you sailing on the River of Gold toward abundance, we'll use one that is even simpler. For now, stop and ask yourself: Is there total harmony in your living and work space? Do you feel harmony or disharmony in your relationships, in your life? Most of us have some of both.

Locating Your Wealth Area

A full fung shui treatment of your physical environment, investigating and making changes, takes time, but you can start putting feng shui to work for you this very minute. First we'll see how the Ba-gua symbol works as an easy-to-follow map of your living space, work space, and life. Then we'll locate your Wealth Area.

The Feng Shui Current is about vibrating in harmony with physical things and your environment, such as money, wealth, and symbols of abundance in the Wealth Area. Thoughts also have a vibrational frequency, the Creative and Rational currents. So do emotions, the Emotional Current. Putting them in their proper place leads to more harmony, flow, and abundance.

Action Step

In your Travel Log, sketch the outline of your entire living space or office, including any garage, patio, or deck that has a roof attached to the main area. For now, leave out the details of the interior walls, windows, and doors. If there are two or more floors, sketch each floor separately, noting the entrance to that floor, the main door, or the top of the stairs to that floor. If you have an elevator, that would be the main entrance. Note on your sketch any windows or doors to the outside.

Begin to float on your Creative Current by slightly closing your eyes and taking some deep breaths. Notice the overall shape of your living or work space. Is the entire space square, rectangular, or does it have some interesting areas that stick out from the basic shape? Are there some areas that seem to be missing? There is a message in the shape of your living and work space. Remember, we mirror our environments. Right now we are just gathering bits of data and taking notes.

Look at the diagram that follows:

The Simple Ba-gua

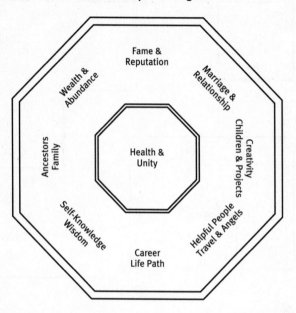

Use an outline of the simple Ba-gua to locate the Wealth Area of your space. Draw a dotted line along the edge of the main entrance, and extend it out in both directions. Then, on translucent paper, trace the simple octagonal Ba-gua and place it on top of the outline of your space, aligning the Career Area along the dotted line by your main front door. You enter your space from either the Career, Knowledge, or Helpful People areas of the Ba-gua. Stretch the Ba-gua, perhaps in your imagination, making it longer (4), wider, or higher, so it fits inside the main shape of your space. Keep it in proportion so that it remains an eight-sided shape. The Ba-gua will indicate useful information as it is stretched to fit the main shape of your space.

Your space may be similar to one of these various shapes:

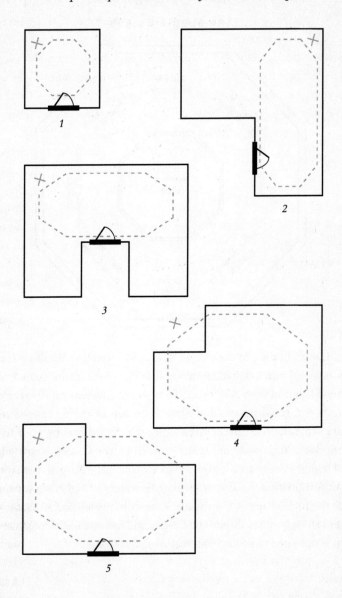

The focus is on whole shapes, squares, rectangles, octagons, and circles, which are considered "lucky" shapes. Irregular shapes, L (2, 5), or U (3), have some area that is missing from the pattern. To create balance and a whole pattern, some action is required, such as a classic feng shui cure found in Chapter 3. Sometimes your main Wealth Area is inside your home or office (1, 2, 3, 5). Sometimes because of the odd shapes and corners poking out, it appears to be missing (4). But it's there; it is just outside the building. Record any thoughts and emotions you experience as you do this exercise.

If your main Wealth Area is outside of the Ba-gua shape (4) in your home or office, just relax. Abundance is *not* beyond your reach. Your Wealth Area requires an advanced step, explained in the next chapter. We will cover how to enhance and create flow and harmony for both interior and exterior Wealth Areas as we go along. Right now just notice where your main Wealth Area is located and record that in your Travel Log. Next think about the general and specific places you have money flowing—for example, your wages, salary, tips if you are a waitperson, bonuses if you're in a corporate environment, and investments. Notice the places where money has stopped flowing or increasing. Include all this information in your Travel Log.

Here is an interesting story about Betty, an artist who came to me for a feng shui consultation. "I was wondering about my Wealth Area being in the yard, beyond the edge of my new deck. My office was in my home in the Self-Knowledge Area. After several weeks I realized I held the belief that my career would never produce the same abundance as my partner's career. I wasn't even aware of how deeply I held that belief until this exercise challenged me. Letting go required disagreeing with my parents' firmly held belief that artists struggle and never really make it. The new thought, that an artist can be successful and create a continuous income stream rather than money being just beyond my reach and enjoyment, was something I had to stretch into over several weeks. Finally I owned it and it owned me! I put a gold wind chime on the deck, a gold reflective windsock in the tree anchoring my Wealth Area, and added a spotlight to highlight the tree.

Now I enjoy the enhancements I made to the yard and I feel confident of my ability to succeed as an artist."

Everything is connected. One day you will look at your sketches and see even more than you think is possible from today's perspective.

The Walkabout

Ready? Let's actually investigate your own Wealth Area.

Now get up, take this book with you, and go stand just inside the main doorway of your home or your office, with the door closed behind you. You are facing into your home, work space, or office. Place your left hand on your heart and just stand there a minute, allowing your breath to flow in and out. Allow your body to relax. Be aware of your breath. Now take a deep breath and extend your left arm, palm open and level with your heart, toward the farthest left corner area of the room or building. This is your Wealth Area for that space. Every environment, every building, and every room has what feng shui calls the Wealth Area, where the energy of abundance is present. In *The Feng Shui of Abundance* it represents the energy of creating abundance with heart. Remember to exhale and breathe normally.

Why the palm up? That is the classic position for being open to receive. A closed fist or hand can accept nothing new. A pointed finger is sending energy away, and a wagging pointed finger points you to the River of Shame, where no love or money flows. Opening your hand to accept what is available is the first step to having more abundance. Connecting your hand to your heart puts you in alignment with open-hearted abundance, where the River of Gold may freely flow. For now, focus on your body sensations and emotional experience. These are the currents that have been ignored by your training and living in the West. Calming your rational thoughts will take several steps, which are addressed in the following chapters. Now just allow your thoughts to flow, note them, and acknowledge that this may seem illogical—for now.

Walk over to that farthest corner of your house or apartment and see where your Wealth Area is and what is actually there. Is it a corner of your living room or your office? A bathroom, your bedroom, or the laundry room? Your child's bedroom, or the garage? Is there a fireplace or back door in that area? Take note of the furniture. What activities occur there? Remember, there is a Wealth Area for each room as well as a Wealth Area for the whole space. The Wealth Area for another floor may be in a different place from the first floor's Wealth Area. The layout of the Ba-gua is based on the placement of the door into your space, the opening that indicates the flow of energy into that space. Noting what is in each room is an advanced step—one you take after you look at your overall Wealth Area.

"I thought Suzan was nuts," Paul, an engineer, said, "until I began to listen at a deeper level than before. This took several attempts, trying to understand that physical things gave a metaphorical message. Hard-headed me said a table or an art object was just what it was—until I bumped into one table for the hundredth time and realized it blocked my movement from one area to another. Rubbing my new bruise, I got the picture!"

Paul moved the table, opening up space and enhancing flow in his environment.

NOTICE THE MESSAGE The most important action to take is . . . Notice. Take note of the physical objects in this space and where you've placed them. Begin to see and hear the message and the metaphor you are sending and receiving from those objects. I have found that directly asking people what they believe about their abundance often results in a different answer from what I get by touring their space and commenting on what I notice. My indirect approach allows them to experience some amazing "A-has."

One businesswoman shared with me, "I work very hard and put in long hours and expect everyone else in my company to follow my lead. Two years ago a consultant had me place living plants around the fireplace in the Wealth Area of my home to counteract what we thought was the fireplace's going-up-in-smoke energy. But it wasn't enough. I kept spending money on business deals that were not profitable. I was resisting making a significant change—and having more ease. Working very hard for many hours a day was also a deeply held belief that consumed my life. While I said I wanted more ease and time to myself, I was actually preventing this from happening. And I had too many things going on at the same time so I never really attended to or finished anything. The working fireplace in my Wealth Area, plus having a home office door that opened into my bedroom, literally spilling work into rest, gave different messages. Those symbolic messages were the ones I lived by—yet resisted acknowledging. I said I wanted more abundance yet I kept putting money into businesses that were not yet profitable, like feeding a consuming fire. I was also wanting more ease and time to do leisure things, but what I was experiencing was more wanting and more and more work."

Well, this is a delicate situation. The woman wanted to talk but not have another formal consultation. So I didn't know what shape her space looked like, or what materials made up her fireplace or floor. And was there water leaking somewhere? Still, I can tell that her Five Elements are out of balance and that she is experiencing a classic Five Element Regenerative Cycle. My question was which element is the most out of balance—fire or water?

In a positive cycle, the wood element, signified by the green plants, actually feeds the fire element of the fireplace. Water, the energy of the Wealth Area, also feeds the wood element, which feeds the fire element so there is energy to create. The cycle flows and she was making lots of money—somewhere in all of her activities. And she was also losing a lot of money. She either had a roaring fire in her Wealth Area from an energy point of view or water was going down the drain. She told me her investments and business deals continued to need more and more money to survive, and several businesses were closed at a loss, as if the money went up in smoke—or down the drain. The cycle was begging to be stopped. And at that point I had more questions than answers. An on-site visit and some more time to talk with her would have revealed a lot.

Water is the first image that comes to mind in creating wealth. If it was water going down the drain, literally leaking away, for this woman, then I suggest checking the faucets, toilets, the pool, hot tub, water sprinklers, and sewer pipes, and having any leaks repaired. Was there water raging through her property, perhaps underground, so she created money but didn't keep it?

If her problem was out-of-balance fire energy, I would want to balance the fire. I would want to slow down the fire, but not put it out, by introducing some water energy, which tames the fireplace energy. Wealth is enhanced by water. Some possible solutions would be to add a black or blue fountain with a pond feeling, on the mantel, in front of, or to the side of the fireplace, or a picture of a lake over the mantel, to encourage wealth to accumulate.

If her problem was with fire energy, "going up in smoke" is indicated by too many opportunities and clients and not making the rounds and completing projects. It is an ungrounded feeling, where things are short-circuited, or light bulbs go out. So I wanted to know if the fireplace was cleaned out, was it aesthetically pleasing, and was there a screen in front to prevent energy from going up the chimney. The plants that were there indicated that there was already a "screen" of energy in front. She indirectly implied that she was too busy, so I wondered what other information was lurking somewhere.

Did she go back to her original feng shui consultant and ask for some more suggestions? No. Did she ask me for a full consultation? No. Did she make some more feng shui changes right away? No, she was too busy. Two years later she was aware and still in the same pattern of consuming work and expensive business deals. Fortunately she had a sense of humor and lots of money. Then much later I learned that she had a leaking toilet in another home and a leak in the pool at her main home, both indicating water going down the drain. So I had the "A-ha!" while she dashed off to another crisis. The cure is to fix the leaks and notice what happens and shifts. If that is not enough, then she could have added a water-gathering energy, with a pond effect, to her Wealth Areas to shift the energy and lead to more accumulation.

You will see and understand the messages in stages, rather like climbing the rungs on a ladder or the steps on a flight of stairs. Getting to the top for an expansive view requires taking the first step.

This book approaches abundance using all Five Currents. Getting you up and moving, to actually observe and ponder with your whole body, is part of the practice of enhancing flow and creating more harmony through feng shui. If we were together, we would talk some, get up and move, go and look at things standing up and from some interesting angles, like on our knees, sitting on the floor, or looking over our shoulders. I would also notice, and mention, what areas of your body are moving or not, and any interesting body movements you make that signal "something is going on" when we talk about money. My questions and suggestions in this book are the best substitute for me being there with you. The most important action you can take is to do the suggested Action Steps. Then you will get the full benefit and develop new ways of understanding your own life and flow. Treat these Action Steps as a walkabout, investigating what is there to see.

Action Step

After your walkabout, take note of what's in your Wealth Area and record your observations in your Travel Log. Also include whatever ideas or images come to mind. Make a new sketch or two of the space and the relationship of the furniture and objects. While you're doing this continue to breathe deeply and steadily. Also make a sketch of your entire living area, including everything that is under one roof, such as your garage or patio. Note also the things that are connected to the building's foundation but have no roof, such as decks, patios, or planters. Pay attention to your emotions and body sensations, and write down your thoughts and imaginings as well. Taking note of your breath, emotions, and body sensations may seem foolish and a waste of time, yet you are connecting to the deeper currents of the River of Gold. Over time this will make a positive difference to your flow and sense of abundance, and you will soon sense that difference.

Maybe you're like Leo, the co-owner of a small communications company. For more than a month he and his partner, Jerry, had been disagreeing about almost every aspect of a new project. The atmosphere in the office was edgy and tense, out of harmony. "I couldn't figure out what was wrong," he said, "until I got to thinking about the layout of my office. When I looked out my open door, my desk faced his, into his office. Our desks opposed one another across the hallway, and I was literally staring him down. I moved my desk diagonally opposite the door to the Wealth Area of my office and things began to shift—on that project and in my career." Leo, who had learned a few things about feng shui, had the answer.

The simple walkabout with your hand on your heart is the most fundamental, easiest way to ascertain your Wealth Area and to connect your heart with your currency and life flow. This system works for discovering the Wealth Area in your living room, your office, your bedroom, and your desk. Each room has a Wealth Area, as does the entire space of a building and each floor of a multistory building. Remember that this is about creating abundance with heart and ease. Now ponder the message: Where does your money go? Up in smoke? Down the toilet? Out the door? Maybe there's a fireplace, a toilet, lots of windows, a back door, or deck in your Wealth Area?

Notice any connection between the room and what is currently happening with your abundance, the message and metaphor, and write that down in your Travel Log. This may take a few days, or not. There is no hurry and no delay. Feng shui is about going with the flow. There is a symbolic message in the placement of your belongings, your Wealth Area, and your abundance. Tune in and you will begin to decipher the message. Remember, you are mirroring your environment and both sending and receiving a message from your possessions.

Arnold, Debbie, and their children stopped at my booth at a convention. We sketched their home and realized their Wealth Area was in their daughter's bedroom. Later Arnold said, "We were spending all of our 'extra' money on our children. We also learned that our children were feeling guilty about how much money their braces, music lessons, and sports activities consumed. All of us were dismayed." They were willing to work with me, and we quickly set a new intention. They made a new agreement with themselves, their children, and the Divine Spirit to accept that the money they spent on their kids would come back to them with ease from other sources. The children agreed to enjoy their activities knowing the Divine Spirit would replenish the flow of abundance to their parents. Debbie attended a weekend workshop based on all the principles in *The Feng Shui of Abundance*. A year later Arnold shared with me, "Our financial reserves have increased! We made lots of feng shui changes beginning with streamlining our space. I'm an engineer. I have a hard time understanding it, but feng shui works."

Streamlining, covered in Chapter 3, had them focus on letting go of belongings they no longer loved or needed. As a natural result, they also looked at how they spent and saved money and made many small adjustments during that time. Movement in one area of their life, their relationship with their children and their Wealth Area, led to releasing clutter, which led to changes in spending and saving money.

What Does Your Wealth Area Look Like?

Read the following questions out loud, taking a deep breath after each one as you consider your answer. Notice your Body Sensations Current and any Rational or Creative Current thoughts or images that arise from asking the questions:

- Is my Wealth Area cluttered? Is it clean?

- Does it give me a sense of satisfaction? The enjoyment of beauty?

- Does my Wealth Area contain furniture or an art object that represents open-hearted wealth and abundance to me?

- Would I be willing to keep the area clean and free of clutter? To treat it as a place of honor?

- How easy was it to say and answer the questions? Did I notice any hesitations or stops in my responses?

If you're thinking, "This is really silly/stupid" or "What value can this possibly have?" thank your thoughts for making an appearance. They represent the flow of Rational Energy, one of the five currents that create the River of Gold. That current is necessary for following through with the logical, step-by-step activities that bring your dreams and goals into reality. Honoring your other four currents creates a great team, one that harmonizes and balances the strengths and shortcomings of each current.

Now focus on the questions again. Write them down in your Travel Log and record what comes to mind. Be open to any nonlogical answers from your Creative Current. You engage that flow with the phrase "Hmmm? I wonder if . . ." You may receive an answer immediately, or understanding may surface later while you are engaged in a nonlogical activity. I often receive insights to my pondering while splashing water on my face, showering, walking, or humming. Remember to record any insights you have in your Travel Log. Any fragments you notice will fall into place—later. Right now observe and record your initial observations on this journey to the ocean of abundance with heart.

Having and enjoying more of anything begins with honoring what we already have. Read that sentence again. I feel so strongly about this concept that I advise writing it in your Travel Log every day for a month and notice what comes up, what other thoughts and images appear in response to a new idea. For some people this may seem to be a strange request. Your early training may have included ideas and beliefs that wealth and money were to be treated as dirty or worse. That having and accumulating money is selfish, and no spiritually oriented person would do such a thing. Just considering some new information may be a challenge. Take some deep breaths and open up to another perspective. This is a nuance, a simple and subtle thing. It also indicates the beginning of significant change in your abundance.

Now consider what reverence means to you. Stretch a bit and consider what revering your abundance would be like. This is a radical departure from the norm for many people who grew up hearing that money and the love of it is the root of all evil. I wonder if we love our money too little, not too much. The sense of awe and holiness that you connect with the highest energy in your life can be applied to your abundance. I actually thank the Divine Spirit for the money that flows into my life.

Now that I have bushwhacked you with a new thought, take the time to log your responses to the idea of honoring and revering your money, your current level of wealth and abundance. For extra measure, ponder esteem and high estimation of your abundance, and log any rational or creative thoughts, emotions and body sensations that appear. This is the basic step of tuning in to our deepest heart's desire and harmonizing with the energy of attracting what we truly want.

Action Step

Once you have observed and recorded your Wealth Area as it currently stands, it is time to ask yourself:

> *Am I willing to take a risk and make the changes,*
> *whatever they may be,*
> *to create open-hearted abundance in my life?*

Remember to log the questions and all of your responses. This is a different question from "Do I want to be rich, have lots of money?" That one's easy. This one is much more demanding; it may involve new and different ways of living. You may feel afraid or experience some other emotion or a flurry of thoughts that tell you this is not possible, at least not for you. Right now you don't know what you will experience on this journey.

Yet this question leads to a choice that is infinitely more satisfying, the experience of open-hearted abundance. Continue to ask the question and record your answers, until you get a full-bodied "yes." This may take several rounds of inquiry.

What represents abundance for you? Is it enough money to pay your monthly expenses? More than enough so you enjoy a sense of ease in your day-to-day life? Does it include an awareness of how your body creates new cells, blood, and bone marrow even as you sleep? Does it include the variety of plants and animals that live on this planet? What about the variety of people you can interact with and the options for entertainment that exist? Are you aware of all of the various ways you can move your body? Abundance comes in many forms.

Action Step

Now ask yourself, "Do the furnishings and objects that are currently in my Wealth Area truly represent the kind of abundance I want?" Record both the question and all your responses, mental and physical, in your Travel Log. This is very important. Stop and do it before you move forward. Much insight can flow from all of these various steps.

If your Rational Current has a lot to say, honor it and record what comes forward. Things like: "Moving things is too much work." "Just spend more time at the office." "Don't believe this soft stuff." "No one I know has done that!" "Things can't talk, everyone knows that." If you experience some or many body sensations, log those as well. If you are off daydreaming, record those images too. You are beginning to identify your patterns of responding to more flow and abundance, to uprising energy. Right now that information may seem irrelevant. It's not. Your patterns are important to your life flow and your sense of abundance. There is gold in your Travel Log; you just don't see it yet. It's okay if your response was "Yeah, fool's gold." It's also okay if you want to stick your tongue out or thumb your nose at me. I've done that to my laptop from time to time. Shocked? I hope not. Being friendly, "honest to the penny," and having fun are also part of the flow of the River of Gold.

A woman once wandered by my booth and stopped to talk. She had heard of feng shui and quickly diagrammed her living space. We discovered her Wealth Area housed her storage space—filled with things left over from a marriage that ended ten years ago. "I just could not face going in there. Clearing it out always seemed like reinforcing the failure of my marriage. So I have kept everything. Now, realizing it signifies my wealth and abundance, I am wondering where to begin." Tears filled her eyes. With some coaching, she took a deep breath, paused, then said, "I am ready to begin anew." We considered several options. One lit up her face with joy. She agreed to go home and toss some coins, with gratitude, into the corners of the storage space. Then as she sorted and let go of her past, little rewards were there, waiting to be discovered.

Even before you understand a lot of feng shui and the connections your belongings have to your life, you can move forward. Insights will come even as you take the suggested steps.

Action Step

Now remove from your main Wealth Area all of the objects that do not represent wealth and open-hearted abundance to you. If the objects are not movable, leave them. Later we will focus on what to do about them. Go ahead and note in your Travel Log what you removed, your responses, and what you think and feel about what is left. Remember to give your Wealth Area a good cleaning before you put anything back or place anything new there.

Now ask yourself: "What do I currently own that represents wealth and open-hearted abundance to me right now?" Write down the question and anything that pops into your mind. Anything, no matter what. This may seem like another stupid question. Thank your rational mind for asking "What possible relevance does this have?" and do the exercise again:

What do I currently own, that I love, that represents wealth and open-hearted abundance to me, right now?

The first object that comes to mind is the one to write down and to place in your streamlined Wealth Area. It may be an art object, some personal treasure, a book, money, or a symbol of money. What matters is what it represents to you. Note that information as well in your Travel Log. Go and find the item, spend a few minutes looking at it, and clean it up.

Remember to record where you found it and what it looked like, whether it was clean and in a bag, or covered with dust, cobwebs, or tarnish, and your body sensations and emotional responses. This whole activity is about enhancing your Wealth Area, enlivening your way of flowing with more abundance, and developing awareness of how you stop your flow.

OBJECTS THAT ENHANCE YOUR WEALTH AREA Enhancing your Wealth Area also includes some classic feng shui enhancements. Here are some items that honor and enhance Wealth Areas:

- Objects that represent wealth and abundance to you, such as a beautiful vase or figurine, crystal, fine stone or brass art objects, a painting or wall hanging

- The colors purple, black, blue, both green and red, or gold

- A colored cloth under an object, or a ribbon around it in the suggested colors

- A water fountain, which symbolizes enhancing and maintaining flow, with a pondlike effect so the energy of money accumulates

- A green plant with lush round leaves, such as a jade plant

Be aware of your breath, body sensations, and emotions as you place the various enhancements in your Wealth Area and record these in your Travel Log.

Ask yourself "What is my intention in making these changes?" Are you focusing on creating more abundance or on something else?

Perhaps "getting rid of" or "moving against" kinds of thoughts? Spend a few minutes pondering the question, noting your responses, and finally state your intention in a positive way. For example, stating the intention of "Getting rid of the lousy job I have endured for five years" focuses on what you *don't* want. That is looking backward and feels like resistance with some anger. As I try on that intention in my body, I feel like I am pushing a wagon up a steep hill. Saying instead, "I am open to a new position that honors my talents and creativity and enhances my financial abundance" is positive enough to draw you forward with ease.

At a convention, Alice walked up to me, very excited. She began asking questions right and left. After a while I realized she was dancing around her real question. I simply said, "I have the feeling in my body that you are dancing around an important issue. Let's create harmony. Just ask what you really want to know." She popped out with, "Is it okay if I put a crystal butterfly in my Wealth Area?" After several more questions I discovered it was her most beautiful, elegant, and expensive possession. And she loved it! Someone from another culture, where butterflies are connected to death, dying, and negative events, told her not to use it, yet to Alice it symbolized rebirth and new possibilities. Her eyes lit up when I said, "Go with what feels most alive and right to you." The way she walked off I knew she would . . . from then on.

SEEING RED I suggest you omit from your Wealth Area the color red unless it is paired with its complementary color of green. In many feng shui traditions, the color red by itself is emphasized for your Wealth Area because in China it represents good luck. It's the color Chinese brides wear on their wedding day and the color of the envelopes used for gifts of money for Chinese New Year and other auspicious occasions. Also, payments recognizing wisdom and a position of honor are given in red "lucky money" envelopes. Red envelopes are used as a sign of respect toward an expert. However, in the United States, "being in the red" indicates serious financial challenges. Other terms that financial people use are "bleeding red ink," "going down in flames," or "going up in smoke." Red is also the color of stop signs, a signal to stop the flow. Allow the Chinese to enjoy their cultural traditions and participate as appropriate when you are interacting with them. However, steer clear of any cultural crosscurrents in your own space.

Red and green together are another story. They are complementary colors that represent fire and wood together, the energies of moving and growing, and as complements they are very calming, since the green adds the grounding earth energy to the fiery red. The green also connects Westerners to the energy of money and growth and the Christmas holidays that symbolize abundance for many people.

One person asked about putting an American flag in her Wealth Area. One question deserves another, and I inquired what that would mean to her. "Freedom!" was the enthusiastic response. The combination of the three colors, the stars and stripes symbolism, and the long history of family flag waving in this person's life gave her a significant message. Financial freedom is a very positive message, one that could release a lot of energy and enhance movement forward. Consider whether your response includes any rebellion or some other crosscurrent and log your responses.

Ruth shared with me her longing for a deeper relationship with her spouse. "I realized my Relationship Area had several mismatched items and nothing that was pink or red and white together. Things were good, but a bit ho-hum. Our Wealth Area was where the red items were, and money had been a strain for a while. I put some red and white in our Relationship Area, removed the red from the Wealth Area and put purple there instead, and put symbols of wealth in the more harmonious area and added symbols of love and passion in our Relationship Area. Later we took the extra money that suddenly showed up, added it to our nest egg, and took a weekend vacation, just the two of us. After a while I realized the strain was gone in both areas!" Yes, things can move this smoothly as you realign the energies in your home and your life.

LAUNDRY ROOM Fine for you, you may say, but what if my Wealth Area is in my laundry room? Do you expect me to remove my washer and dryer? No—feng shui is easier than that. Moving plumbing is a major event, a very advanced step. First, thoroughly clean the area and keep it neat. You could put an art object in that area, or you might create a collage or Treasure Map (see Chapter 6) representing abundance and hang it on a wall as a constant reminder of the River of Gold with which you are beginning to flow. If a collage seems like too much for the laundry room, put some pennies in a colorful, attractive bowl and place it in a visible spot. Tape some play money to the wall or put up a poster of a pond or lake to reactivate your intention to accumulate wealth each time you walk through the area. The important thing here is getting started, taking beginner's steps toward flowing prosperity.

OFFICES AND DESKS Creating abundance is the focus of most offices. For commercial buildings, the three places of power are in the back in the Wealth Area, the Fame and Reputation, and the Relationships and Marriage areas. The layers of people near the front screen the challenges so that the larger and more important issues filter back to be addressed in the places of power. On the other hand, home offices are best placed near the front door, not in the back of your home and especially not in the more intimate Relationship Area. An office in your bedroom means you never leave work and cannot truly rest as work is always staring you in the face. Leaving your computer plugged into the wall or turned on is too much subtle electrical energy near your bed, and that electrical current will eventually disturb your sleep patterns.

Notice the placement of your desk. Where you sit in your office influences how much ease you experience as you work. Sitting so you can see who comes into your work space, whether the person makes any noise to announce his or her presence, is key to the position of your desk. Look at the following sketches. In figure A, the area diagonally opposite the doorway is a position of power and command. Place your desk in this position so you can easily see your doorway. Allow your assistant or secretary to sit closer to the door. Then he or she will be avail-

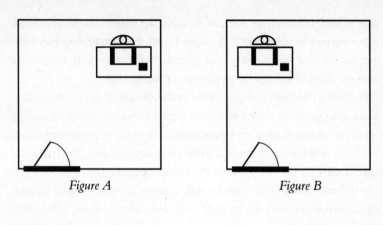

Figure A   Figure B

Figure C   Figure D

Figure E

able to people passing by and can attend to the numerous interruptions, allowing you to concentrate, focus, and work with more ease. Remember to enhance the Wealth Area of your work space with something that makes your heart sing—yes, even at work.

While the desk in Figure B is in the Wealth Area of this office, even with the door closed your concentration will be compromised by all of the energy passing by. You'll experience many more interruptions, and you will have less command of your time, energy, projects, and career than if you were to sit in the corner opposite the door.

If you share an office with a colleague, as shown in Figure C, then sit as coworkers, with the front of your desks aligned along the sides of the eight-sided Ba-gua. Sitting facing opposite one another pits your energy one against another. You literally are staring each other down. One of you will keep track of the other playing one-upmanship. If you are unable to move your desks, place an interesting crystal in the Fame Area of your desk to soften and deflect the adversarial energy, and enhance the Helpful People Area of your desk and the office.

In Figures D and E, sitting with your back to your door invites unexpected people and unfortunate events to sneak up and surprise you. In this position you are always jumpy and putting out fires rather than accomplishing things. Placing a mirror on the wall, so you can see your doorway with your peripheral vision and only move your eyes slightly to see with more clarity, allows you to relax and focus on your task at hand. If your desk is configured so that it can only face the wall, hang the mirror on the wall above your desk, or place it on top of your computer monitor or on the windowsill so that you can see the door.

If you sit with your back to an interior window, say in an interior office, you may feel as if things are going on behind your back. We each have a "guardian" energy that is on watch. This is true when we work and sleep and as we go about our daily lives. Cooperating with this energy, rather than turning our backs on it, allows us to relax. When we guard our own situation—our backs—we accomplish more. Move your desk so your back is to a solid wall. Hang a mirror so you can see what is going on behind you without having to shift your position. Seeing behind you with ease is the goal.

Figure A is the ideal setup, where you sit with a solid wall to your back so you feel supported as you work. In a corner office, where there are windows on both sides and the doorway is diagonally opposite the power site, sit facing the door. If you sit with your back supported by the solid wall and you look out the windows enjoying the view, as in Figure D, then place a mirror on the windowsill, so you can see the doorway and whoever stands there. Harmonize with your guardian energy and give yourself more ease.

Remember your desktop contains each of the nine areas of the Bagua. The Career Area is where you sit, so your Wealth Area is the far-left area of the top of your desk. Enhance your Wealth Area using something as small as a piece of ribbon or paper in the appropriate color (purple, blue, green, or gold), or an item that represents wealth and abundance to you. If your employer would frown upon even as little as something in the appropriate color, then place something inside your desk as a reminder to you and to help align yourself with the appropriate energies.

Dancing Pennies

Now it's time to take a moment and let go of any judgments, old assumptions, and attitudes from your Rational Current and just experiment.

The following simple action connects all five currents and can have profound results: Honor your feng shui Wealth Area every day with a small increase, a penny. This subtle move, with the right intention, allows you to experience on a fundamental level more abundance on a daily basis. Your Feng Shui, Body Sensations, and Emotional currents are all enhanced. In addition, your resistance or openness to coaching is revealed very quickly by how you participate in the following exercise.

I call it the Penny Dance. It is a very small and subtle thing, yet it signifies a huge change. I ask you to save a penny a day. In my workshops, I give each person a penny, usually one that I have polished and blessed. It's a gift from my heart to yours and from my sacred penny bowl to yours. While a penny seems almost insignificant, it actually signals the tide shifting if you are quiet and listen spaciously. (Chapter 6 covers the art of spacious listening.)

Choose a container that you already own and absolutely love. Round, square, oval, or some other shape—it is your choice. This container represents wealth and open-hearted abundance to you. Place your container in your Wealth Area and put the penny into the container. Every day take another penny, go to your Wealth Area, and hold the penny in both hands. Give thanks for the abundance you already have and for the open-hearted abundance that is coming to you. Place the penny in your container with gratitude. Notice over time how the pennies flow together in an interesting dance.

Remember, you have a Wealth Area for your whole living space as well as one for your living room, your bedroom, your kitchen, your desk and office. You decide which Wealth Area to honor with the Penny Dance and how public you want to be with your activities. If you place the container for your Penny Dance in your living room, people may ask you to explain what you are doing, and why, as they enjoy your hospitality.

While the Penny Dance may seem odd or silly to your Rational Current, there are four other currents to consider. Is your Creative Current happy with the change? Can your Body Sensations Current touch the pennies and the container with appreciation? What about your Emotional Current—is your heart singing?

Why a penny? Why not something larger? Well, pennies are still made out of copper, although a smaller amount than in the past. Copper is used for conducting water and electricity, the common currents and energy around the world. Connecting with the "coppers," the pennies, puts you in touch with a subtle energy flow that goes back to the U.S. Mint and the various sources for electricity and water around the country. This is where the power is located! A subtle thing, yet very powerful. Now ask yourself: "Am I willing to connect with the source of flow and energy?" Remember to note the questions and all of your responses in your Travel Log.

Paying attention to, and being aware of, the pennies in your life enhances paying attention to these nuances. The Penny Dance reminds you to tune in to the smaller or quieter messages in your life, such as hunches. Many of your Body Sensations are very subtle, and your Creative Current and intuition whisper. Remember, everyone has his own pattern of enhancing abundance and of blocking it and sending it away. Your own pattern is uncovered little by little as you notice and pay attention to nuances, the small and quiet things in your life.

As you go about doing the Penny Dance, notice your other behaviors with money and your accumulation of it. Are you faithful or do you often forget to do the dance? Is this similar to your interaction with loose bills and change: Do you put your money back into your wallet, or stash it in various pockets? Are your bills in one area or scattered around? Do you remember to pay them on time, or is your life a mad dash from one missed due date to another? Do you regularly set aside some money, even a small amount, so that it can grow? Notice any other connections with your finances and how you participate with the Penny Dance.

My friend April shared with me that she knew just what container to use as soon as I spoke the words. However, it took her a while to find it. In a wink it was clean and sitting in her Wealth Area with her first penny. This was something she could do even on her unemployment check. Her next position came only two months after the first one ended—with a much higher salary and a nice pile of pennies in her fancy dish. Eighteen months later, still Dancing with her Pennies, April's salary had doubled.

If you're doing this at home and have children, consider doing the Penny Dance together. You also can do it with a partner; however, each of you will grow tremendously, at your own pace, if you go solo. If you already have a container or a pocketful of coins stashed somewhere, add these to your Wealth Area.

Does it matter if you put in more coins or larger coins? No. *Intention* is what counts. Remember to add coins with great love, gratitude, and awareness every day. If you miss a day, just begin anew.

RECIRCULATE When your container seems full, put your pennies back into circulation with love and gratitude, and use this as a great time to review your financial situation and the flow of your five currents. Notice how easy it was to accumulate your pennies, and see if it was just as easy to refocus your flow: reducing your spending for some items, paying down your debt, and enhancing your accumulation for a six-month cushion.

I have been dancing with pennies for a long time. Occasionally I forget to do the Penny Dance. When I remember, I laugh and start over again. You will too. Everyone dances to her own penny tune. Enjoy the dance, and notice when you are having fun—and when you are not. Circulating pennies includes depositing them in your savings or checking account or spending them on something that would make your heart sing. The log of your responses and your purchases will be very interesting reading—someday.

3

Clearing Clutter, Getting Unstuck, and Stopping Your Wealth Drain

for some people, the energy in their space is stuck or moving too slowly and needs to be released and speeded up. Here streamlining is the first step. For others, energy is moving too quickly, or leaking out, so containing and slowing down the flow are necessary. Still others have "missing areas" to be augmented. Various feng shui "cures" are used to speed up, slow down, collect, or contain flow.

Ease and flow define the term "streamline." You can move easily and change directions quickly when things are streamlined. It is more of an experience rather than a destination. You should be able to go fast and stay in control, maneuver quickly and stop on a dime, effortlessly, all the while looking as if you gave no thought to how you and everything else look. This is the very essence of feng shui.

Vibration

Everything has its own vibration, its own energy signature. For energy to move, it requires both open space and real objects to move through. The more stuff and clutter, and the less open space, the more energy slows down, then stagnates and finally comes to a stop. Ever lay something down and then a couple of weeks later realize you have quite a pile of things accumulated around the first object? This is another variation on the theme of like attracts like.

The more possessions we own, the greater the amount of our personal energy that goes into maintaining them. We use energy in cleaning them, insuring them, and seeing that they have a roof over them and are safe and warm. Beyond a reasonable amount, our possessions actually slow us down, consuming our energy or creating a detour that slyly directs us away from our best path, our life purpose. Moving quickly, stopping on a dime, and changing direction without losing your hat and balance all flow from establishing clean lines and little or no clutter. When we let go of the things that no longer make our hearts sing, it's like releasing a heavy load we have been carrying or throwing useless items overboard. There is more space and we can move with more ease. Clearing our space is not something we do with glee or do often; we resist more freedom and flow. Usually it takes a big kaboom! in life to face the fact we have far too many things to dust and insure. What's a kaboom? Maybe a relationship or job ends in an unfriendly manner, or a valued object breaks. Or someone, often you, trips or becomes seriously ill. All of these are calls to remove what is outdated and blocking the flow in your space and your life.

Feng Shui Clutter: The Deeper Message

Clutter. Energy that is waiting to move is, in reality, stuck. Things saved for "someday" are the classics that take up your space. How will you know when "someday" announces itself? Does a trumpet blow or lightning strike? Stuck energy must be released so it can flow again. Clearing your space also clears your mind. You can literally see more clearly. More open space means more options to move around and to consider new ways of doing things.

Many people hold on to things and also hold their emotions in check. Holding on is a particular vibration that shuts down the flow of energy. Letting go of a long held "treasure" also means letting go of the emotion that is connected with the item. The usual ones are sadness and fear. Most people focus on the fear and loss, the "what if I need this in the future and it's gone?" question. We associate the object with the event and person who gave it to us. If we are open and flow with our emotions that are connected with the person, then we can thank him or her for the item, recognize it's no longer in our best interest to keep it around, perhaps offer it back to the person, or to a favorite relative or other friend, and let it go. We can also just let it go to some favorite organization. When our emotional energy is not flowing, then taking any of these steps can be quite challenging. And if the person who gave it to us is no longer walking with us in this life, then we may keep it as a reminder even if we no longer want the item. Clutter and stuck emotions go together.

Fred was working as an emergency medical technician. The crew got a call for help and charged off, only to find an old house where every room was filled with stacks of newspapers, some over four feet tall. The pathway to the person in crisis was narrow and snaked through the maze of these papers. The odor of garbage, cat litter, and old papers was horrendous! More than once Fred had to dash outside to catch his breath as he attended to this elderly person. The stretcher didn't fit. The technicians had to create a cradle with their hands to carry the elderly person through the maze. Later, Fred learned it took several dumpster loads to empty the house of the clutter. Upon hearing this, he went home and began clearing every room of clutter. While telling me the story, Fred shuddered. His contorted facial expression said it all when he mentioned the odor. Yes, clutter can have an aroma, musty and stale. Quick! Open a window and let in some fresh air.

Love It or Let It Go Living with things that you love is an up-lifting experience. Everywhere your eye rests or your body touches sends back to you your own energy of love and acceptance. Contrast that with seeing and touching things that you associate with painful memories, with the energy that causes you to wince or worse. As you walk through your space, you have the opportunity of replaying, in your head, the movie or audiotape that may cause you to contract. You begin to see the value of streamlining, of having your space filled with things you love and use, and of releasing things that have other associations.

Action Step

As you look at your own belongings, ask yourself the following questions:

- Do I love this?

- Does it fit into my lifestyle as I am currently living it?

- Does it bring me joy and ease?

- Am I saving it for someone who loves and wants it?

- Is it of great value to me for sentimental reasons?

- Will I use it in the next couple of years?

- Does it make my heart sing?

- Does it speak to my soul?

If your answers to all of the questions are no, then ask yourself where the item fits in your life. If you want to live your life with joy and ease, some things will not add to your movement and flexibility. Let them go with your blessing to someone who will find them joyful and easeful.

GETTING STARTED You may be asking yourself "How do I get started?"

That is a great question. Begin with the easiest and the smallest. The easiest item, space, room; just begin. From the easiest you will have the fun, experience, and courage to move to the next item and the next, until the very thing you thought you could not "face" is already accomplished.

This is a step-by-step process that will take time. Consider it a two-step-and-rest process. And once you have done it, you will feel joyous and ready and able to look again at the things you surround yourself with and ask the questions again. I have found over time that my tastes and my tasks have changed. What served me well visually and task-wise at one time no longer fits the bill. It actually serves someone else wonderfully once I release my hold on it.

SPACE CLEARING Clearing a space of stuck energy after streamlining and cleaning it includes some actions you might consider mystical or downright odd. Since everything has its own vibration and is part of some series of frequencies, then enlivening that vibration with sound is an obvious next step. Using bells, chimes, drums, and clapping your hands in corners and throughout a room breaks up the stuck energy. These actions are best taken after centering yourself, setting a clear intention to raise and release stuck energy, opening some windows, and moving around the space in a methodical way. After a space clearing, I also smudge the air with a combination of sage and sweet grass to bring in harmonious energy. Afterward, I play some beautiful music.

Sprinkling sea salt around the perimeter of a room also absorbs stuck energy. Always buy new sea salt to use to absorb energy. Again center yourself, send gratitude to the salt, set an intention to raise the energy and create harmony, then lightly sprinkle the salt methodically around the perimeter of the room, beginning in one corner and ending in the center. Leave the salt in place for no more than two or three days, then vacuum or sweep it up. Remember to dispose of the sea salt so that it is outside the space you have cleared, not sitting under your sink absorbing even more energy.

There are several books on the subject of space clearing. There also are training sessions to teach people to feel energy, clear a space, and leave it feeling harmonious. Call in an expert if, when you read this information, your body contracts, your breath hesitates, and you wonder what to do next.

CLASSIC CURES Over the centuries, classic cures to feng shui challenges have been discovered, used, and found to be reliable. These cures collect, raise, speed up, and slow down energy, once you have streamlined and cleaned an area. There are nine basic cures, eight of which involve everyday objects that are easy to use and to understand, plus the other, nontangible cures:

1. Light-refracting or bright objects: lights, mirrors, or crystals

2. Sound-making objects: wind chimes, bells

3. Living objects: plants (artificial or real), flowers (artificial or real), an aquarium or fish bowl, or bonsai

4. Moving objects: mobiles, fountains, waterfalls, whirligigs, windmills

5. Heavy objects: stones, statues, rock gardens

6. Electrically powered objects: computers, stereo systems, televisions, air conditioners

7. Bamboo flutes

8. Colors

9. Others

Lights can be used to encourage ch'i circulation inside a building or to square off an awkward space or missing space outside. A light installed at the bottom of a steep hill and aimed upward toward the building's roof will stem the flow of money rolling away from a Wealth Area by recirculating the ch'i back to the building.

Mirrors, the larger the better indoors, bring in good ch'i, light, and good views as they repattern the flow of energy. They also can fill in and correct the energy of missing areas and create depth when a space is confined. Outdoors they reflect back the often negative energy of other buildings, especially the corners or traffic flow that points directly at a home, thereby protecting the home and its occupants from outside influences. They symbolically straighten slanting interior walls and generally enhance the energy of the Ba-gua wherever they are hung. Think of them as aspirin useful for many situations. Be careful with how you use mirrors. Hanging a mirror so it appears to cut off the top of people's heads as they look at themselves lowers their energy when they pass by and eventually leads to headaches and tension. Little mirror tiles also distort images and lead to challenges. You appear to be broken or cut up when you look at yourself in them. Smoky or dark mirrors seem oppressive.

Wind chimes and bells hung on an entrance door announce someone's arrival and serve as a simple alarm system. Hung on the outside of a business, they attract ch'i, customers, and profits, while on the eave of a home, they improve the house's ch'i and the residents' finances. In general, they moderate the circulation of ch'i and can disperse strong energy that flows along a long corridor or the road that aims at a home.

Plants and flowers are symbolic of growth and bring nourishing ch'i into a space. Plants placed in front of harsh corners that jut into a room soften and resolve the challenging energy. Flanking and outside an entrance, they serve as beacons attracting clients, business, and ch'i. Growing outside, they are indicators of the ch'i of an area, good ch'i if they are thriving, and negative if they are not. Building in an area where no plants or trees are naturally growing may end up drawing energy and money out of your project and your bank account. Plants also can be used to balance the shape of a building or a plot of land. Place a large plant at the junction where the corner should be located. Artificial plants can be used as well as living ones, indoors and out. Keep them clean and place them with clear intention to raise the ch'i. Let your personal taste guide you here. Dried plants and flowers are dead. Avoid them. Fish bowls and aquariums are positive interior cures, symbolizing the wealth-enhancing properties of water in nature. Focus on the colors of the fish, harmonizing them with the colors for the Ba-gua area being enhanced. Use black, purple, green and red, or gold for Wealth Areas.

Moving objects, electrically or wind powered, create active positive ch'i. Used outdoors they deflect and disburse the negative or "killing" ch'i of arrowlike roads and neighboring overbearing buildings. Both home and business finances are enhanced by water fountains, waterfalls, geysers, and harmoniously placed ponds. Gently flowing water that accumulates like a reflecting pond is the goal. Take caution when a sharp corner of a pool points at a building; the cutting ch'i can be softened by a large plant or planter placed near the corner.

Heavy objects, stones, and statues, placed in the appropriate Ba-gua area, stabilize unsettling situations and harmonize unbalanced shapes. They also serve as a support for Wealth, Career, or Relationship areas that appear to be hanging out in midair or seem to be missing.

Electrically powered objects, used indoors in the appropriate Ba-gua area, can stimulate that area. A computer in the Career Area, a stereo system in a Wealth Area of a business to stimulate profits, or to raise a business's profile, or an air conditioner in the Fame Area all create alignment and harmony.

Bamboo flutes are classical Chinese cures. They were used to announce peace and good news in ancient China and symbolically enhance safety and stability. They are hollow and segmented and are seen as funneling the ch'i up when used to uplift the energy of an oppressive beam or slanting ceiling. Hang them with red ribbons so they slant upward, creating an octagon shape like the Ba-gua. As protection, like crossed swords, they are hung in Chinese homes, stores, and restaurants to guard against robbers and evil spirits. Many people hang angels for similar reasons.

Colors are often the first thing people notice. Used symbolically as well as emotionally, they enhance energy in the eyes of the beholder and are used as often as mirrors to correct and enhance the energy of an area.

"Others" are the nontangible cures that include your own intention, the infusion of energy from your hands or altar, and the mystical blessings, chants, and ceremonies done by a feng shui consultant.

All changes and enhancements to your Wealth Area are put in place to create more harmony and flow, so use objects that are in alignment with your personal tastes and decorating style. Using feng shui does not mean you must have Chinese symbols in your home, especially if they do not harmonize with your décor or you simply don't like them. *The Feng Shui of Abundance* is about flowing with the River of Gold and creating open-hearted harmony and abundance, not about creating a particular decorating style. Remember to remove any clutter and clean the area before putting anything in place. Spend some time energizing the cure; perhaps place it on your own altar if you have one or take it to a place to absorb positive spiritual energy. Open your heart and send gratitude to the abundance you already enjoy. Invite the flow of abundance into your hands and your bank accounts as you put your objects in place.

Leaking Energy

I once visited a corner office where everyone oohed and aaahed about the two walls of windows, except me. I had serious reservations about the Wealth Area's abundance of windows, the feng shui of the office and the whole space, but with only a couple of years of self-study under my belt, I was hardly an expert. The office manager believed the expansive view would inspire everyone to work harder and the company would flourish. When I walked into the main event room, the three walls of floor to ceiling windows caused me to pause and comment on the major energy leak issue. I was told, "We'll just close the shades." Then the square pillar in the Relationship Area and the matching one in the Helpful People Area stopped me in my tracks. The sharp corners pointing into the open area where everyone sat, representing

Health and Unity, sent cutting energy, called cutting ch'i, into every-one's heart. I wouldn't have signed the lease, and I asked the manager to get an expert's opinion. The response was "You're too sensitive. Everything will be okay." Two years later the financial situation was strained. Four years later the company closed that office and nearly went out of business. I was glad I was not an employee. That space is still empty several years later. From that experience, I learned to trust my first impression of a space, grateful for my sensitive awareness.

Energy leaks out of windows, gets flushed down the drain with toi-lets, runs down a stair and out the door, and goes up in smoke in a fire-place. In a Wealth Area any of these items, if out of balance, can be a major challenge. With stairs and grounds sloping away from a Wealth Area and draining the money, the cures are different, but the idea is the same: contain and uplift the energy.

BATHROOMS: ENERGY DOWN THE DRAIN Bathrooms in your Wealth Area are the biggest challenge. You already have water, symbol-izing money, going down the drain several times a day. This is a red flag. What to do if you have a bathroom in your Wealth Area? First, keep the toilet lid closed. Open toilets are powerful symbols of energy, and cur-rency, going down the drain. Every time you flush your toilet, you forcefully activate the down-the-drain energy. Is your toilet lidless? Please get a lid, put it in place, and keep it closed! You can laugh and en-gage your Creative Current imagining Dave Barry discussing feng shui, men, and toilets. Yet the only way you will learn to trust these feng shui actions is to take little steps and experiment with the enhancements.

Second, place a full-length mirror on the outside of the bathroom door. This is the strongest cure. Bathrooms also contain sinks, bathtubs, and showers. This is where we let go of all kinds of waste, sending it down the drain with lots of water. The full-length mirror on the out-side of the bathroom door in the Wealth Area is to contain all of this down-the-drain energy. Set an intention and ask the mirror to contain the energy and prevent it, and your money, from flowing into the bath-room and down the drains. Keep the bathroom door closed to allow the mirror to both contain and stabilize the energy flow in your space and create a new pattern with the mirror.

If the door to the bathroom opens opposite your front door, then without any cures, you and your guests will want to use the bathroom as soon as they enter and often during their stay. Remember to keep the mirrored bathroom door closed and the toilet lid down.

If there is an open bathroom area that is off of or part of a bedroom, and you cannot add a door that you keep closed, hang a crystal in the doorway or archway between the bathroom and the bedroom, or create a barrier with a curtain of beads between the two areas. You can also create the illusion of a barrier with some fabric hanging down from the ceiling. Midway between the toilet and the opening, hang another clear, round, multifaceted crystal from the ceiling. Use a colored string or ribbon that harmonizes with the area of the Ba-gua you are enhancing. The crystals and draped fabric are to hang down in increments of nine—either nine, eighteen, twenty-seven, or more inches.

Closing the toilet lid is the most important first action step to take. It's one small step for abundance. Then step out and get a full-length mirror for the bathroom door and keep the door closed. This book is not about rushing headlong to correct everything in one day, possibly creating a flood, hurricane, or tsunami. It's about flowing with the current. Step by step and easy as she goes are the watchwords.

I am reminded of a story that still pains me. In 1997 I visited a lovely jewelry store on Madison Avenue in New York City. In talking with the owners, all men and lively storytellers, I learned that they once had five stores but were now down to one. Wonder what I noticed as I walked around? In their Wealth Area was a bathroom with a lidless toilet. It was only for the staff, all men. In a place of honor, on the Wealth Area wall facing into the store, were pictures of one owner's nephew and his horses, riding school, and stable. The bathroom was on the other side of this wall of honor. The nephew was prospering while the jewelry stores were going down the drain. After much talk, I brought up the subject, but the owners had no interest in feng shui, and I walked away with a heavy heart.

WINDOWS Here's an example of a leaky vessel: Modern office buildings are not built with the idea of containing energy, especially the energy of a Wealth Area. A wall of floor-to-ceiling windows creates an expansive view and also allows energy to leak out. Would you leave your money lying around for people to take whatever amount they wanted? Walls of too many windows in a Wealth Area allow your energy to be taken; in fact, you are sending it away.

To contain the energy, place green plants along the windows or place credenzas or low furniture in front of the windows. To totally block chaotic energy from entering, perhaps from fast-moving traffic, close the shades or create a "wall" of green plants. To diffuse energy from the outside, hang faceted round crystals in the windows with a colored cord, in increments of nine, that harmonize with the Ba-gua area you are enhancing. Add a valance, again hanging down in increments of nine inches, half-inches, or feet to contain some of the energy.

Too few windows create a boxed-in or cavelike feeling. Make sure there is adequate lighting, and add plants and pictures of the outdoors. Change the pictures to harmonize with the seasons. Place a picture of a pond or lake in the Wealth Area to enhance wealth accumulation.

DOORS Doors are important! Energy enters and leaves through doors and doorways, and the Ba-gua is oriented from the main entrance to a room, building, or plot of land. Notice whether you have a doorway in your Wealth Area. Here you want to accumulate the energy and control how fast it leaves, so place a small mirror above the inside doorframe to slow down the exiting energy. Back doors symbolize indirect opportunities, so make sure that your back door opens up to a wide pathway, symbolizing the broad potential for financial growth and abundance. If the Wealth Area door is directly opposite the entrance door, place a screen or plants between the two doors to block the energy that is racing in one door and out the other. If your Wealth Area door is obstructed or bangs up against another door, increase the flow, ease, and accumulation of abundance by removing the obstructions. Enhance this area with colors and other symbols of wealth and abundance. If you have several other doors to the outside, consider keeping your Wealth Area door closed and create a special place in that area that collects energy, such as a table with a fountain or several items with special meaning and value.

Here is something that is unique to my approach to creating abundance. Consider blessing everyone as they come and go from your home. Place an item that symbolically pours a blessing—for example, a cherub or a pair of them with a blessing bowl—above the inside of the main doorway to your home. Then every time you look up or go past the door you are reminded, and feel yourself blessed and perhaps grateful for the reminder. East meets West and both are changed.

STAIRS Ready for some fun? Using your Creative Current, imagine yourself standing at the top of a flight of stairs with a handful of marbles and a Slinky. Now gently release both and watch. Where and how do they flow? Take note of where they came to rest. Most of us spend little time noticing how energy actually flows down stairs. It doesn't just flow where we walk, it moves and careens from one area to another.

Energy flows down stairs and right out the door that is at the bottom. It flows especially fast out a door directly opposite the stairs. The goal is to contain and even slow down the flow. Gently curved staircases actually slow down the flow of energy, as do landings. Open stair steps allow the energy to slip between the steps and crash to the bottom.

To uplift the energy, hang a round crystal halfway between the bottom stair and the doorway, again in increments of nine from the ceiling. If you cannot reach your ceiling, then place a small mirror above the doorway. A round or octagonal mirror, as large as is aesthetically pleasing and centered above the door, is ideal. Do not use a convex or concave mirror in this area. Both focus the energy too much. You want people to use the stairs to come and go, but not at a fast and furious rate. Various feng shui schools caution against using a painted Ba-gua mirror in the house. I agree. Why? Such a mirror is small and usually convex or concave, so it focuses a lot of energy back at the stairs or any other space inside your home. Being comfortable inside your living space is also a basic tenet of feng shui.

SPIRAL STAIRWAYS Spiral stairways are challenging, because the energy flow is not stable. Like whirlpools and drastic stock market adjustments, spiral stairways bore energy downward from the upper floor. Getting to the upper floor is difficult, like trying to go upstream without a paddle. Spiral stairs also allow energy to slip between each open stair step, fall and crash to the bottom area. Whatever energy is still flowing on the stairs rushes down very quickly on the small pie-shape steps. These pie-shape steps are also very dangerous for people to walk on, especially when they are carrying things.

To ground and stabilize the energy, place some green plants at the bottom. The next cure is to wrap some upward-flowing material, fabric or ivy, on the hand railing to encourage moving up to the next level. Last, hang a crystal above the bottom stair, in nine-inch increments from the ceiling, to raise the energy. For an extra boost, place a light near the top of the stairway to uplift the energy. Leave the light on for several days to raise the energy flow.

SLOPES Sometimes the land slopes away from the Wealth Area inside a building or where the building's Wealth Area is missing. Here it's important to contain the energy and stabilize it. Uplifting it would be ideal. Leveling the ground is an option for a missing Wealth Area. Stabilize the sloping land with a patio, large rock, planter, or tree in keeping with the other landscaping and the style of the building. A working fountain or a light shining back up toward the building would uplift the energy.

For a missing Wealth Area, planting a tree or installing a patio or light would work nicely to square off the corner. A working fountain with a pond and plantings in purple, or green and red combined would be outstanding. When you first complete the cures, leave the light on and the fountain running for several weeks to set the energy in motion. Later you can turn the light off during the day.

FIREPLACES Fireplaces are not necessarily challenges, yet if one is out of balance it will become an issue. I include fireplaces because of the going-up-in-smoke or going-down-in-flames comments about money.

Fireplaces influence homes and, indirectly, businesses. The Wealth Area of a business owner's home is most important, while the homes of major officers and managers are less important. Fireplaces where the Five Elements are out of balance can be a challenge, and energy can shift very quickly.

Let's walk through this step by step, a type of fire walking. To produce any heat with a fireplace, you first have to put the fuel, such as wood, in place and open the flue for air or wind to enter and exit. When you light the fuel, smoke goes up the chimney and you get some heat. To keep the fire going, you have to add more fuel, more wood, feeding the fire to keep it going while some energy goes up the chimney with the smoke. Air is also sucked from the room up the open flue with the smoke. Then once the fire is cool, you throw the ashes away.

Remember all the fuel that goes up in flames . . . are you getting the drift? An out-of-balance fireplace in a Wealth Area can symbolize fuel—money—going up in flames with a raging fire, while you keep feeding fuel to keep the fire going, like feeding more money to keep your life or the life of your business going. You either buy or chop your own firewood so your money or life energy literally goes up in smoke in your Wealth Area!

What to do? First laugh. Then pay attention to what is happening in your life and your business. Are you literally feeding money to a business and seeing no or very little results, as if it is going down the drain? Or is your money being consumed as if it is going up in flames? This would be much faster than going down the drain with a leak somewhere. Take some deep breaths and set an intention, in very positive language, for your money to grow and the actions you take to cure this imbalance to be for your highest good. Then close the flue, empty the ashes out and bury them in your yard so something can grow from them, even symbolically. Keep the flue closed when you are not using the fireplace.

Center yourself, bless your fireplace, and set an intention that only actual fuel goes up the chimney and that your money and your wealth continue to grow even as you use the fireplace. Look at the Five

Element Regenerative (Destructive) Cycle on page 31 and notice what element is missing and which one is in abundance around your fireplace. Then enhance your fireplace Wealth Area with a containing cycle of the Five Elements, where fire is supported by wood, which is supported by water, which is supported by earth. Adding several elements, water to wood to fire, create a gentle cycle; try adding a fountain with a pondlike effect and several green plants. Adding water alone would put out the fire, the movement of energy and the passion.

Note in your Travel Log what you did and pay attention to your money flow, your business, and your life. Be prepared for cycles of change. You are repatterning an area and flow. If within six months you do not see any difference, your fireplace is very powerful and your own actions and intention alone are not strong enough to turn the tide. You need a professional to symbolically close and seal the flue, to look at your situation to see if you overlooked anything, and to add a very powerful intention using energy from the lineage of the ancient feng shui masters. Yes, I could include this information in this book, but for it to really work, you need to be connected to the feng shui lineage, and that takes a connection to a teacher over time where information, energy, and blessings are exchanged.

HELPFUL PEOPLE, ANGELS, AND BENEFACTORS If you do need additional help, there are always people who are eager, able, and desire to be of assistance. Few of us have done anything major without some assistance from other people. Even fewer accomplish things without the help of the Divine Spirit—whether we recognize it or not. The larger the idea, desire, and project, the more assistance is required to move forward with ease toward your dream.

Align yourself with the energy of a great and wise team and consider enhancing this area at the same time or even before you enhance your Wealth Area. Use black and white or gray to honor and draw the energy of benefactors to you. Place pictures and symbols of the highest beings of a Divine nature that you can imagine and believe in to assist you in achieving your heart's desires. Then add those of many other people, perhaps in a collage or picture album that you place in your Helpful People Area.

One woman I know set up an altar with a gold cloth for wisdom and statues and pictures of angels, Christ, a golden Buddha, several black leather-bound books of wisdom, and a candle to represent the light. That very week, several people offered her assistance and things shifted in a positive direction for her regarding her Wealth and Abundance.

Career, Fame, and Reputation

Two other areas of the Ba-gua that are influenced by and affect your wealth and abundance are your Career, and Fame and Reputation areas. The challenges and solutions for them are similar for your Wealth Area, except for the colors and symbols you use to enhance these areas. Use black and gold for your Career Area while red, purple, and gold (for wisdom) enhance Fame and Reputation. We roll out the red carpet to really enhance the energy of your reputation and add the necessary fire energy so you can step out and shine in your career and life. Career and Fame areas are also great places for a Treasure Map with your long-term dreams and a list of your short-term goals. If you place a fountain in your Career Area, consider putting it on a timer that keeps business hours. Leaving it running 24/7 gives the subtle message that your career also runs even when you are at leisure. That is fine for accumulating wealth and a positive reputation, but those long hours will leave you little time for anything besides your career as you continue on your journey to abundance. Having your fountain rage 24/7 in your career area may be your undoing. You may have so many opportunities and so much work that you truly accomplish very little, your expenses may grow out of control, and your entire life will become unbalanced. Feng shui and the Ba-gua are about creating balance, and this includes time away from your career.

Bottom Line

What is your own bottom line, your final answer, where everything is reduced to your most basic response? Here are some questions for your Travel Log. Give yourself permission to feel all of your emotions and body sensations as you consider them. Listen to all of your thoughts and imaginings, ponder them, and log your responses.

- Am I willing to do the exercises and tell myself what is true for me?

- Am I ready to set sail in a vessel that is rock solid and watertight?

- Am I willing to experience more integrity in my life?

- Am I willing to begin streamlining my space?

- Am I willing to enhance my Wealth Area?

- Am I open to abundance?

If so, the River of Gold awaits you.

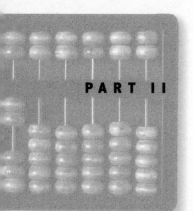

PART II

THE RIVER OF GOLD

In this section the other currents come into focus one by one, showing off their strong points and challenges, their individual patterns, and then all of the currents combine to create the River of Gold—the flow of abundance into your life.

4

The Body Sensations Current

When you are in the womb, the Body Sensations Current is the first to engage, and it bursts forth on the scene with your first breath and cry. This is the most active current during your early years, delighting your caregivers with your first eye contact, finger grasps, words, and steps. It is also the current that contributes to your early challenges in recognizing and appropriately responding to your full bladder or bowel as you enter the Terrible Twos. Some of the major challenges of your later life arise from the potential conflicts around these events. Once those milestones are passed, your Body Sensations Current is often dismissed as not important until puberty. Then the unmistakable body sensations and sexual energies show up, adding to the interesting stresses that arise during the typical challenges of becoming an adult.

Sending this current underground leads to many interesting complications in adulthood. People who do this do not recognize the early warning signals from their body regarding tension and discomfort from particular sitting or standing positions. These signals of tension, tingling, aches, or stiffness alert you to possible trouble down the road. If you ignore them, you take no corrective action when the problem is small. If you freeze this current out of your awareness eventually you'll end up with a restricted flow of energy, a limited range of movement in your body, and a more limited range of options in your life. You'll have to spend your money and time on the accumulated physical stresses and breakdowns of your body rather than taking expansive action to create more abundance and have fun.

Your Body Sensations Current contributes to

- When and how you take action

- Your ability to integrate your intuitions and emotions

- Your preferred style of doing new and innovative things

- Sensing ch'i, the flow of energy in your environment

- Feeling and enjoying a sense of abundance

My goal in this book is to enhance your inflow of money, increase your net worth and wealth and your experience of abundance. Increasing your money flow begins with being sensitive to the energy flow in your body. Participating with more money means participating with more energy, opening up to more flow rather than shutting it off. This is true for your environment, your bank account, your body, and your profession. In this chapter I will address some intangible and subtle things you may have never associated with your bank account.

Feeling Sensations

Everyone can develop a way of perceiving alignment and harmony. It begins with feeling at ease in your own body: the feng shui of the self. Noticing what is moving, even subtly, and seeing if there is any pressure, tension, or any other sensation that signals any blockages to flowing more freely, is part of the feng shui of the self. Gently flexing and moving parts of your body as you breathe, sit, or stand creates harmony with the subtle flow of all life. Sitting or standing rigidly upright, stiff and tight, as if nothing is moving, is out of harmony with reality. There is movement and flow in your body all the time. Your blood flow, heartbeat, and breathing in and out confirm this, as do all of the neurological impulses that occur as you simply sit or lie down.

Right now, scan your body, noticing whatever sensations are present. Sensations include tingling, tightness, pressure, a flow of sensations like an electrical current, heat, twitching, cold, tension, spasm, throbbing, an itch, hunger, and aches. You may have a much larger list. I purposely did not use the term "pain." By itself, "pain" does not convey much information, as there are no qualities included when you name it. The term "pain" also has become attached to the judgment of negativity, as if all pain is bad. Your body sensations are trying to get your attention. They say "Pay attention to me" and imply that you have been ignoring something important. Paying attention when the signal is small and subtle, and taking some positive action, can head off a much larger signal later, preventing what is often termed "pain." Paying attention will lead you to discovering your own particular body signals.

Your five senses—smell, sight, touch, taste, and hearing—are all body sensations and add to the richness of your life. Your breathing, your movement preferences, as well as how you respond to challenges are all body actions. Making decisions when you are tired, which is a full-body sensation, can lead to missed details in an analysis and less than ideal results. The late founder of Sony shared that he figuratively "swallowed" a business deal to see how it would "sit" with him. If he had indigestion, felt ill, or "off," he took that as a valid signal and did not pursue that course of action.

Feeling Energy

Our bodies feel energy flow, whether there is more or less, and they can identify a particular flavor, frequency, or signature. Not being sensitive to the energy flow means we miss some subtle signals from our bodies. Sensitivity to energy flow and its different nuances is a body sensation. For example, hunches, often called gut reactions, are a very subtle sensation in your body that signals "pursue this" or "danger there." Hunches are, in fact, credited with many financial successes if you hear the story behind the official story.

Action Step

A quick way to feel energy flow is to rub your hands together back and forth, palm to palm, until they tingle and feel warm. When you stop, hold your palms very close together and feel the sensations. Then slowly move your hands farther apart and then closer together. Notice and feel any changes. Doing this with your eyes closed allows you to focus on fewer stimuli, to become more sensitive to just your palms. Rubbing your palms in circles may give you different sensations. Try it.

Doing this with another person is even more interesting. Rub your own palms together while he rubs his palms, then place your palms very close to your partners', but not touching. Feel any sensations, then slowly move your palms farther apart and then closer together. Do this several times and notice any differences. Try this over several days, and notice the sensations. See if a different partner causes a different sensation.

You feel more alive when your energy flows. Allow the feeling of tingling and streaming sensations of energy on your skin to open up the tap of your Body Sensations Current into your life. Remember trying to wake up a hand or foot that has fallen asleep due to constricted movement and blood flow? The tingling sensations signal you are waking what had been asleep.

Practical Uses: Detecting Dubious Business Deals

Tuning in and using your Body Sensations Current to make decisions about money matters may seem odd to you right now. Yet once you have learned to read the signals and to decipher the messages, your Body Sensations Current can save you heartaches and money.

Your body sensations are what alert you to the early stages of the con game. Here someone is taking you into her confidence so she can eventually take advantage of you and your money. Early on something may signal to you—some body sensation—that things are not quite right. It may be a tingling sensation in a specific place on your body, or certain muscles may twitch or tense up, or you may have the sensation that your hair is standing on end. It is not a big deal at this stage, but information is beginning to trickle in. Later, when you go over the situation, the signals will be more obvious, but the earliest ones are very subtle. You may simply feel a bit "off" as you listen to the person. If you were to say something at that stage of your information gathering, the con artist or other people would say how odd you are, and she would continue with the transaction. Only later, when there are lots of signals and clues, does the game become obvious.

Lucille shared with me that she had been taking her car to the same repair shop for many years and knew the owner. The shop was sold and the new owners hired several new employees. She felt okay with most of them, but there was one that just put her off. He seemed nice enough, but for some reason—she couldn't explain why—she just had an odd feeling, as if her skin was itching, whenever she was near him. It took extra effort, but she made sure she didn't allow him to interact with her or her car. Over time he did several things that were dishonest and was let go when they were discovered. The new owners had been taken in as well, and were surprised when Lucille shared her information with them. They had experienced no "extra" information. Later Lucille spoke with another customer and learned that he also had had a strange body sensation when interacting with the man in question, but had ignored it, much to his chagrin.

Being sensitive to and honoring your own early signals and sensations is often a trial-and-error process. The errors will include financial losses. Ugh! Maybe I can save you some money and some unpleasant experiences by alerting you to pay attention to your early-warning signs. Signals like a tingle along your spine that shows up repeatedly, or the way a muscle pulls slightly, perhaps the twitch of your eye, mouth, or cheek, some particular itch, or a pressure in your "gut" are some other body sensations that you may begin to notice. All of these are signals to pay more attention to a message or activity that is not what it seems to be.

Another place where your early, subtle signals come into play are with deals that seem to add up, even very nicely, but are disasters waiting to happen as you turn the corner. Here your rational mind goes through its motions and the numbers add up when you read the literature, but there is something that nags at you, something that seems to be not quite right when you tune in to your sense of your body and flow. You may be feeling a pull or tug in your torso, or you feel out of alignment from your head down your spine—and this feeling goes away when you consider not moving forward with this transaction. Other signals are feeling as if you are pushing something up a hill, or you have the sensation of falling down when you consider this financial situation. Perhaps you experience a sense of hesitancy that is different from your normal sense of caution, where your body sensations may become active and are different from just feeling afraid to take the plunge. Notice whether you have an old pattern showing up, one that you might call procrastination or avoidance. Pay attention to the subtle signals from your own body as you move toward this financial opportunity and as you move away from it. If these sensations go away when you consider not taking the planned action, pay attention. None of us can see into the future with any real accuracy, however we can feel energy and how it flows or stops. We can feel the tide turning if we are sensitive to the subtle influences all around us. If taking action doesn't feel right, honor and go with that.

For example, Ralph shared with me that he felt a very subtle shift inside his body as he was listening to a sales pitch about a new product—one that he "had" to buy for his company, according to a new sales representative. It worked well, the documentation seemed to be in order, and the price was reasonable, yet he paid attention to his odd sensation and said he would consider it again—later. A short time later it turned out that the product was discontinued. It seems that there had been some misinformation within the company about the product's reliability and the new rep didn't even know what had happened. An odd sensation from the Body Sensations Current alerted Ralph to a very subtle situation and saved him some money and grief.

STRENGTHENING YOUR SENSES Here are a couple of games you can play to hone your Body Sensations Current.

- Stand at a bank of elevators in your building and tune in to yourself; decide which elevator to wait for by using your body sensations to indicate which elevator door will open next.

- Tune in and sense when to call a friend and notice whether she says that she was just about to call you.

- Pause and consider who is calling you before you answer your phone.

- When you have the idea to contact someone, pay attention to if and when he contacts you.

Another way to develop your own awareness is to notice your own signals when you read something, perhaps a mystery, or attend a movie. With mysteries, the main character may have a particular body sensation that signals something is not quite right. When watching movies, your own body sensations are very alive and flowing, and there is little financial risk involved. Pay attention to your own early and subtle body signals about what will or will not happen next.

When you begin to trust your sensations more, you can use them to make larger life decisions, such as when to buy a small asset. You may go to buy something and find that it is on sale. Or you may feel an impulse to go for a walk that connects you with an answer to a nagging issue at work. Keep track of your signal and the results in your Travel

Log. Later, when you have tested your signals and found them to be reliable, use them to decide when to buy or sell a larger asset when there are few other financial indicators. Relying solely on something new and untested is not wise, yet including your subtle signals as part of your analysis will lead to sounder decisions and more long-term abundance.

Notice how you interact with subtle signals, such as a penny lying on the ground. Consider Alan's experience. "I had been grousing to Suzan about the lack of opportunities in my current position when she scattered a handful of coins on the floor and asked me to pick them up. I went for the quarters first, hesitated, then picked up the dimes. I left the rest without a second glance and sat down. Suzan allowed the silence to fill the space. I finally told her, with quite an edge to my voice, that I thought the little ones were not worth my time. She smiled and asked me what I was paying her, by the minute. I was dumbfounded, then angry, and exploded, 'How can you expect me to pay attention to all of the worthless little things that go on?' I shook for a while, took several deep breaths, and realized my dad used to say that to my mother—about us kids.

"Suzan then asked me to pick up the rest of the coins, moving first like my dad and then like my mother. After shifting back and forth for a while and pondering some questions, I realized that I was missing out on the little signals from my boss and colleagues that would translate into more opportunities and eventually more money. Instead I had been holding myself aloof and rigid, like my dad."

Alan was not focused on his priorities, ignoring coins, subtle signals, and smaller opportunities for abundance. We created some games for these issues, including what was missing in his career and in his life so he could play with each of these areas. Alan began to see the connection among his thoughts, body movement patterns, and ability to take action regarding his financial abundance. You also will be able to see some of your own patterns and make connections as you ponder and integrate this information.

Each of us moves in recognizable patterns. We also respond in predictable ways, called habits or patterns. We function on automatic pilot based on prior patterns that were set down early in our lives. Recognizing where you engage your own pattern allows you to take some deep full breaths and open up space in your mind and body, so you can engage in a new way. The phrase "If you always do what you've always done then you'll always get what you've always gotten" comes into clearer focus. If you desire more financial abundance, then moving in an abundant manner, flowing with the vibration of abundance, means you have lots and lots of movement options. You can then take action quickly when the situation calls for that energy pattern and go slowly when that is the wise response.

Interacting with Money

Where do you keep your cash? Have you embraced it, or do you keep it at arm's length—or even lose it? Do you keep your bills and loose change close to your body and in some sort of order? Is it neatly tucked away in a wallet and coin purse? Or do you have to look through many pockets of your clothes and/or little sections of your purse to find your money? Is there any correlation between how you embrace with your body and how you embrace your money, checkbook, and keep your financial records?

"How you do one thing is how you do your life" is an interesting concept. At first you may argue with it. That's okay. Just realize that you are revealing a part of your preferred pattern. Pay attention to how you embrace and interact with your family, your friends, your life experiences, and your money. You have a pattern in each of these areas.

Consider using a money holder/container that your heart embraces, one that feels abundant, so that you have a tangible experience of open-hearted abundance when you touch your own money. If your cash flow says "Stop! don't buy anything right now," then honor that awareness and use the money holder that you currently own. Adding to your debt or creating a financial constriction is not the goal. Go with the flow and the abundance that is happening right now. More is coming.

Interacting with money constantly involves your Body Sensations Current. Someone puts money in your hand. First it was your parents, maybe grandparents and other relatives, then perhaps an employer from a part-time job, then a full-time one. You may combine your income stream with your partner's. You began by putting money into your wallet, handkerchief, or other safe place. Eventually you have a checking account, savings account, credit cards, and accounts at other companies and institutions. All of these require some "handling" by your body, whether physical or verbal.

Action Step

Now ponder how your body responds to this flow of financial energy. How do you handle your money? Do you engage your rational mind and place this energy in a safe "container" where it can grow and where it is available to use for maintaining your life and your lifestyle? Or do you quickly scatter this energy, purchasing all kinds of things you either do not wear or use, or imbibe large quantities of food or spirits? Do you lose your money either somewhere in your home or in your clothes or money container? Or do you lose your money with your pattern of investing it?

Remember, money is energy, and the flow of money is a current of energy in your life. How you honor, use, and protect your money is how you embrace it. Open-hearted embracing of your money is the recommended pattern so that you can flow with more ease and have some breathing room in your life.

Breathing Room

Knowing how your Body Sensations Current flows leads to being able to step outside of the box of your known responses into new patterns and create abundance with greater ease. These steps will also lead to new methods of saving and investing your money. That awareness ought to give you some breathing room and an inner sense of abundance. Now take a deep breath and ask yourself: Are you ready for some new information? Ready for some things you have not considered connected to your flow of abundance?

Breathing is one thing that can go on without our attention, and it easily responds to the gentlest focus. It is also something that stops dead on a dime in times of high stress. As a protective mechanism, people hold their breath when they perceive danger. Imagine suddenly facing a tiger; your life is in immediate danger. Freezing and holding your breath are natural and immediate responses. That split second of freezing allows you to identify where the danger is and in what direction and how fast it is moving. However, continuing to hold your breath as you run away leads to feeling breathless, and you tire very quickly. Running away requires a huge amount of air. If your old pattern is to hold your breath when you experience a challenge, you will be limiting your ability to respond. Becoming aware of your patterns with your breath allows you to expand your range of movement and options when a financial challenge appears.

How you breathe also has a direct effect on your clarity of thinking. Connecting the two may be a totally new idea for you, a leap from point A to D or beyond. Breathing affects how much oxygen is in your blood, which affects how clear your thinking can be, which affects the clarity of your financial analysis and your decision making, which all contribute to your abundance. Ever say "I just can't concentrate"? One contributing factor to your ability to concentrate is how much oxygen your brain is receiving, and that is influenced by how deeply you breathe.

Here is how it works: Your brain cells use oxygen as their primary food, much more so than sugar or protein or carbohydrates. The cells in your brain are surrounded by a network of capillaries, so small that they allow only one red blood cell at a time to stream through, in single file. Picture a barge going up and down the river, one vessel at a time passing through the locks, picking up and releasing "cargo" and then starting over again, as in the circulation of goods and the flow of currency. As your red blood cells flow through the capillaries in your lungs, they release carbon dioxide and pick up oxygen molecules. The cells now carry that oxygen and release it in your brain and body, feeding your brain so you can think clearly. Your red blood cells do this more times than you can imagine as they circulate in your bloodstream. Now this is important. The way you get oxygen to the red blood cells is by taking a breath—literally filling your lungs with air that contains oxygen. Not having oxygen available for your red blood cells means your brain and body cells will eventually starve. Now here's the catch! Notice the subtle movement of your eyelids. What happened? Did you stop all other movement to pay attention to your eyelids? Including holding your breath? Take notice. Are you now breathing, deep and full, or still holding your breath? Something so subtle as saying "Stop!" can also stop your breathing! Now gently exhale, then take a breath and relax.

Most people pay no attention to how they breathe. Fortunately, breathing just happens. Breathing is also one of the activities of the body that the Rational and Emotional currents can influence by increasing, deepening, or holding the breath. Let me show you something—I call it "Living on a Teacup." This may be fine for high tea at some fancy restaurant, especially if you have a new, outrageously beautiful hat and an entourage of servers waiting on you. But breathing up high, just under your shoulders and collarbones, is a lot of work with very little benefit. The lobes high up in the lungs are narrow, somewhat pointed, and smaller than those below. There simply are not enough capillaries in your upper lobes to oxygenate, in one breath, all the blood that is in your lungs. Instead only about a teacup's worth of blood receives fresh oxygen. The rest of your blood carries on without refreshment. No wonder you feel tired! You're starving for more air and more breath. Compensating by breathing faster doesn't do the trick. What to do? Use the lower lobes! Breathe down into your belly, allowing the larger lower lobes to fill with air first. Then the smaller ones will fill automatically.

Breathing. Right now lightly place your attention on your breathing. Resonate with what is happening right now with your body. How deeply are you breathing? Have you changed your pattern just by noticing? What are your elbows doing? Can you sense them? What about your waist? Now notice your shoulders. Notice your rib cage. Is anything moving as you inhale and exhale?

Notice how much of your body moves, and where, as you take in a breath. Feel the air move into your nose and down your windpipe. Notice your shoulders. Do they rise and fall with each breath, or are they relaxed? What about your abdominal area? Does it expand with ease as you breathe, or is your waistband so tight that nothing could move if your life depended on it? Notice how you exhale. Do you simply let go, or do you use a lot of effort to blow your air out?

If your shoulders rise and fall and your abdominal area is still, you are breathing into your upper lobes and expending a lot of effort in the process. Most people breath up high in their upper lobes. This is upside-down breathing. Take it easy! Use the lower lobes and allow your diaphragm to do the work.

Taking a full abundant breath, also called diaphragmatic breathing, is easy. It begins with relaxing and breathing down first into the lower lobes of your lungs. You can see this gentle expansion of your abdominal area. Here is a place where bottom up is preferable to top down.

ABUNDANT BREATHING Abundant breathing is the easiest form of drawing and releasing a breath. In fact, you are just remembering that you breathed this way as a baby in the womb. You probably continued until your first big event, where you held your breath and shifted into upside-down breathing. Time for another shift—to the breath of life, abundant breathing, that is deep and full. Many people assume they know how to do this, until they actually give it a try. Laughing kindly at yourself is advised. You can do this while sitting or lying down— whichever feels more comfortable to you.

Sitting. Move slightly forward in your chair, sitting on your "sit bones" rather than your tailbone and your slumped back. Uncross your legs and allow your waist to relax and air to flow into your lower lobes first as you inhale. Rocking forward on your "sit bones" and slightly flexing your pelvis as you inhale gently exercises your hip joints and allows your abdomen to expand. A very subtle motion is all that is needed. Allowing your head to turn upward, lifting your chin ever so slightly as you take in a breath, enables your rib cage to open up and expand more easily. Your windpipe also flexes slightly. Your lower belly expands and your lower lobes fill at the same time. The middle and upper lobes of your lungs will automatically fill in sequence and without effort. Then as you exhale, you let go and look slightly downward, causing your spine to flex in harmony as your pelvis begins to rock the other direction. You can do this sitting, standing, and lying down. These movements can be very subtle if you are in public and you want your breathing to seem invisible. You also can have lots of fun with a larger range of movements. One of the complaints people have as they age is their lack of flexibility. Abundant breathing gently flexes your spine and hip joints while clearing the cobwebs out of your mind.

Your diaphragm is a muscle—one you probably ignore until you have the hiccups. Then you experience the force of this muscle. You use it to breathe deeply into your lungs by letting go of your belly so your diaphragm can flex down and your lungs can expand from the larger lower lobes. The only place your lungs can expand to easily is down into the open space of your soft belly. Taking a deep abundant breath down into your abdomen also gently massages all of your internal organs.

You may wonder about your belly losing its tone and going flabby. Actually, holding a muscle tense all of the time leads to muscle fatigue. After a while the tensed muscle will be unable to respond again. Once it has rested and recovered, then it can respond and tense up when requested or required. Keeping your diaphragm flexible and moving adds to the ease in your life.

Breathing Flat on Your Back. If you are having trouble coordinating all of the movements to breathe more deeply, lie down on your back, preferably on the floor or a similar firm surface, with your arms at your sides. Flex your knees so your feet are flat on the ground and spread as far apart as your hips. You know you have your feet in the right place when your knees stay up effortlessly—even if you doze off. To begin, gently rock your pelvis in an arching motion, forward toward the ceiling, and then relax and release. This is very subtle; not even an inch will appear between your back and the floor. If you place your hand in the small of your back, you will just feel the pressure lift when you have it right. If your hips are stiff, this may take a few repetitions before you move freely.

Once your pelvic movement feels smooth, then coordinate it with your breathing. Your arms are down at your sides with your hands relaxed. As you rock your pelvis forward, inhale fully, then release your efforts, let go, and exhale as your pelvis relaxes to the floor. One motion flows into the other. Your head also will move slightly, following the rocking movement from your pelvis up your spine if you allow it. You may notice your hands gently move, palms turning outward, away from your body, as you inhale and rotate in toward your body as you release and exhale. Allow that motion to enlarge slightly so your hands are palm up at the peak of your inhale and palm down toward the floor as you release and exhale.

Whenever you realize your breathing is out of sync you can reset yourself, doing either the sitting or the flat-on-your-back exercise. Resettling yourself through the lying-on-your-back breathing exercise every morning before you begin to dress and again at night before you go to sleep, will take a lot of kinks out of your body and your life. Over time you will continue to dissolve any blockages and smooth out the flow of energy through your body with these breathing practices.

BENEFITS OF ABUNDANT BREATHING Paying attention to your breathing and all of its changes will lead to many benefits. Your breath connects you to the energy of feng shui, the movement of the energy of the wind and how it flows and stops. Your sensitivity to your own ch'i is enhanced by your breath, and you can experience larger and larger amounts of energy as your breath smooths out the blocked places in your own body. Noticing your own breath as you enter and move through an environment assists your awareness of the energies that are there and how they flow, whether fast, slow, or blocked. Your body is signaling a significant change when there is a shift in the energy as you move from one area to another and you "catch your breath" or "can't breathe." This sensitivity to the flow of ch'i continues to be enhanced as you regularly practice these breathing techniques.

Breathing deep and full, all the way down into your belly, enhances your blood flow and brain function. No longer will your brain feel nitwitted or befuddled. Inspiration, literally and metaphorically, allows for visionary thinking and opens the door to your natural intuitive gifts. Self-inspiration is not only possible; it costs much less than other people's workshops and books.

With abundant breathing you can enliven yourself at meetings, in airports, when flying, and anytime during your day when you feel tired. Just doing the sitting deep abundant-breathing exercise will allow you to scan your body and reduce any tension that is building. With it you can increase the flexibility of your hip joints and your spine. You can also refocus your thoughts with more ease if your brain is already functioning with a good supply of oxygen. If there is a kaboom! during your day where someone, including you, becomes very sad, angry, or afraid, you can use abundant breathing to flow through the wave of energy and calm yourself. It's great to use when you are considering an issue, looking for a new way to approach something. Abundant breathing, deep and full, also enhances exercise and strenuous effort.

So a short review. Breathing affects thinking. Deep abundant, diaphragmatic breathing provides nourishment for your brain so that you can think more clearly. To clear the cobwebs from your brain, take some easy deep full breaths. For more ease in learning something new, take a deep abundant breath, or several. Remember to breathe down into your lower lobes, with a soft and happy belly. Experience the flow of ch'i, the energy of wind, as it moves with and through your body.

Breath and movement go together. When you are short of breath it is difficult to move quickly. When you experience an out-of-breath sensation then sitting down or stopping all other movement allows you to recover quickly. Abundant breathing enhances a freer range of movement and represents the action component of the Body Sensations Current. Once you begin to breathe abundantly, you can then enhance your movement style and resonate with the energy of an abundant range of movements.

Action Step

Here are a series of questions to ponder and ways to play with and expand the range of your movement style and release the grip of your old patterns:

- Where does your breath begin?

- Can you feel the air moving in and out of your nostrils?

- What is the quality of your mental state?

- Where are you contracted in your body and your financial activities?

- When was the last time you changed the way you wear your hair? How similar is it to what you have worn for the last ten years or what you wore your last year of school?

- Where do you keep doing the same thing over and over even though you are unhappy with the results?

- How do you get up from a sitting position?

Allow yourself to play with your movement patterns and try doing something different every day.

- Where do you collapse or take lots of action—but have little to show for your activity?

- When you take quick action, are you happy with the outcome?

- Where do you block your flow?

- How do you interact and participate with other people's money?

Do some free-form movement every day. Keep changing the way you move with every movement, exploring different styles, tempos, and fluidity. Do this for five minutes or more every day. Notice any tendency to repeat a motion before you move to the next one. Notice where your body is tight, tense, or experiencing a contraction. Notice when and where you lose your balance. Pay attention to any change in these sensations as you play with your range movement styles: fast and jerky, slow and smooth, fast and smooth, slow and jerky, controlled and jerky, marching quickly or slowly, waltzing around, then free-form slow dancing.

Do you see a correlation with how you have gone about creating a savings or spending plan in the past and your body movements? The feng shui of the self is about being in balance as you create harmony and flow from one situation and experience to another. Awareness of your breath, breathing deeply, creates harmony with the cosmic ch'i, the breath of life and abundance.

Now consider how you would like to envision your life and abundance.

5

The Emotional Current

I t may seem odd—even scary—to allow an accountant to engage in emotional communications. We accountants are supposed to crunch numbers and talk about money, not delve into the murky world of emotions. Yet in reality, financial decisions are driven by emotions. Speak to people's hearts and dreams, and their wallets will follow. Many people take action with their money without understanding the emotional component of their reasoning.

Your emotions influence your behavior regarding money, whether you understand what your emotions are trying to communicate or not. Two classic examples are the selling panics of the stock market and buying something on a hot tip from someone who has no established credibility with you. With the first event, the selling panic, people are afraid that they will be left holding something that is worthless as the whole market drops in value. While with the latter, the noncredible hot tip, they are afraid that there is not enough time for them to be included in the upswing, and they will be left out of the loop. Both of these examples also include a bit of anger or suspicion that other people might be getting more than their fair share. There is also, underneath all of this, a tacit understanding, an unspoken agreement, about what is a "fair share" of abundance. And "fair" can range from everyone having the same, to you having more than me but less than some people, or to the extreme where you have more than anyone else.

Learning the language of your emotions allows you to speak, understand, and take action with authority and clarity. Unfortunately, many of us have either ignored our emotions or thrown them away, forgetting that our emotions are part of us. In essence, we have been telling ourselves—that part of us we can't communicate with and don't understand—to shut up and go away.

THE BIG FIVE

Everyone has emotions. Even people who claim they don't experience certain emotions in fact do, but they are not aware of the signs and signals. Emotions also have many nuances, subcategories, and levels of intensity. Learning to recognize and experience these nuances and intensities and how they affect your decisions is the purpose of this section and of the book.

There are five main or core emotions. People, of all ages, around the world, experience, express, and resist these five core emotions. While you may call these core five emotions something different from what I call them, the emotions are still the same.

The Big Five are:

1. Joy

2. Anger

3. Sadness

4. Fear

5. Sexual feelings

These are the basics that combine with one another and with the Creative, Rational, and Body Sensations currents to create all of the various emotions people experience. All of these emotions present opportunities to go with the flow or to set up a dam and let them accumulate, pushing them underground until you have an undercurrent or freezing them and your life energy. And each emotion has a particular vibrational bandwidth of frequencies that includes a range from its subtle to intense levels. Recognizing these vibrations allows you to resonate with them, allows them to pass through you, leaving you transformed into a more harmonious wave of energy and flow.

Love or a Reasonable Facsimile

You may be wondering why I did not include love with the Big Five. Of the range of emotions, love is the highest vibration. It also has the widest bandwidth, which can and does encompass all other emotions. Picture a very wide bandwidth of frequencies like all of the colors of the rainbow. Along this bandwidth there is the love you have for a friend, a slightly different quality of love for your siblings, somewhat different love for your parents, a notch different again for your pets and your favorite objects, a still different quality for your partner, different again for your profession, and another notch different for your hobby. Your relationship with the Divine Spirit is another place on the frequency of love. In the West we call all of these things love.

There is even the admonition "Love your enemies" that many people try to integrate into their lives. Now, that is a different quality from the others! Vibrating in harmony with the love that the Divine Spirit offers to us—what is called unconditional love—allows us to resonate with the love that encompasses everyone and everything. It is an unconditional and nonjudgmental love beyond what most of us have experienced. We can think about it, engaging the flow of our Rational Current, as we wonder how many angels can dance on the head of a pin. The experience of love, that sense of awe that leaves us speechless and tingling with something almost overwhelming, is the combination of the Body Sensations and Emotional Currents flowing freely.

TRANSFORMED INTO LOVE All of your other emotions can be transformed into love with inspiration. It may take a few or many deep abundant breaths, yet coming into harmony with the inspiration that the Divine Spirit gave us, that deep connection to creativity and possibility, causes a fundamental shift inside toward living in wonder and abundance. At its grandest, love is the atmosphere we are surrounded with. We may not recognize it, but it is there. Even in the midst of unbelievable anger, love is there. And where love is, there is creativity, inspiration, and abundance just waiting to resonate with you.

The wealth that you seek is connected to your own sense and experience of wealth and abundance in your body, mind, and emotions. The symbolic winds and waters are all connected. Thus, enhancing one current's flow enlarges your capacity to experience and remain balanced with any other flow, including that of money. Money is energy, ch'i, flowing energy that is just a different frequency from your breath, your own wind energy and ch'i. Feeling and experiencing a lack of love in your life slows down the flow of wealth and your heart's desires to you. Here is one important exercise you can do on a daily basis to keep love in your life.

OPEN-HEARTED LOVE PROCESS Sit comfortably with your feet on the floor, eyes open or closed, and breathe deeply for five or six breaths. Allow your body to relax and your thoughts to flow on by. Now think of someone or something that you know that you love. This could be a person, an object, or an animal. Experience the love that you feel for and give to that person, object, or animal. Now open your heart and send your love to that person, object, or animal. See your love wash over and fill that person, object, or animal. Continue to breathe deeply and allow this love to return to your open heart. See this love enlarged and enhanced as you send it out to them and receive it back into your own heart. Sit quietly for a minute and experience this flow of love. Now increase the intensity of this love you are giving and receiving by ten times. Fully receive and enjoy this love while continuing to breathe deeply. Let this love wash over your body and fill your thoughts and send it back to wash over them. Enjoy this for a couple of minutes. Now increase the intensity of the love again by ten times, feeling it flow in through your own heart and through your body and out over your entire life. Open your heart even wider to receive all of this cycle of love as you continue to breathe deeply. Surround your love object with a pink bubble. See the energy flow between you cease and allow it to flow back into your open heart. Sit quietly.

When you are ready, gently stretch, wiggle your toes, tap your feet on the floor several times, open your eyes, and come back to the present.

The energy of unconditional love is actually much more intense and much more expansive than this experience. You may or may not be ready to allow that much more energy to flow through your body and your life. Since the focus of this book is on maintaining balance and being grounded as you enlarge the flow of wealth and abundance in your life, I stopped with this level of intensity. One way you will enlarge the flow everywhere in your life is to come back to this experience regularly.

Reexperience this Open-hearted Love Process as often as you choose and as often as you can maintain to your sense of harmony, balance, and ability to do the everyday things—work, laundry, buying groceries, and paying your expenses—in your life. Consider doing it every day for a week or a month and notice how your life and your flow of abundance change. If you seem out-of-sorts from "too much," also do the Cross Crawl in Appendix A to come back into a synchronous flow.

Recognizing Emotions

All people have an outer or public language that they use to communicate their emotions, as well as an inner language they use only with themselves. You communicate the intensity of each emotion by the words you choose, your tone of voice, and your body actions. Emotions are waves of energy. Unfortunately, if your cycle is interrupted—that is, if you do not feel or experience your emotion's full cycle—you will not "get over it." Wherever you hold an emotion back, it will seem to go underground and persist as an energy block in your body and environment. The pressure of a backlog of emotions builds until eventually you cannot contain it. Then the emotions resurface from time to time—when you least expect it—first leaking and then flooding over you and perhaps spraying anyone nearby.

Your awareness and compassion increases when you realize that no one else uses exactly the same words for the same intensity or for the same emotion. Your "irritated" for a low level of anger could be a colleague's word for a level 9 intensity, assuming 10 is the maximum. Here the feng shui question of "Where do you have that emotion placed?" steps into the spotlight. Are you feeling a low level of intensity and ignoring your emotion, or a high level and trying to contain the wave that is crashing over and through you? Imagine a flood with the water rapidly rising, or a gale of hurricane force, to help you see why most people avoid making the connection between money and their emotions. They feel scared. And they imagine they will lose control and drown with the flood of emotions they are holding at bay, if they recognize and actually experience any of them.

Recognizing your emotions so that your inner experiences match your inner and outer words takes practice. To get you started here are some common names many people use for each of the Big Five:

JOY: happy, pleased, overjoyed, tickled pink, ecstatic

ANGER: mad, annoyed, peeved, irritated, torked, pissed, ticked off, enraged

SADNESS: blue, down, depressed, grief-stricken

FEAR: scared, concerned, worried, scared witless, frightened, stressed, terrified

SEXUAL FEELINGS: twitterpated, aroused, "come on, baby, light my fire"

You also have your own preferences.

Action Step

Begin to collect the words you use to express your own emotions. Some of these you use in public, other words are your private stash. Gather them together. You can scatter them randomly on a few pages of your Travel Log or neatly collect them in five separate piles, one for each of the Big Five. Begin to collect your common actions, the things you do and buy, when you are experiencing each of these emotions. Some examples: some people avoid paying bills when they feel afraid, or buy extra goodies to eat when they feel sad. Other people give themselves an expensive present that they can't afford when they're angry, indulge in an expensive and provocative item when their sexual feelings make an appearance, or spend money they've saved on their heart's desires when they feel joyous.

JOY Living in joy, feeling bliss, and experiencing the thrills of life are where most people want to hang out in their emotional life. Many people think the other emotions, such as anger, sadness, and fear, are to be avoided because they are judged as bad or negative. Yet they all come out of the same faucet and are part of the Emotional Current. Constrict and block one and you impact the flow of all of the others.

Some of us were taught that too much joy is dangerous. We close off the nozzle, shutting down the flow, and experience life at a low level of intensity. Eventually we reduce our ability to flow with more energy for all of the currents. We settle for less in all areas of our lives, including money and wealth. You may list people like this under the heading of tightwad, stingy, skinflint, or just poor.

Some of us were taught to grab all there is in one big embrace, turning up the heat and the volume, unsettling ourselves and everyone else around us. We literally take up our space and move into any available space around us vibrating at full force. Joy! Joy!! Joy!!!!! And we wonder why people run for cover when we show up. Our nozzle is wide open all of the time, spraying everyone in range. Probably we never learned how to moderate it, to turn it up and down ourselves. You may call these people overspenders, big-deal chasers, or wild and crazy with money.

Living in joy all of the time is an ideal that we don't often reach here on earth. Someone may be able to do it beyond this place, but not too many flesh-and-blood people have come back in my lifetime to report there is no other emotion besides joy. Stuff happens. Our other emotions still flow and move us up and down the vibrational range. Be careful not to become frozen in any emotion, or to deny what is really happening inside you. Go with the flow. The goal is honesty with yourself and among people who are close to you so the energy can flow freely, and abundance will flow to you. When you feel joy, breathe and vibrate with it, and don't worry about feeling joyful when you are experiencing something else. Breathe into what is happening so the energy cycle can be complete. Abundance comes in many ways, including times that are less joyous than others.

ANGER Anger is an emotion many people deny to themselves and to others. They resist experiencing it in their bodies, shutting down the flow of energy in their lives as well. Anger comes from within your body in response to your boundaries being crossed. Anger also arises in response to other people's boundaries being crossed and our own interpretations of what happened. The training you received from your family, teachers, religious leaders, and playmates affects how you go about expressing your anger. If you learned that having any anger was something bad people did, then in order to be accepted, loved, and thought of as "good," you probably deny your anger—unless you decided to rebel. Then having and expressing anger fits your agenda, your persona, and your intention to rebel. You are probably quite unfriendly when you express your anger.

Feeling and experiencing the full cycle of your anger is neither good nor bad. However when you live with anger, you send it out with every step and action that you take. The energy of such constant anger attracts and gathers the anger that is denied or sent out by other people. You can tune in and feel its heavy, prickly, and sticky energy as you walk through some homes and businesses.

How you go about expressing your anger can have results that you prefer or ones you do not. Whether these results are good or bad, positive or negative, are value judgments. Feeling angry can lead to you judging yourself as bad—unless you deny what is happening. I'm feeling my body contort even as I write this. Since you are angry some of the time, denying that you are is the same as lying to yourself. Lying results in contortions of your mind and body as you hold back the flow of emotional energy. You can fool some people some of the time, yet people who have embraced their own anger cannot be fooled. They know the vibration of anger and how it leaks out when it is suppressed and denied. They also can feel in their body whether someone is smooth or contorting him- or herself.

Men are often more comfortable in acknowledging and experiencing their anger. Yet I know plenty of women who are "anger energy waiting to erupt." Everyone feels angry from time to time. Not embracing your anger—resisting it—means you will draw more anger to you. Embrace your anger, love it, and feel it deeply. Then let it go. Tell yourself the truth—"I feel angry"—and breathe into the hot, prickly energy that flows through your body. Tell yourself the truth when you want to hit, strangle, or injure someone, then breathe deeply and take no outward action. When the anger cycle has passed, then you can talk about your experience. When the energy cycle is complete, you can decide what steps you will take to reestablish your boundaries. Take no action when you are angry. Just breathe and vibrate with the energy.

Taking action with your money when you are angry sends both your money and your angry energy out into the world. You will get back that energy, like attracting like, and the things you purchase will hold that angry energy. This is true whether the money is yours or whether you are working and creating money for someone else, in business, finance, or commerce. Yes, abundance can come with anger attached to it. Just ask anyone who has inherited or received money with lots of rules about how it can be spent. Beneath some of those rules are some anger and the thought "How dare you!"

Anger is a signal that says "Pay attention!" Your anger indicates a boundary has been crossed—yours or someone else's. Heads up! Your current anger is connected to all of the times in your past when your boundaries have been crossed. All of the times in your life that you dismissed your own anger are piled up on top of this current event. Until you clear the backlog, your current response will be out of proportion to the actual event. Allow yourself to cool off before you say or do anything with this current event. Acknowledge your anger to yourself and really consider what it is you want and are willing to receive to reestablish your boundary and flow with abundance. Taking action and spending or withholding money to reestablish boundaries may not be in harmony with your goals and heart's desires. Ask yourself what your goal is. Is it settling an old dispute over your boundaries? Or inner peace and abundance, more wealth and balance in your life? The focus of this book is on maintaining balance as you enlarge the flow of wealth and abundance in your life.

Action Step

Here you're looking for the beginning of a pattern. Has someone ever spent money on you when he or she was angry with you? Has anyone ever withheld money from you when he or she was angry? Now consider how you spend or withhold money when you are angry. Remember the last time you spent money this way. What happened just before you spent the money? Allow yourself to really feel your anger through the full cycle, and let it go. Flow with your experience of anger and begin to separate it from your experiences with money. Allow abundance to flow free of your anger.

SADNESS Many people view sadness as a weakness and avoid it at all costs. Avoiding feeling the sadness from the losses that happen in your life, resisting and denying them, blocks your energy and reduces your aliveness. People move away, friendships end, pets die, people are injured, they die, careers end, whole industries die. People experience disappointments with friends, relatives, coworkers, bosses, and religious leaders. Loss is a real experience of life. Leaning into and breathing through the emotion of sadness, the tears and sense of loss and aloneness, allows you to flow through the experience. Denial and resistance keep you stuck with your hands pushing against the wall of tears and loss, sometimes for years. Allow your tears to flow. Feel and experience all of your life!

Dave, a busy executive, said, "I was becoming aware that I bought a latté every day. I got off the subway and stopped at a fancy shop as I walked to my office. Later in the morning I noticed a burning sensation in my stomach. When I stopped drinking lattés the sensations subsided. I also realized that I didn't even like coffee. Hmmm? I wonder how I got started. Then I remembered the morning subway rides with my dad. We always stopped for a doughnut and he bought a cup of coffee. It was a togetherness ritual we had when I was a child. I resumed it as an adult. He's been dead five years and the latté was a way of connecting. I felt waves of sadness in letting it go that lasted about a week. I also hugged my children more, each time feeling a wave of sadness. By the time I let the waves of sadness go through me, I was feeling that deep connection I used to have. Then I decided to really honor my dad. I used the money I saved from releasing the lattés for some very special outings with my children."

Sadness is an energy that spirals downward and occupies the lower range of the emotional frequencies. Eventually the resistance to feeling sad will weigh you down and cover you like a heavy blanket. Some people say they are "drowning in sadness." And yes, your abundance can flow back to you overlain with sadness. You can work in an environment where you feel sad, such as hospitals and the funeral industry. Relief organizations deal with loss and sadness even as they bring help and hope. Some people inherit money and feel sad about the event that started the money flowing. Money often comes with sadness. Resist your sadness and you may be resisting more money.

Some of us, myself included, feel our sadness first. Tears flow easily. When I walk into an area, I can feel the sadness that a space holds before I register any other emotion. I have to center myself, tune in, and allow myself some time to pick up and resonate with the other emotions that are still there. Working with people, I also tune in to their denied sadness first. Men cry easily in my presence, especially if we are working alone on their challenges with relationships and creating abundance. Many times they admit that they haven't cried in years and are amazed that I consider it natural for a man to cry. There is a cultural prohibition against men crying, with Americans labeling them weak if they do. As a result, many men hold back tears and block the natural flow of a bodily fluid. The feng shui of the self includes flowing with the waters, creating balance and harmony.

Spending money when you are feeling or avoiding your sadness can quickly add up to a large amount. For example, I've noticed some divorced fathers who spend lots of money on their children for toys, things, and fun experiences while denying their own sadness and tears around missing their children as well as the end of their former relationship. They may allow themselves to experience their anger, yet they don't realize that they take their sadness with them to the shopping mall. Some children have never seen their dad cry. For these fathers there is the actual money that is spent plus the hidden cost of not recognizing and experiencing all of their emotions, the full range of life energy. Another example where sadness may be paired with spending lots of money is on funerals, especially for someone you loved. Pay attention and consider expressing your emotions, love and sadness, clearly when you can do it in person. Underneath your spending may flow the message: Spend money and avoid your uncomfortable emotions.

Action Step

Take a moment, get up, and actually push against a wall with both hands. Feel the energy in your body as you try to move this wall. Feel the wall as it resists your efforts. This action anchors in your body a realization about resistance that is deeper than simply talking about resistance. Here you create resonance, where you vibrate with the experience of resistance and eventually find the resolution to the resistance. The issue you are resisting can then dissolve.

FEAR Everyone feels the energy of fear. Many of us are afraid of losing; afraid of being hurt; afraid of being lonely; afraid of old age; afraid of not having enough money, food, clothing, or shelter. Afraid of looking bad, like a fool, afraid of making mistakes . . . what did I miss from your personal list? Fear is an emotion that is denied and avoided in this culture. Yet many of our actions are driven by fear and we continue on, unaware. The energy of fear goes with the actions you take when you feel afraid.

The energy of fear goes with us if we spend money when we feel afraid. Many, many people buy things to cover and deny their fear—things like new clothes, fancy food, or meals out. Some buy new vehicles or boats. They may see their business or industry about to take a downturn, and they buy something just in case they won't be able to afford it later. Underneath their action flows a huge amount of fear. Many people sell investments when they feel afraid. The stock market drops, and suddenly you may decide to sell something that you recently bought with the idea of adding it to your long-term buy-and-hold investments. A classic response to fear is trying to buy earthquake insurance just after an earthquake or flood insurance when there is a flood watch. Some people reach a certain age and suddenly start buying things—motorcycles, fancy trips, sports cars, facelifts—afraid that they no longer measure up. They try to shore themselves up with material items. Many people keep things because they are afraid that they will need them in the future and not have the money or energy to buy them. They might be afraid that the person who gave it to them will be angry if they get rid of the gift. Afraid, afraid, afraid. Much clutter accumulates from denying our fears.

Fear is an energy that spirals downward. Eventually you feel so afraid that you are overwhelmed with this energy. Either you take enormous action to avoid your fears or you freeze. Simply breathe deeply into your fear, giving it some time and space for the wave to crest using the cycles of your breath. Pay attention to the smallest signal that you are feeling afraid, tell yourself the truth, be honest to the penny, and say "I feel afraid." Five deep breaths later the Divine Spirit has filled you with air, begun to clear the cobwebs out of your mind, enlivened the flow of energy through your body, and perhaps inspired you to take some action steps forward.

Action Step

Look around your living space for things you've purchased when you were feeling afraid. Now locate those things that you're afraid to put in storage or to release. Do you love these things? Do they represent open-hearted abundance for you? If not, by when will you take steps to release them and allow them to flow toward someone else?

Where else do you spend money—food, hobbies, entertainment, investments—when you are experiencing or resisting waves of fear? Note these in your Travel Log.

SEXUAL FEELINGS Taboos abound about sexuality, sexual emotions, and body sensations. We either don't touch our sexuality with a ten-foot pole or we are totally out there and in one another's face. We are simply too afraid to face and enjoy our own sexual energy. Most people deny they are experiencing any sexual energy when they are in public. What will other people think about us? Even when it is obvious to anyone around that there is a current of sexual energy between two people, still the charade goes on. "Who, us?" Yet sexual energy is just another frequency of emotional and creative energy, and it's just as important as the other emotions and other currents when it comes to wealth and abundance.

Few of us vibrate with sexual energy, clean and clear, simply enjoying the aliveness of this emotion. Our sexual energy is often coupled with other energy, such as fear; other people overlay their sexual energy with anger. Then there are all kinds of judgmental thoughts surrounding our sexual energy, things like: Nice girls don't. You're just like your philandering father. Only a whore would wear red like that. Men think only with their penises. Nice girls don't enjoy that awful black deed. Everybody knows that men only want one thing from a woman. No man can resist what a woman like that has to offer. These thoughts contract our energy flow and our bodies, tightening the nozzle and leading to a buildup of pressure that eventually leaks out at the most inappropriate time.

You can be overwhelmed by your sexual energy if you deny it exists. When you are in denial, you don't notice the subtle signals when the intensity is low. Your classic response to uprising energy, your Four F Preference, engages, and then you take your classic action steps, either fighting, fleeing, freezing, or fainting. Denial can have some very unfriendly outcomes.

Many of us have done things in response to feeling overwhelmed by our sexual energy, and we judge ourselves harshly. Few of us have been encouraged to embrace all of our thoughts and emotions, to give up judging ourselves and deciding we are bad people, and simply to love ourselves. The Divine Spirit is without judgment. It simply is unconditional love. Embrace yourself and all of your sexual experiences and energy.

Many people have experienced sexual energy and money energy together. A failing marriage or intimate relationship is a classic example where the finances are intertwined with sexual energy. Many people also have experienced the linking of money and sex in other ways. One friend shared with me that her mother believed that earning more money was bad because she had to earn by interacting with men who were sexually inappropriate at her workplace. She saw no other connection and no other way of increasing her abundance. The mother also thought that people should keep quiet about sexual harassment; she said it was "just the way things are done and you just endure and keep quiet." So her mother stayed in the same job at the same place for years—frozen in the combination of sexual energy and money. Separating all of this intertwined energy is a challenge. Recognizing and flowing with your own emotions is the first step.

Silence and denial flow through the combination of sexual energy and money, creating a vicious cycle. Understanding this cycle reveals how and why some of us take strange actions with our money when we are sexually active adults. You now may understand some of the reasons why people prefer celibacy or poverty. Money and sexuality are powerful energies by themselves, and separating them once they are entangled takes an even more powerful energy. Allow yourself to experience all of your emotions and breathe into them. Go with the flow and allow your cycles to complete. Embrace and enfold yourself with love. Do the Open-hearted Love Process.

Repressing the combination of sexual energy and money often leads to avoiding creating abundance or creating it and sending it away. The old linkage of sexual energy with money is too frightening and too hidden to allow you to enjoy your abundance. You also are experiencing too many intense emotions. I often see people who barely glance at abundance, living instead on the edge of poverty, frozen back in time when earlier experiences overwhelmed them. These people rarely call out for help since those around them denied their earlier experiences. They live with lots of old things, including their denied memories. For such people, streamlining is a major challenge; enhancing their Wealth Area and focusing on their heart's desires are major achievements. Now take a deep breath and allow these challenging energies to flow through and out of you.

Some people are flamboyant with their combination of money and sexual energy, and their spending patterns are just as flamboyant. They have lots of showy things but have not accumulated enough money to last for six lean months, let alone money that is growing for their future. "What future? The time to enjoy it is now!" they often say about creating abundance.

Action Step

Imagine what your life would be like if you simply realized and acknowledged your sexual energy when it rises. Imagine just experiencing the sensations without judgment or embarrassment. Imagine taking action only if it is friendly toward you and everyone else. Imagine if your sexual energy was welcomed by everyone involved, and especially by you. Imagine enjoying the flow of your own energy cycle, however it shows up. And resonate with the vibration of such abundance.

Embrace Them

Embrace your emotions! Claim the energy they represent when they show up and flow with them. Breathe deeply three to five times, be silent, and give your emotions some space. Be with and experience what is happening in your body. It is a wave of energy that will pass through you if you go with it. Allow the Divine Spirit to transform your emotions with your breath. Calming yourself and your troubled emotional current comes through connecting with your deep abundant breath, your quick connection to the Divine Spirit, rather than catching and holding your breath. Remember, love is more powerful than any other energy or experience.

Once you have embraced your emotions, feel free to express them to others with comfort and ease. Don't worry about overwhelming someone or making them feel uncomfortable; you can experience or express any emotion in a civil and friendly way. Simply use "I feel . . ." language that includes your body sensations and your emotion, such as "I feel joyful!" or "I feel sad." Remember, emotions are like ocean waves that can't truly be held back. Allow them to flow rather than getting stuck resisting or controlling your experience.

Where Emotions Are Lodged

Each emotion has some common lodging places and corresponding sensations in all people as well as ones that are unique to every individual. Here are some common sensations and lodging places you may associate with an emotion. Remember, you probably have your own to add to the mix.

Sadness is often revealed in the quivering of the lower jaw, a heavy feeling in your upper chest, and the tearing up of your eyes. Intense levels lead to sobbing where you hold your breath as you try to stop the intense flow of sensations.

Fear is a queasy feeling in the area of your stomach, often called the pit. You may quiver, and your breath becomes shallow. With more intense levels you also may hold your breath, and your body may shake. Fear also produces a particular odor, one that unfortunately humans have tuned out; animals, especially dogs, can smell when a person is afraid.

With anger your skin may prickle and become hot; you may shake or want to kick and lash out with your arms or legs. Your face and neck may turn red. With more intense levels of anger, your blood vessels may bulge. Anger is also felt in your lower abdomen. Very intense anger, called rage, is felt low in the belly.

Joy is a full-body experience of tingling and smiling. With intense levels you may become spacey and feel overwhelmed. You may feel like you are floating, or you may want to jump around.

Sexual feelings may begin with tingling and warmth in the genital area. You may also squirm inside your body, and your Rational Current may flood you with various mental comments to bring down your sexual energy. With increasing intensity your whole body may tingle or become warm, fluids may begin to build and eventually flow, moistening your underwear, and your particular odor may waft. You may experience other sensations and emotions as well.

People also lodge emotions in the things they buy and keep in their living and work space. When you look at or use an item and you reexperience an emotion or are reminded of a memory, you are reconnecting to the emotional energy lodged in that item or space. Some of your things are associated with joy and some with other emotions.

Action Step

Look around you at the things you have purchased when you were feeling an intense level of emotion. Consider whether you wish to keep being reminded of sad events or reexperiencing your anger or fear. Would you be willing to let go of some of these items and the emotional backlog that they represent? Streamlining also applies to your emotions and their energy in your environment. If you are willing, by when will you begin to take action and release these items?

Sometimes people think that the way to discover where their emotions lodge is to pay close attention to all of their body sensations all of the time. This is doable, but it will take a lot of energy to be constantly on "red alert." Checking in with yourself five times a day is an easier way. A slower and less demanding method than the five times is to notice your body sensations when your emotions are less intense. Your Rational Current is very good at checking in with yourself randomly throughout the day. Here you pair your Rational Current with your Body Sensations and your Emotional Current so they begin to communicate as allies.

Note where your emotions lodge in your Travel Log to add to your understanding of your own signals. Tune in to your own frequency, whatever emotion you are experiencing, and resonate with it with some deep breaths. When your emotional intensity is fairly subtle, as few as three deep breaths will allow you to resonate with your emotion and get back to whatever task is at hand. For very intense levels of emotion, you may need to take several deep breaths to give yourself some time and space to acknowledge your emotion. I often say to myself "I feel _____" to make sure I am in harmony and resonating with what is true for myself at that moment.

Paying attention to your body's signals and your emotional state before you go off to buy, invest in, or sell something allows you to avoid or deny an uncomfortable experience that may end up costing you lots more money than you planned. In the midst of an emotional cycle, your rational mind is very busy trying to understand or deny what else is happening. It's not fully available to analyze the financial repercussions of what you are about to do with your money. By paying attention to the subtle signals of your body, eventually you will tune in to the subtle changes in the energy flow around you. The heat you feel in your body could be related to your anger—or perhaps the sunlight streaming through your office window, the fact that you just got back from the gym, or your hormones. Or perhaps the subtle heat in your body when you read the financial news is connected to the hot air that is flowing through the financial markets about some impending change—either for your benefit or as a caution to take very little action. Noticing the sensitivity of your body's signals can enhance your awareness of your wealth and abundance and lead you to spend and save in ways that allow you ride on the River of Gold in a new way.

Uncomfortable Emotions

When your emotions make you uncomfortable, you resist the flow of that energy. You may add to this mix judgmental thoughts that decrease your energy and flow. Here I shift the focus to emotions that other people treat as uncomfortable. Every family, religious or military organization, and business group has some emotions that they consider outside the bounds of acceptable experience. Usually this view comes from one person, often the leader, resisting an emotion and judging it to be "wrong." By announcing to the group in various ways that "we don't do that emotion here," the person forces others to omit part of the range of frequencies people experience and broadcast. Fear is a big challenge for the business community. So is sadness. Absolute terror, which is fear at an intense level, is often outside the bounds of acknowledgment and acceptance even among close colleagues. Some members of the military also fall in line here. Yet the possibility of losing a large sum of money or going deeply into debt is the stimulus for large emotions to show up—and for taking huge steps to avoid those emotions, which can be very detrimental to your well-being.

Business news, for example, is full of stories about actions taken that turn out to be the undoing of the businesses, while below the surface of the activities are unacknowledged emotions and perhaps thoughts about getting even or avoiding losses or poverty. The actions have at their core the very emotions—fear, anger, sadness—that the leader and much of the group are ignoring. Remember that what is sent out comes back with increased energy, like attracting like and resonating together.

Action Step

Do your spending patterns signal some old sadness? Or some old anger? Your emotions are actually driving your money patterns. And they can drive them away from accumulating and creating wealth and abundance. Right now notice what you are experiencing, flow with it, and allow it to pass. Here is where your breath comes into play. Breathing into your emotion and allowing the wave of energy to gather, rise, crest, and subside is a form of resonance. You can simply "be with" your cycle. And when it has passed you can again resonate with wealth and abundance and spend your money where it harmonizes with your larger goals.

Combinations

Your emotions can show up one at a time or in various combinations with their accompanying body sensations. Each emotion of a combination registers its own level of intensity, and all can affect your approach to abundance. A classic combination is the emotion feeling of "hurt." Consider the various methods your family and friends use to stop their feelings of being hurt. Some people take action to end their hurts by spending money, some by eating or driving, working in their garden, reading—the list goes on. Have you noticed that those solutions actually work? They don't. All of these actions are *doing* kinds of actions. People are called human beings for a reason; we effectively address and resolve many of our experiences through "being with them" and the energy instead of "doing" anything.

Three particular combination emotions can affect the way we think about abundance in a profound way: bitterness, compassion, and gratitude.

BITTERNESS. Someone has done something that is beyond the boundaries of what is acceptable. The breach is so large that it can not be repaired—not by the usual means anyway. Nearly everyone you talk with agrees that "it" is way beyond what any rational person would forgive. They are right. So are you. Your anger, sadness, and fear are justified. However, unless you allow yourself to experience these emotions, to resonate with them and let them go, you will dam up your emotional current. Becoming frozen is the ultimate cost of resisting your emotional experience, and frozen bodies cannot resonate with ease and abundance. Bitterness can fill your entire life, freezing your dreams and your joy.

You are keeping an account—a bitterness account—one in which you keep track of the event and all the other offenses that go with it. You also keep track of how it could be repaid, the actions "they" could take and the things that could be said to make amends. These are the costs to "them." They owe you. For example, the explanation might read: 10/5/92 _____ said the following hateful things to my face. Cost/repayment: demand an apology, no dollar amount. You will be able to assign a dollar amount immediately for some things but not for others.

With each offense there is a cost that you put down on the imaginary paper that is a part of the person's account. The costs include the things you want done or said to make things right, and the emotional wear and tear on yourself. These costs can be the money you actually spend to keep the whole affair going, like doctor's appointments, time spent talking about the event, legal fees, vehicle accidents, long-distance calls, letters to the editor, and indulging in your favorite addictions. The longer and more intense your engagement with bitterness, the higher the costs and the less likely you or they will be able to repay.

At some point, you're going to realize the huge costs that accompany ongoing bitterness and how much energy you are spending and wasting by not letting go. Imagine how it would feel to abandon the grudges you have kept alive and free up the energy. Think of the abundance that could be created with all of that newly available energy!

Forgiving the debt is in your best interest. The benefit of finally releasing the cost and freeing up the drain on your energy is for you, not them. Take a deep breath and feel the bitterness deep down, so deeply that you are shaken to your core, so deeply that you open up some space in your body, your mind, and your heart. Then let go. Cut the ropes, free yourself, and float on down the river. Abundance cannot flow to you if you are resisting its vibration and flow. Look at your space in a new way. See any items that lead you to remember your bitterness and let everything go. Clear your physical space as you relinquish your position in this adventure. Cancel your debt.

This has nothing to do with accepting what was said or done. Because the debt cannot be repaid, set right, or made whole, you canceled it to become whole again and to return to your journey down the river, with your flow unencumbered.

Forgiveness Process

Now you know enough to begin to cancel some debts. Spend some time with your Travel Log acknowledging who and where you are resisting canceling debts. Choose one person and write out the whole scenario as you see it. Feel your emotions. Write a letter to the person, saying how he or she hurt you, and forgive the person. Write a letter to yourself and experience all of your emotions. Tear up or burn both letters. Now do the Open-hearted Love Process for yourself. Forgive and free yourself from debt, and just let go!

COMPASSION. Compassion is a process and it happens after you forgive the debt. It is a driving force in creating abundance. Extending compassion is about opening your heart and offering more flow than you have received or can expect to receive. It is about cutting the strings or the ropes that compel you to "get even" and detour on to the River of Shame. Compassion flows with the River of Gold. You decide which river you prefer and where you are eventually going.

Compassion is extending your warmest and kindest of feelings to some person, event, or thing that has not earned and does not deserve your blessing. With compassion you become a source of the flow that warms and melts people's hearts, a flow that leads people to give up defending themselves against you. You do more than declare the fight over; you now live as if there has been no fight, no cause to uphold. You extend compassion knowing it will wash over many more people than you can fathom. Do the Open-hearted Love Process and send love to this third person. You become the flow of energy called compassion. And abundance flows to you imbued with this energy.

One friend shared that she stepped into compassion toward her former spouse and let go of extracting any more child support money from a very messy divorce after five years. She also let go of trying to limit his relationship with their children, refocused her energy on her own life, and experienced a flowering of her business. In one year she earned twice the amount she was trying to demand from her old relationship.

GRATITUDE. Gratitude is the most important experience of all. With gratitude you cover yourself with your own warmest and kindest feelings: your emotions and body sensations. You do this for no reason and for every reason. Gratitude also includes your Rational and Creative currents. You give thanks with your Rational Current for those things the Creative Current sees in your future, your heart's desires.

Again, gratitude is the most important feeling, and it is the one that is most blocked by unresolved waves of emotion. People who are angry, sad, and afraid and have frozen those emotions into bitterness cannot expand with any warmth. They have no energy and no space left to vibrate directly with gratitude. Facing the unresolved waves of emotion is the first step in extending gratitude to yourself. The second step is extending love to yourself for being frozen and unwilling to let go. Use the Open-hearted Love Process. This little step will allow enough warmth to begin the process. Once you cover yourself with gratitude, you can extend it to whomever and whatever you imagine.

Right now feel gratitude for no reason at all. Do this several times a day for no reason. Become a force field of gratitude. Now feel gratitude, focusing it on what your heart desires.

Whom do you want to do business with, a smiling face or one wearing a frown or a scowl? Gratitude changes your face and your body in many ways. You appear to be more approachable, and so business comes to you with more ease. Do you want to talk with someone who is grateful you showed up or who treats you like you're an interruption? When you have a challenge that you can't solve, are you eager to go to someone who treats you like a crisis or like a friend he or she is glad to see? Think about where you invest your abundance. Do you want to interact with those who are grateful for your business, or not? Gratitude and abundance vibrate in harmony and create more flow and ease.

Buyer Beware

When you are experiencing an emotion, its vibrational frequency is felt by your body and in the space around your physical body. Whatever you touch is also connected to that frequency and that intensity. So spending money when you are in the grip of an intense emotion imbues and locks that vibration to the object or the project. This is not so bad for joy, however consider the result with other emotions and their combinations. This is serious business!

When you are resisting an emotion, that frequency is also in and around your body. You connect that energy of resistance to whatever you touch or are near. So if you are clearly experiencing one emotion and resisting another, you vibrate with both frequencies. Now consider that backlog of emotions you have been resisting. Perhaps you get a picture that is quite muddled with lots of conflicting vibrations being broadcast out into the world. Taking this muddled energy as you go about creating abundance is quite a challenge. Nothing is clean and clear as it goes out into the world. No wonder your heart's desires have not yet shown up.

Now consider all of the projects and business dealings you have and multiply them by, say, ten. That's quite a lot of action going on. Then multiply that number by one hundred. Pretty significant, and it's just you. You get the idea of how much emotional baggage your projects and purchases can carry with them. Emotions you are resisting are also moving around with you, in your body, and in the space around you and connecting with everything you touch and the things you work on. It is important to experience your emotions and allow them to pass; allow yourself to resonate with the present energy and then allow it to dissipate. Purchase things when you are emotionally congruent and current with your anger, sadness, and fear. Otherwise you will just overlay whatever emotion(s) you are resisting onto the item you are acquiring. Did I hear someone say "Bummer!"? When I first learned this I had the same response. Now resonate with that feeling . . . and let it go.

Everything has its own energy and can be imbued with other energy, especially emotional frequencies. Streamlining and keeping only the things that you love may now take on a new significance, and open up some space for more creative energy in your life. Are you ready to focus on your Creative Current?

6

The Creative Current

i t is with this visionary, imaginative creative current that we think with our hearts, hear with our eyes, see with our sense of touch, and use love to measure the true cost of something. Our Creative Current allows us to see, experience, integrate, and "get" a new pattern before our Rational Current has figured it out and can explain it logically. With this current you see and integrate the map of the River of Gold and the benefits and challenges of each of the metaphors. Your Creative Current understands that doing the Penny Dance is the first step toward creating abundance in your life—long before you have enough pennies to interest your rational mind.

This current sees connections that the other

ones miss and jumps over the logical, step-by-step approach. It makes meaning out of vague information and allows you to create with abandon. Nothing has to make sense to this current or be real in the moment. "Just do and see what happens" is its motto. The Creative Current is well suited to tasks of innovation and creativity, forward and future thinking, and holding a vision of what is possible. This is the place where new ideas and things emerge. It is the energy of possibility, where "I can!" is the rallying cry.

The Creative Current also gives meaning to your own life and to what other people have said and done. You can literally imagine your own life story, and if you imagine something unpleasant, you can reimagine it. Your beliefs and your own sense of self come from your Creative Current, while your Rational Current supports these creative thoughts with practical, logical reasons. And remember, it is the Creative Current that allows you to believe, know, and trust.

Seeing

The Creative Current is the place where you can imagine your dreams and desires as if they were real. You do this by "seeing" in your mind's eye a color picture of what you strongly desire. Rolling the pictures like a movie, in full color, with intense positive emotion creates an energy field, a vibration that goes out into the world to attract to you what you are imagining. This is manifestation at its most basic, vibrating in harmony with the positive experience. You don't have to make it up, or go looking for it, or figure out how to get it. It already exists as a vibrating energy out in the world. Being aware of and using this Creative Current is a different way of living. And with it you step up onto a higher plane and dance with a different and powerful energy field.

You also step into a very powerful creative energy flow by calling out to something that is already in existence by stating "I am." Restating your "I am . . ." phrase with deep feeling is your Creative Current's forte:

- I am financially abundant.

- I am enjoying my larger income.

- I am at ease with more wealth.

Pay attention to when you use the "I am" energy. Many people use it for creating lack, for example, saying, "I am hungry" or "I am thirsty." Shift and use it to create financial abundance.

Rational adults often ignore the Creative Current or, worse, discount it as something from childhood, until they wonder why there is little that is new in their lives or why they are always wanting and feeling afraid. As children we pretended and the imaginary became real for hours at a time. Then we became adults and left our child's play behind and became dull and stoic. Bah humbug! Life without dreams and dreamers, visions and visionaries is drab and dull. It's important to revive the flow of your imagination, especially if it has gone underground.

You may wonder why you would want to do this. Or even how. How shows up later in this chapter. Why? is the immediate question. Everything that has been created—jobs, more wealth, new products and movies, various investments, different businesses—all began with some pictures and some idea in someone's mind. And after pictures and the idea came some words to describe and explain "it" because no one else knew about it. Then it became more words, or a diagram that could be talked about and shared. So out in the area of your life called the unknown resides whatever you are not currently experiencing and long to have in your life, like more wealth and abundance. It is not present right here, right now, within the vibrational frequencies that allow you to touch it with your body. It may not yet even exist in physical form! There may be no words to describe "it," if it is totally new. Creating it means you move out into the unknown. You imagine and picture it with your Creative Current; use words to describe it; create a picture model so others can see it too, perhaps a small-scale model; and finally the real deal presents itself—and positively influences your bank account.

Enhancing the Flow

Enhancing the flow of this current means stimulating your senses—your eyes, ears, skin, tongue, and nose. Looking at a sky full of moving clouds or art at a museum or gallery, watching the movement of traffic as it flows or a nature scene—all add to the energy of this current. Personal creativity feeds this current's flow using the free-form creation of shapes, colors, and interesting media. Most people think of painting with oils, acrylics, or watercolors. Working with wood, clay, charcoal, or any other medium also applies. Free-form hand movement using any writing instrument, commonly called doodling, enhances this energy. Listening to and playing music plus adding pleasant aromas to your environment keep this current flowing.

In business, you can use this current to visualize a new product, new clients, a more harmonious team, and everything you want the future to hold. Remember those moving clouds! Stepping up to bat in your own field of dreams is what makes "it" happen.

Creative movement of your body also opens up this channel of flow. Many adults have restricted their movements to a few forward-and-backward or up-and-down patterns: walking, running, sitting, and standing. Whatever happened to moving one part sideways while another twirled and still another part patted or stroked? You were probably told you looked like a fool. Perhaps you were asked the classic question: "What will the neighbors think?" As an adult you probably added "What will my customers or clients think of me?" Looking like a fool is an anathema to business and professional people! How do you move creatively in a gray suit? Creativity in business is now highly prized, and one very successful financial group even refers to itself as Motley Fools. Combining both wondering and your own creative movement, where you let go of knowing what is next and move from your inner impulse, is also a key that unlocks the flow of your Creative Current. Your currents are more connected than you realized. Flowing with one can begin the flow of another and another.

Stopping the Flow

You stop the flow of the Creative Current by holding your breath, contracting your muscles and holding your body unnaturally still, and constricting the flow of your emotional energy. Limiting rational thoughts also constricts your body and your energy flow. Holding your body tight eventually will lead to some ache or pain registering in your brain. Your mind's eye will stop the moving pictures, and the imaginative energy field around you will collapse.

If you end with the thought, "This will never work," you also shift the energy field around you, and you send that energy out with whatever emotion you are experiencing—probably something like fear or anger. The universe interprets those energies as a signal to stop the flow of your dreams toward you. This is why visualization seems to not work for some people. It is working, but they are not aware of how their other currents are working against their creative flow.

The Creative Current also responds to your desire for something by providing the experience of wanting. Wanting is not the same as having. Everyone forgets this from time to time. When you say you want something, then you are resonating with the energy of lack, of not having, rather than flowing with the energy of abundance. When you say you want something, you're also, at a very subtle level, complaining. You are actually blocking the flow toward you because the universe responds to clear requests, not complaints. You create a clear request when you see yourself in the picture with what it is you want, whether that's more money, a better job, or a larger house and you experience gratitude. Using your Creative Current, you send that image and energy out into the universe. You also enhance your experience of having "it" with both your Body Sensations and Emotional currents by combining these positive emotions and energy.

"I wanted more time and money," Amy, a business consultant, shared. "Time for myself to just be and to think about things other than business and financial crises. Time to consider some new services, and more money to cover my expenses while I was away, more money to buy some new equipment and to enlarge my financial reserves. I heard myself saying 'I want.' I didn't see the connection to my current experience of lacking more time and more money but still wanting them. My complaints were numerous and the wanting continued. When I tuned in to myself, I felt terrified that I would never have the time and money that I wanted. I eventually faced and experienced that terror, then felt a sense of completion and letting go. I began to realize how powerfully I had kept in place what I said I did not want. I felt at peace and simply said, 'I am at peace with time to just be, time to create new services.' It worked immediately! I began to experience less time pressures during my day. I had forgotten to release my 'wanting' energy around money. I laughed at myself then, and still I chuckle over my lack of awareness."

Her new awareness led to major changes in her life and business. Amy's focus on her fear of not having enough money lasted less than thirty minutes. This may seem like a long time for an emotion so intense, and yet allowing herself to feel it, for her body to shake for a few minutes, led to a full release and movement forward. Amy also became aware of her language, her use of various phrases, and how much or little of her emotions were in alignment with her language and her heart's desires. Amy refocused her energy, let go of the word "want," created a collage around financial abundance, and added the missing creative visualizations of experiencing more money in her life. She also shifted and experienced gratitude as she paid her expenses. Within a month there were some positive shifts in her day-to-day life and her bank account. During the next six months she created some new services, connected with both old and new clients, and increased her abundance.

Wanting is also similar to resisting. Your main focus is on what you do not have right here and now. You are literally vibrating with the frequency of wanting, and that is what you are attracting to you. You are also indirectly resisting what it is you long for because your energy is focused on your lack and your subtle complaint. The goal is to refocus your energy and what you send out into the world from wanting and feeling the lack to imagining you already have it and feeling gratitude.

Your blocks around having more money will begin to dissolve as you stop using the word "want." You increase the flow by adding the creative visualizations for more money and financial abundance. The universe can now bring to you your heart's desires. You have shifted your energy flow and your experience toward abundance—you have literally put out a clear request. You also will notice that you interact with people from a more positive place. You have stepped into the energy of knowing that at some level you already have "it," and your self-confidence will radiate that out around you. Other people will notice the positive shift and respond to you and your everyday requests so that the things just seem to flow toward you—requests for information, for new contacts who become clients, and for new sources of services that you use. And when you seem to encounter a glitch, do the Cross Crawl in Appendix A or Abundant Breath exercises and just shift into the energy of knowing that something better is coming to you.

Action Step

Notice when and where you use the word "want." Pay attention to the actual things and events that are connected with this word. Let go of using the word "want." Several times a day just focus on your heart's desire. See yourself and "it" in the picture, experience having and interacting with it, resonate with the image, and feel gratitude. Once a day spend a longer period of time—three to five minutes—resonating with the whole experience, and send this energy out into the universe.

Wondering

Using your Creative Current to wonder about things can be enormously rewarding. Imagine that you have a financial challenge and you want an answer that will make a profound difference in your life.

Instead of making a list or thinking about this for a while, you step into a different energy flow where you ask a question and let go. Stepping into this energy begins with wondering, with giving up the idea that you already know why something has or has not happened. When you begin to wonder about a challenge, you then have the opportunity to step into the flow of creative energy of your own life. I call it stepping into the wondering move because you move and walk around as you say the questions to yourself. And then you let go. You don't even wait for something to show up. You shift and go about your life. The wondering move works for questions you have about your financial situation and for challenges with your money, your job, and your sense of abundance—and any other area in your life. It also works when you are sure nothing can happen and there is no solution.

So what is it and how does it work? Wondering begins with a question or challenge. The goal is to engage your Creative, Rational, and Body Sensations currents to solve this issue. The process begins with saying the humming sound, "Hmmm?" out loud as a question, connecting and unifying both sides of your brain and allowing them to work in harmony as you consider your question. "Hmmm? I wonder . . . ?" while you get up and move around the room for several minutes. Then you go back to your regular life. You let go of your current answers, the ones that glibly roll off your tongue. The wondering move opens up space in your mind and body, so you can access all of your stored information for something deeper to emerge. When you step into the wondering move, some answers may show up right away. Most come later that day, and some the next. The key is beginning with saying out loud "Hmmm? I wonder . . ."

For example, your challenge may be "Why is my account so low? I'm sure I had enough money!" Your Rational Current probably will respond with "Because you spent the money!" Yes, this is true, and you want a solution to your spending pattern. So you decide to engage the wondering move. You say out loud to yourself as you begin to move around, "Hmmm? I wonder how my account balance dropped so low. Hmmm? I wonder how I cocreated the lowering of my account balance." Then you pause and allow a deeper current to surface and present you with something other than the glib answer that you spent the money. Instead you open up to a deeper answer, something that has not surfaced before, or a new awareness and perspective on something you thought you already knew.

A classic challenge is not having enough money, week after week, so you begin with "Hmmm? I wonder how I am cocreating this situation. Hmmm? I wonder how I keep this experience going." You let go and allow the deeper answers to arise from the wisdom that is stored in your body and your mind.

One day Elizabeth shared with me after she did the wondering move on just that question that she realized underneath everything she believed money and abundance were evil. It wasn't just a strange belief from her parents or her church; she felt it in her body. It was figuratively the rock she stood upon. She was shocked. When Elizabeth looked deeply into her patterns, she realized that she did several things: She quickly spent any extra money on experiences that would not last, and she accepted very little money into her life with her career choices. And she had never, as an adult, even opened a savings account. Money was "evil," so she sent it away. That week she took action: She opened a savings account, canceled her attendance at an upcoming workshop, and added the refund to her new account. She also refocused on using the affirmations listed in Appendix A.

When you are stuck in any area of your life, saying "Hmmm? I wonder how I am cocreating my stuckness right now" allows you to step into the creative energy flow of the universe, which will restart your own flow. Taking some deep abundant breaths will help, as will shifting and moving your body. You then realize you are part of this creative energy, and you can ask "Hmmm? I wonder how I cocreated this situation in the first place" or "Hmmm? I wonder how I am participating in this." Both of these are good beginning phrases for the wondering move.

Action Step

Focus on a financial challenge. For example: a contract falls through, a client becomes angry, your business connections are not working for you, or you lose a major client. You're asked to put in more hours for the same amount of money, or no one is calling you to participate in their new ventures. Whatever it is, take a deep breath, stand up, and begin to move around and say any of these phrases:

> "Hmmm? . . . I wonder how I can solve this issue."

> "Hmmm? . . . I wonder how I can create more abundance."

> "Hmmm? . . . I wonder when this first began."

> "Hmmm? . . . I wonder how I contribute to keeping this going."

Remember to pause after each question to move around to open up space in your mind and body, so more than your habitual answers can float to you. Allow yourself some time for a deeper answer to float to the surface of your awareness. Let go and notice what shows up over the next couple of days.

Collages and Mind Mapping

There are several ways to use your Creative Current to assist you in sending your heart's desires out into the world for more abundance and attracting those things back to you in physical form. These techniques will help you focus on the indirect approach while continuing to live your life. For example, say you would like $20,000 in your savings or investment account. What are the images, emotions, and sensations that this amount represents to you? Perhaps it means financial security, peace of mind, or the ability to weather a downturn. Connect with the images, emotions, and body sensations that accompany this amount of money.

Another example would be a new car. What are the things you want to do and experience with this vehicle? Haul bags of concrete and pieces of lumber? Buckle your children in the backseat? Open a moon roof? Carry your golf clubs? Touch leather seats? Drive to the theater or out to dinner?

Now consider another job or a different career. What things would you like to actually do? What would your day look like? What service would you be providing to the people you interact with and to the universe? How much money would you like to earn from this position? What kind of colleagues would you like to interact with?

After considering questions like these for your own desires, focus on the following steps to create a collage and do some mind mapping to bring the experience into your life. Remember to keep this collage focused on creating financial abundance.

With a collage or treasure map, you create a visual image in physical form. It is a collection of pictures that symbolize the feelings, and experiences, and images, the essence of your heart's desire. You create a collage from the images you collect from magazines, newspapers, photographs, the Internet, and other sources that visually represent the things and experiences of your focus. Remove the parts of any image that do not resonate with your own inner image. Arrange and paste the pictures together on a large sheet of paper. Freely add other things besides images. I've seen ticket stubs, travel brochures, dried flowers, tokens, and sports memorabilia. It is also very important to include your own face in the picture to tell the universe that you are open and ready to receive—and that you actually expect these things to show up physically in your own life. Sign and date your collage. Some people have created collages yet left themselves out of the picture; months and years later they wonder why collages don't work for them. Remember that like attracts like, so if you leave your own face off your collage, you are telling the universe to send "your" things to whoever else is pictured on your collage. Put your collage where you can see it upon arising and going to sleep. Or create a smaller one that you can carry with you; again, look at it every morning and evening. Spend some time every day looking at your collage and experience your feelings and the plea-

sure of your heart's desires already in your life. Doing so both recon-
nects you with your own desires and adds to the energy that you are
and have been sending out into the universe. You are both focusing and
increasing your energy and concentration. And keep track when your
heart's desires actually show up, perhaps in a special section in your
Travel Log. Create a new collage for your abundance when all the
things and events pictured have come into your life.

Mind maps are useful for creative problem solving and for innovation. Agree with yourself to include whatever comes to mind, regardless of how it looks or whether it seems to fit. Just go with the flow of
ideas for at least twenty minutes. There are two variations to this
process. First write the issue or challenge, using one or two words in
the center of a page of unlined paper. Draw a circle around the word(s)
and, before you lift the pen off the page, let it flow away from that
word, as if you're creating a map. Write the first idea that comes into
your mind, and move your pen again. Continue to free associate, writing ideas as they show up. Some will connect back to the circle, and
others will seem to be connected with other words. Write down every
word and idea that comes to your mind as they appear on this map,
then sign and date the map. You also could make a mind map with your
spouse or partner. Some of these ideas will immediately flow onto your
to-do list, while others may be a step or two removed. Look at this map
every day for the next week and then weekly until the challenge is
transformed.

Another variation is to write the word or words that represent the
challenge in a circle in the middle of the page, then extend several lines
out like spokes. Add words and ideas as they come to you to the end of
the spokes, creating a hub. Add to that hub or other word hubs all of
the ideas that come to mind. Keep writing for at least twenty minutes.

With these techniques your Rational Current may want to focus
on the questions "What steps do I take and how will this come to be?"
Right now the "what" and "how" questions cannot be answered—you
are out in the unknown area of your life. You literally don't know right
now. While you're creating your collage and mind map, focusing on
the details of how your solutions will show up is like checking things

off of a list. Doing so stops the flow of your creativity. Adding to your to-do list will happen during the next few days or weeks.

Visualization

The Creative Current helps you send out energy riding on the waves of very specific images, called visualization. And you will get back what you send out based on the Law of Attraction—like attracts like resonating in harmony. What limits visualization from working for some people are the constrictions and crosscurrents in their Emotional, Body Sensations, and/or Rational currents. You may send out a beautiful image that is overlaid with a strong energy from thoughts that say "I don't think this is possible," or "There is no way this can happen," or "I am not worthy of this much good." You get the idea. What to do? Let go of your visualization and turn your focus on "seeing" and experiencing yourself as someone *worthy* of receiving. You replace the negative image with a positive one, and focus for several days on being worthy of receiving and having. Fighting or resisting the "negative" thoughts and images actually gives energy to them, and they remain firmly in place. These negatives will dissolve from gentle neglect while you're focusing your attention and energy on a more positive experience.

Action Step

Here is a visualization you can read out loud to yourself, or better yet, slowly record in your own voice, and listen to and actually experience it:

Sit quietly, with your feet on the floor, in a place where you will not be disturbed for twenty minutes. Notice if you are comfortable and warm enough. Place your hands in your lap. Relax your body, close your eyes, and breathe deeply. Notice if you have any tension in your feet or ankles. Tense and relax them. Continue to scan your body for areas of tension and let go. When you feel relaxed, notice your mind. Is it quiet? If not, slowly count the length of your deep full breaths for several minutes: inhale one-two-three-four, exhale one-two-three-four. Now in your mind's eye see yourself walk down some steps and into a nature scene where you are safe and comfortable. Look around. Now notice a place to sit. Walk over to it and sit down. Enjoy the scene. Really look at all of the details. As you look around, you see some money lying on the ground. Get up and go and pick it up. Hold it in your hand and then look around you. Notice that the very thing that you long for is just a few feet away. Walk over and experience your hand touching it. Begin to examine it. Now begin to use it and work with it. Notice your body sensations and emotions. Now see yourself in your everyday life experiencing and enjoying it. Hold it close to you. When you are ready, see yourself walk back up the stairs. Now notice you are sitting in your seat back in your room.

When you are ready, wiggle your toes, stretch gently, and open your eyes. Take some deep breaths and touch your right hand to your left elbow. Then touch your left hand to your right knee. When you are fully back in the room, stretch again and get up and move around as someone *worthy* to receive.

Creative Meditation

A dual meditation practice allows you to tap into and flow with your creative energy. You tap into it and you express gratitude, creating in the morning and feeling grateful at the end of your day. You honor the alpha and the omega, the beginning and the end of a cycle of creation. And with the name, alpha and omega, "aah" and "om," you have the sound of the meditation. This meditation is very old and flows through many traditions.

"AAH" CREATIVE MEDITATION. Here are the instructions for this creative meditation practice. In the morning, before you begin your day, sit quietly, placing your feet on the ground, since you are focusing on things actually showing up in the material world. Do the deep abundant breathing for three to five minutes as you feel your body relax.

Then begin to imagine with your mind's eye that the bottoms of your feet open so the energy from the earth can enter and rise up your legs and torso. Imagine a green cord fall from your heart through your body and out the bottom of your feet to the center of the earth. Imagine and sense the earth's emerald-green energy coming up your feet and legs as you inhale.

Quietly say "Aah" as you let go and exhale. Inhale again and continue to visualize the earth's emerald green energy coming into and filling your body, and quietly say "Aah" as you let go and exhale. Inhale and visualize the top of your head, your crown area, opening. Visualize a tube or a funnel connected to the top of your head and going up into the sky. Say "Aah" as you let go and exhale. Inhale and see the golden energy from the heavens enter and flow down this funnel through the center of your head, down your neck and spine, and on down into your feet. Continue to say "Aah" as you let go and exhale. Inhale and see this gold energy filling your chest area and your entire body as you exhale and say "Aah." Inhale and see these two energies, emerald green and gold, meeting at and filling your heart as you breathe. Exhale saying "Aah." Inhale and feel your heart swell and visually open your heart so these two energies can flow out with love and gratitude as you exhale with the "Aah" sound.

Now let go of the visuals and continue to inhale and say "Aah" as you exhale. You can say it very quietly or not. Allow your sensitivity to your living situation and your body guide you. Repeat this pattern for three to five minutes. Now see the gold and emerald-green energies coming through your body from the heavens and the earth, meeting at your heart, and going out with the "aah" sound of your exhale. Float out on these colors an idea, or a visual of something you desire, and resonate with it, feeling its essence. Send it out your heart with the "aah" sound on your exhale. Do this for five to seven minutes as you continue to inhale deeply and say "Aah" as you exhale, sending the energy out your heart.

Again, drop the visuals and just focus on saying "Aah" as you exhale. Do this for three to five minutes. Feel gratitude and resonate with gratitude as you exhale with the "aah" sound. Then imagine your crown, the top of your head, closing and any excess energy leaving your body through your feet. See the bottoms of your feet close and experience gratitude. Exhale with the "aah" sound, allowing it to become more and more quiet. Silently, for three to five minutes, say "Aah" as you exhale, like a hum. Let go, and if any thoughts or visuals float through allow them to pass. End with experiencing the silent hum of the "aah" sound as you feel gratitude. When you are ready to come back and reintegrate, stretch your body and open your eyes, take your left hand and touch your right forearm or knee, then elbow. Take your right hand and touch your left elbow, then forearm, crossing your midline. Touch your toes and the floor with both hands. Take some deep full breaths and rise. Add the Cross Crawl in Appendix A if you feel ungrounded or "out there."

Doing this for twenty minutes is ideal. Feel free to make a tape for yourself, pausing often. Go with the flow. If you only have ten minutes, enjoy the energy and the process. Why do you focus on placing your feet on the ground and connecting with the energies of the earth and sending them out your heart? Well, this is about attracting the things your heart desires into your physical space here on earth. Those people, things, and experiences are already out there, somewhere. Perhaps just over a rainbow. With your heart and the "aah" sound, you are connecting with them, attracting them into your heart space. Now enjoy your day, knowing that you have called out to the universe and resonated with the energy of creation and your current focus. Energy is moving! Let go and allow this energy to move things so they show up in your life. Continue to live and focus on your daily activities and be at peace.

Are there other uses for the "aah" sound? Yes. I use it with the "aah" meditation to open up to a creative solution to a question I am wondering about or to a creative solution to a challenge I am facing. In my mind's eye I imagine the question or challenge and experience the solution as a feeling. Then I let go and do the "aah" sound meditation without a visual. An answer usually comes in a day or two, when I am doing something else, as an idea or the sound of a very quiet voice

making a new suggestion. Sometimes I get up from the "aah" meditation "knowing" the solution.

"OM" CREATIVE MEDITATION. The "aah" sound is the beginning,
the alpha of this meditation. There is also the ending, the omega, the
"om" sound. So at the end of your day, again sit quietly with your feet
on the ground. Do the abundant breathing for three minutes. Imagine
your feet open and a green cord drop from your heart, through your
body, and on down to the center of the earth. See the emerald-green
energy of the earth as it rises up this cord, into your feet, through your
legs and torso to your heart. See and feel it filling your entire body.
Now open the top of your head, your crown, to the golden energies
of the heavens and allow them to flow down to your heart. See this
golden energy filling your entire body. Imagine both energies combining, filling your body, and going out through your heart on waves of
gratitude as you exhale saying the "om" sound. Then allow the visuals
to drop away. Just breathe deeply and say the "om" sound as you exhale. With this sound you simply let go and feel love and gratitude.
Allow your mind to relax as you say the "om" on your exhale. Feel
gratitude and do this for five to seven minutes.

After a few minutes see the energies of both the earth and heavens
flow through your body and out through your heart to the earth as you
exhale. Say "Om" and feel grateful. Then imagine your crown closing
and any excess energy leaving your body through your feet. Imagine
the bottoms of your feet close and experience gratitude. Let go, and if
any thoughts or other visuals float through allow them to pass. Simply
experience gratitude for your day and your life. Say "Om" on your exhale, becoming more and more quiet as time passes. Finally say "Om"
silently for about five minutes. End with experiencing the silent hum of
the "om" sound as you feel gratitude. "Ommmm."

When you are ready to come back and reintegrate, gently stretch
your body and open your eyes, take your left hand and touch your right
forearm, then elbow. Take your right hand and touch your left elbow,
then forearm. Touch your toes and the floor with both hands. Take
some deep full breaths, relax, and go to bed.

Breathe and say the "om" sound for about twenty minutes total. Your heart's desires have gone out into the universe on the vibration of creation in the morning and completion at the end of your day, the beginning and end of a creative sound meditation. Be at peace. The Divine Spirit is listening to your heart and your desire for abundance.

Constantly Creating

You are and have been creating constantly all of your life. Now you are becoming aware of how to do it and how to focus on what your heart desires, rather than drawing to you what you don't want. You are a magnificent cocreator. How do I know? Because you are here breathing and have been all of your life. Your breath is your connection to the Divine Spirit. With every desire you have breathed energy, yours and the Divine Spirit's, as you have gone through your life and sent your energy out ahead of you. This is the essence of the Creative Current—opening your imaginative mind freely to your fundamental longings and heart's desires.

Your Rational Current has patiently taken in all this information. Let's turn and allow it to surface, shine, and shape your finances accordingly.

7

The Rational Current

this current, which I call the Rational Current, analyzes and determines whether something is logical and rational and whether things make sense to it. Thinking is its main purpose—dealing with concepts in your mind. When you want to get something done in an orderly fashion, the Rational Current is what you turn to. You use the energy of this current to:

- Analyze

- Calculate and compute

- Compare

- Decide

- Discern benefits and differences

- Count

- File things

- Gather details

- Keep a list

- Logically review

- Maintain order

- Remind yourself

- Track details

Your Rational Current favors order and is used when you complete tasks, require discipline, take things in a step-by-step pattern or sequence in a rational, linear manner. It seeks proof; it measures and compares the good with the bad, what's better than and superior to, and what's right or wrong. It seeks input from others, and it also dismisses information and people.

Your Rational Current can race in circles, thinking the same thoughts over and over attempting to do more with less—the classic insomniac pattern. The give-it-a-rest solution is suggested, but like the rat in the wheel, people's Rational Current just keeps going until it drops from exhaustion. Here sleep is fitful and the person rises to step back into the pattern from the day before.

Here is where the *W*s reside: the Whys, Whens, Whats, Whos, Worries, and Wants that fill your thought patterns with lots of downward-spiraling, negative energy. This current also holds judgments, sees errors, and overrides all of the other currents. It just shuts down when there is an overload of stimuli and emotions and you have gotten too little rest or sleep for too long.

Innovation is not the Rational Current's strong suit. It judges ideas before they have been allowed to unfold and flower, which stops most innovative processes. In fact, relying on your Rational Current for new ideas could leave you standing out in the cold.

The West favors the Rational Current. For centuries, westerners have preferred this current to all others. Few of us even realize that our rational mind turns on and engages almost as soon as we open our eyes. For many of us, our mind continues to race late into the night, keeping us awake and dominating our lives. We notice and categorize, make decisions, think about things, drive ourselves crazy with the rehashing of old ideas, criticize and judge. We especially judge ourselves, deciding if we are right or wrong. And many people conclude that they are wrong or fundamentally flawed deep down inside. Imagine the contortions in our minds and bodies trying to move forward and create a life of abundance with the thought that we or they are fundamentally wrong. Help!

Man as Machine

The Rational Current was the darling of the Industrial Revolution. This current created the measurements to indicate output, efficiency, financial well-being, and return on investment (ROI) during the Industrial Revolution. Great strides forward resulted in new machinery, buildings, railroads, telegraphs and telephones, automobiles, and roads. Most of the tenets of the accounting profession flowed from this current.

Financial analysis also comes from the Rational Current. However, when you look at the financial information for companies, the output of machines and people, the lack of information about their valuable employees is amazing. This industrious era was a time when people were thought to be interchangeable with machines, able to run long hours day after day with minimal adjustments to produce more efficiently and increase output. Emotions were thought of as something weak and ridiculous and were to be ignored. These ideas are still quite pervasive. You may have encountered many of these ideas—and even have them lurking in your own mind.

The myth that the Rational Current is the be all and the do all of business and of creating abundance still exists. Pay attention to when and where it shows up in your life, and then expand your possibilities and pair it with one of the other currents. When you think about your own spending and financial health, remember to consider your heart connections, your dreams, and your other currents.

Consider the multitude of thoughts that run through your mind as you dash from one idea to another. All of them are filled with unacknowledged and unresolved emotions. And many of your thoughts contradict one another. You desire something, and your rational mind comes up with all of the reasons why you cannot have or do what you desire. You want and you don't want at the same time, thereby sending a confusing message out into the world, such as wanting a new job but feeling angry or afraid that you cannot have what you want. When you project too many confusing messages, nothing moves toward you. Your goal is to become clear and focused and to pack your thoughts with congruent emotions.

QUIETING YOUR MIND PROCESS Quieting your mind, the continuous flow of thoughts that creates a raging river, is a challenge for many people. Taking a direct approach would seem logical, yet an overactive mind is unable to focus and quiet itself. Engaging your other currents will quiet your mind. Use this process whenever you have an over abundance of thoughts.

Sit comfortably with your feet on the floor and your spine straight. Take several deep full breaths. Notice how you are breathing, whether your chest or abdomen expands, and just be aware of your thoughts and let them go. Close your eyes and notice any tension in your body. Just notice. Now begin to count your breaths. Inhale while counting one thousand and one, one thousand and two. Exhale while counting one thousand and one, one thousand and two. Inhale, one thousand and one, one thousand and two. Let your thoughts go. Exhale, one thousand and one, one thousand and two. Keep your inhale equal to your exhale. Inhale, one thousand and one, one thousand and two, one thousand and three. Let go of any judgmental thoughts. Exhale, one thousand and one, one thousand and two, one thousand and three. Your Rational Current is happy to count and keep track.

Gently flex your hips and spine as you breathe abundantly. Inhale and roll slightly forward, one thousand and one, one thousand and two, one thousand and three, one thousand and four. Exhale and roll back on your sit bones, one thousand and one, one thousand and two, one thousand and three, one thousand and four.

Continue for several more minutes, counting your deep full breath and letting your thoughts just flow on by. Now notice your body. Are you relaxed? Is your mind quiet? When you are ready gently stretch, wiggle your toes, open your eyes, tap your feet on the ground, get up, and refocus on your life.

Language

Words are symbols of the actual object or experience. Words also have energy and vibrate at the frequency of the thing they represent. We attract the things we desire by resonating at the frequency of the actual thing through using words, thoughts, visualizing, or experiencing the frequency as we breathe and meditate. We also send the thing away or block it from coming to us with our language.

We send things away with our own words by saying "I can't believe this"; "This could not be happening"; "I don't know why this would be true"; "I can't afford to keep this"; "This is too good"; "I don't deserve this."

The more often we say these things and/or the more intense our emotions when we do say them, the more we push and send the energy and the person/event/thing away from us. Again, like attracts like. You do not and cannot embrace these things, resonate with them, and feel gratitude when you say statements like this.

Action Step

Notice your language and release your speech patterns that send things away. Do this for thirty days and see what happens in your life.

Use your Travel Log to collect your old phrases so they can rest in peace.

Create more positive and inviting language. Express gratitude and use "I'm delighted this showed up" and "I gladly accept."

Blocking Movement

We block abundance from moving toward us by saying and/or thinking "This will never happen"; "I don't believe this can happen"; "I can't afford to buy/rent/lease this"; "I can't imagine this will ever happen"; "I'll never get ahead." The list goes on. Few people are aware when these words come out of their mouths. They have heard these things and said them so often they just disappear from their awareness and control. Yet just becoming aware is simple. You decide to become aware. Then you make the commitment to release these phrases from your speech and thinking patterns. Remember, commitment is just gathering yourself together and sending yourself forward on a journey. The journey to abundance is the one we are focusing on. Again, the more intensely we say these statements, the more energy they represent. Think of them as creating a large wall with a KEEP OUT sign posted. The universe honors what we say and do, our vibrational field, even if we are not aware. What do you say that blocks energy, people, and things from flowing to you? Become aware.

Action Step

For one week, focus on becoming aware of your language and thoughts that block the flow of your abundance. Note them in your Travel Log and commit to releasing these things from your flow. Create affirmations similar to these: My heart's desires freely flow to me. I'm enjoying my heart's desires. I am open to the flow of abundance into my life. I accept the abundance that is here now in my life. Begin to incorporate the affirmations in Appendix A in your life.

Keeping Accounts

Everyone is an accountant. We all keep accounts with our Rational Current. We count or keep track of whether someone said one thing or another, whether she did or did not do what she said they would do. We each keep account if the "something said" was a promise to do something, especially if we're invested in the outcome.

Everyone has an account. You have an account with each of the members of your family, your friends, your neighbors, and the people in your spiritual community. You also keep an account on each of them, your private stash. In addition, you have an account with your employer and coworkers, your community, the local newspaper, dry cleaner, at the grocery store, and where you buy your shoes/clothes/computer/vehicle. Some of these accounts are obvious, and some are not.

While the things we enter into the columns vary, each of us has a balance. You instinctively know with whom you have a positive balance and with whom you do not. Just now, think about who would buy you a birthday present today. If you're invited to a birthday party, do you want to go and do you want to buy them a gift? Who bought you a present or called you for your birthday last year?

Now let's up the ante. Whom would you lend money to, no questions asked? Whom would you not lend money to, for any reason?

Those are just a few of the accounts you keep. We keep track of one another and one another's behavior. Stepping onto a deeper and more solid foundation of integrity assumes that we acknowledge and accept the things we are really doing. The game is up! No more lying to yourself—or to anyone else. You can still smile when someone asks you about his account balance; you just cannot continue to deny to yourself that you keep track. Telling the truth in a friendly way keeps the current flowing deep, wide, and smooth.

Without Reasons and Excuses

We deny what is going on with our Rational Current, making up reasons and excuses instead of facing the thing or issue straight on. Here the classic phrase "The way it is, is the way it is" comes into focus.

With denial, the Rational Current comes up with lots of reasons and excuses why what is cannot be. These reasons are repeated as a defense and to bolster the growing barricade that blocks out what is really going on. Repeating the reasons prevents you from turning, facing, integrating, and taking positive action steps in line with reality. Integrating the Rational and the Body Sensation currents allows you to turn and face your denied issue and to say what you have been avoiding. Living without reasons and excuses is a challenge and very liberating!

Action Step

Your mission, should you care to accept it, is to live without reasons and excuses. Try it on for thirty days, repeating to yourself "without reasons and excuses" as you go about your days. Once you decide to abandon denial, your Rational Current will remind you whenever you step back into that energy, remind you that you have released that thought pattern, and assist you in facing your issue. Make your Rational Current feel happy and useful and team up with it in areas where it excels.

Make no excuses and give no reasons for the increase in abundance you experience. When more money shows up or an item costs less, simply acknowledge the increase and feel grateful.

IDENTIFYING AND FLOWING ON By Your Rational Current can learn to identify the flow of your emotions and what is happening with your body sensations. It can remind you to experience your emotions through four or five deep abundant breaths and allow the wave of energy to subside. When an innovative idea arises, it's your Rational

Current that goes round and round with all the reasons why it won't work, while you feel various emotions, especially your wide range of fears. Yet you can turn your Rational Current around, engage its best characteristics, and assign it the task of keeping track of any and all new ideas. Opening new files and filling them with useful data delights your Rational Current.

Elizabeth, a project manager, relayed to me her recent experience with Roger. "No, that won't work!" was his first response to her project idea. He then launched into a long list of reasons to support his position. She said, "That's interesting, tell me more." And he did and ended with "and I don't have the time to do it." "Oh, John has already volunteered," she told him. Somehow Roger had assumed that he was the one appointed to the task rather than simply in on the informational loop. It turns out that he was already carrying a fairly heavy load, feeling overwhelmed, and afraid that he was being asked to do more. His Rational Current had no trouble taking over, providing plenty of reasons why the project was a bad idea.

"I just wanted you to know the process," Elizabeth told him, "and to hear any ideas you had that would improve it."

"Oh," Roger replied. It took him a while to respond to her real request for advice and wisdom.

Left to its own devices, the Rational Current will focus on the reasons why something should *not* happen. It can overpower and stop the other currents, damming them until they're just a trickle or they dry up completely. It shows up in responses such as "Don't bother me, I'm busy doing something much more important," sending the Emotional, Body Sensations, and Creative currents far underground. Yet in Elizabeth's case, a little insight into Roger's emotions enabled her to open up the flow of ideas again.

The Language of the Ws

Language is symbolic. The words on the page are not the thing itself but an agreed-upon representation of the experience. The Rational

Current prefers words and mathematical and scientific symbols. Using words and symbols is at least one step, in some instances several steps, away from the experience. Yet using language allows me to communicate my ideas and you to begin to experience and play with them.

For example, take some *W*s: Why, When, Who, and Worry. Each one leads to some initial questions, probably a decline in your energy, maybe even to a stage of negativity that can spiral you into a deep pit. There are also two interesting and more positive *W*s: What and Want. With them your energy can spiral upward and lead to taking steps that move you forward.

WHY. Why? is a classic question, often the first asked when something goes awry: Why did you do/say that? Why did this happen to me? Why did I go this way? Why? asks the question and demands an answer right now. We then get an answer and think we know the truth, the definitive answer that will solve our dilemma and allow us to move forward with our life. With "why" we ignore the emotions that precede the questions, preferring to only engage the Rational Current. In fact, we are looking for a way to avoid experiencing the hurt, sadness, fear, and anger that goes with deeper exploration. And the bigger question we avoid is "What will you do with that information and where will it lead you?" Knowing why someone acted as she did does not, in fact, tell us very much, but it allows us to judge the person as being wrong and avoid more complicated emotions. Any argument requires a defense, and the I'm right/You're wrong battle takes a lot of energy and goes nowhere.

Action Step

Pay attention to your own "why" questions, especially about spending and saving money. Notice when you use this energy, asking "why" when you are engaged in creating abundance, say at work or on a project that will reduce your own expenses. Become aware of your emotions and how easy it is to get back in the flow and accomplish something when you ask or are asked a "why" question. Does asking yourself "why" enhance your own flow of energy and sense of worth?

WHEN. When did this happen? When did you say that? When did you buy this? These are variations on the why question. Most "when" questions lead to very little information that can move you forward toward your dreams and heart longings.

WHO. "Who did this?" The accusatory tone implies "I'm going to get you/them and punish them till they can't . . ." You fill in the blank with the common threat you heard as a child or a new one that you like better. "Who did/said this?" leads to blame and punishment, to people running for cover and dodging the experience of their emotions. What will you do with this information? Assume someone actually gave you an answer. Will you use the answer to defend your position, or to attack the other person's position or his very self?

Action Step

What emotions are you experiencing now? What thoughts are flowing through your mind? Are you aware of your own abundance and your flow? Is there something that you want, or don't want, that shows up and comes out as a "when" question? Notice your own issue and question hidden under your "when" questions.

WORRY. Worry is something that the Rational Current does very well. Worry begins with judging something that happens in our life as "bad." We may have a thought that something will happen with our money out in the future, and we judge it as bad. Then we heap on more and more thoughts that increase our worry, and our sense that "This is really bad" increases. When we worry, there is no space between our thoughts. They just jam up against one another. We spin ourselves in a downward spiral of more and more negative thoughts and sensations so that the negative energy repels people and things. Worry especially repels money. We feel so bad that we contract and freeze ourselves, unable to take positive action steps, unable to complete tasks or to climb out of the pit we are in. Worriers also breathe shallowly, which causes a buildup of carbon dioxide in the blood that leads to feelings of anxiety. And so it goes.

Action Step

You stop the worry cycle by tuning in and recognizing that you are worrying, acknowledging that you are just imagining the worst that could happen. Then take a few deep breaths so you can begin to oxygenate your blood and brain and create some new and more positive thoughts. Creative movement when you realize you are worrying shifts your vibration and begins a new flow of energy, as does the Quieting Your Mind Process.

WHAT. What? begins the upward spiral of energy. It starts with pondering "What will you do with that information?" It stops the flow and allows some air and space between the automatic responses. Few of us spend any time wondering what the payoff is to a line of questioning. We have heard and experienced a particular flow of questions, and we simply use them again, engaging our Rational Current's storehouse. Here the idea is to stop the familiar pattern and open up, to get our creative juices flowing, to pair the Rational Current with the Creative Current so some new thoughts can emerge.

Asking the open-ended question "What happened?" invites an inquiry into your responses to the stimuli, your body sensations, your emotions, and your thoughts. You begin to unwind from the contracted response that led you to the bottom of the pit you spiraled into.

"What happened?" allows you to start breathing and moving. Once you open up and notice your prior responses, sort through them, experience them to their fullest extent, and complete the cycle, then you can entertain the questions "What do you want?" "How would you like it to be?" You then engage both your Rational and Creative currents so you can imagine taking steps toward something better than what you currently have happening.

Practical Uses

Your Rational Current is great at analyzing, making lists, and reminding you to do things. Allow it to team with your other currents to remind you to breathe abundantly and fully, move creatively, create and repeat your affirmations, schedule a time to create a collage, meditate, feel gratitude, and read uplifting materials when you are finding your vibration at the lower levels. Invite your Rational Current to team with your Creative Current to actually do the various Action Steps, the Penny Dance, the feng shui sketches, streamlining, and feng shui cures. The Rational Current also checks in during the day, scans your body, and keeps track of your own subtle responses. Invite this current to team with your Body Sensations Current so you stay limber and well oxygenated.

Action Step

What do you actually think?
For thirty days keep track in your Travel Log the answers to these questions:

- What thoughts regularly flow through your mind?

- Which ones hang around when you are happy?

- Which ones do you hear over again when you are feeling stressed?

- Which ones are your own thoughts? Your father's? Your mother's? Your grandparents'? The teacher you admired? The teacher that deflated your life?

- Which ones come from your religious training?

- Which ones are in your mind's flow by your choice?

- Which ones are you willing to let pass on by?

Recirculation Action Step

Now consider with your Rational Current how you interact with your Penny Dance and the way you go about putting your pennies back into circulation. How will you know the right time to recirculate? Listen to your heart; notice your body responses. Does your body feel tight and constrained, or does it contract anywhere when you think about emptying your penny container? Do you feel sad or joyous? Are you suddenly eating or drinking more than you usually do? Are your pennies overflowing in their container? Pay attention to your Rational Current's activity. Is it wandering down the path littered with signs saying "There is never enough," "You'll be sorry," and "A fool and his money are soon parted"? Pay attention to all of the currents to know when the time is right for you to put your pennies back into circulation.

Allow Your Rational Current to Shine!

Your Rational Current can accomplish many things. Allow it to shine and point it in a positive direction. The negatives, all of the you-do-not and you're-not kind of thoughts, will just dissolve from lack of energy, focus, and attention. Growing up in the West, your Rational Current has been working very hard and carrying a heavy load for a long time. Lighten up its load! Tell your Rational Current that it is important and that you value and appreciate all that it has done for you.

For example, use the Rational Current to keep track of all of the good memories in your life, remind you of when you did something right, analyze your financial situation, and keep track of where you have your money saved and invested. The Rational Current will remember the times your hunches were correct and what signals you received. It reminds you to meditate; to appreciate yourself, your work, your colleagues, your living space, your vehicle . . . and it, five times a day. Put your Rational Current in charge of keeping track of the wins in your life. Remind it to put out a memo to yourself to celebrate all that flows into your life. Ask it to keep track of your body sensations and emotions. Allow it to remind you to fully experience a wave of energy and to keep track of how often you check in with yourself.

Your Rational Current can keep track and file away the ideas and information from the imaginings and visions of your Creative Current. Allow it to keep track of when "good" things flow into your life, and let it remind you to focus on your collage twice every day and to stay balanced and enjoy the flow of abundance into your life. It can keep track of when you set in place your feng shui cures and the results. And put it in charge of seeing that you eat, work, play, rest, and sleep in a balanced way. When it comes back to ask for more, thank it and ask it to accompany your Creative Current out to look for a rainbow and the pot of gold that just fell into the river.

8

The River of Shame

the Rational Current encourages our judgments to flourish and flounce around with great abandon, forgetting that they are connected to the Emotional and Body Sensations currents. These three currents can work together to create a separate, lonely stream, the River of Shame. This one is not connected to the River of Gold nor does it flow to the ocean of abundance with heart. It's not on the map; rather it flows underground below the light of day. We hide and go underground when we experience shame. We may feel so much shame that we withdraw our energy from our own life and flow. Most people have traveled on this river at one time or another, and many of us have participated in events that keep this river

flowing. Rarely do we want to remember the event, the things leading up to it, or the thoughts, imaginings, and emotions that combine
to create the experience of humiliation that floats on the river's current. You will know if this is true for you.

The classic game on the River of Shame begins with one person
who is absorbed with the energy of self-righteousness. Feeling superior
over someone else is based in fear and a subtle message that we are not
good enough, that there is something fundamentally wrong with us.
Eventually the critical person gathers followers and begins to condemn,
shame, and cast out a third person. Classic examples are the comments
by someone who appears to be wealthier than you, at a nice restaurant
or an upscale store, criticizing your clothing or appearance. Some employees at upscale resorts, restaurants, and shops play this "superior"
shaming game when they treat you like you cannot afford the mer-
chandise or service they offer. And gossip, especially the vicious kind, is
about shaming you and cutting you to your core. For example, "I
mean, how could she possibly think that she could even fit in."

Some of the experiences on the River of Shame that people have
labeled as emotions are actually thoughts or mental concepts with lots
of judgment attached. A classic is feeling dumb or stupid, especially
with handling money. Here the mind has judged some action or comment, often very harshly. I am imagining that the emotion of fear might
be combined with the judgment of being dumb or stupid, depending
on whether your early experiences had that combination.

Other judgmental words include: clumsy, awkward, humiliated,
dumb, dorky. Although we may have some emotion connected with a
word or experience, these are mental constructs with lots of judgment
attached to them, not clear emotions. So release the judgment, the
thoughts and images. If you instruct your Rational Current to remember more favorable comments about your abilities with money, then it
will, with delight!

Using the word "should" sends people underground where the
River of Shame flows. "You should do this" indicates not only that you
are not measuring up but that you probably will not in the future. You

also flow with the River of Shame when you say "You are making me. . . ." Fill in the blank for the emotion and the actions. This language blames someone else as if he is controlling your experience. Such language also attempts to shame him into feeling guilty, diminishing his sense of self. Heads up! Remember, emotions are your own response to various experiences and stimuli. Many people have similar responses to a particular event, yet many people do not! You step into the energy of shame and blame when you expect other people to change their behavior because you are uncomfortable with an emotion or event that they are experiencing, similar to saying "You can't do that, I won't allow it!" to someone who is experiencing sadness.

The River of Shame must be purified and distilled, to see any of its gifts. That is done with love. It's difficult to create a warm environment and to open your heart to the experiences and gifts after being harshly treated as you previously floated on the River of Shame. The good news is that the heat from an open heart will eventually warm the Emotional and Creative currents so they will embrace the judgmental flow of the Rational Current with love. No one is without redeeming features. No one is beyond being welcomed back onto the vessel that floats on the River of Gold. Having your Rational Current embrace the rest of your experiences on the River of Shame is most challenging yet provides the most rewarding outcome. The appreciation of one current for another creates beautiful music, and all can flow in harmony to the ocean of abundance.

Action Step

When you realize you are cringing or pulling back, check in and notice whether you are reliving an old experience of shame. Remember to breathe and allow the wave of emotions and images to rise, crest, and subside. Then call to mind someone or something that you love and wash that love over yourself. Do the Open-hearted Love Process. Then extend those warm sensations to your money and your current activities. Become a generous field of energy.

Responsibility and Accountability

These are juicy words! These two words signal that you are danger-ously close to traveling on the River of Shame. Both words can be used to open up to a new way of living, to police the activities of other peo-ple, or to lay blame at someone's feet. When people do the latter two they use the classic phrases: "Who is to blame for this?" or "Who did this? I want to know right now!" or "Why don't you take more re-sponsibility?" "I'm holding you accountable for this!"

Most people treat responsibility as a heavy burden, something to be shouldered when nothing else will do or is available. Just feel the extra weight on your body: "Here take more, and more, let's just load you down. You can handle it; you're one of the responsible ones around here." In fact, the person speaking may be looking to add a part of her load onto the "shirker" just for good measure, as in "I work hard around here and it's time you did your share!" Ugh! Lots of energy and suppressed emotions in that sentence. No wonder people duck out and go looking for something easier and more pleasant than shouldering more responsibility. Shall we join them for a different perspective? Now, wonder what a pleasant or even exciting approach to responsi-bility would be? How about stepping into a new vibration, something outrageous like celebrating responsibility? Now, that is a totally different perspective, like looking from above rather than from underneath. "Hmmm? I wonder how I could celebrate responsibility?"

With the burden approach, one person is energetically underneath, carrying and paying more than his portion or share. If I, for example, insist on paying more than my share for a group gift or the support of aging parents, then you must carry less of the share than I do. The gift or financial support costs only so much to carry, and there is no more to apportion. I may be trying to get extra points for being the "good guy" and doing more. So two halves try to equal a whole and in reality cre-ate a hole in our equal relationship. It makes sense when we add up the numbers; one-half and one-half equal one. But often something else is going on when people and projects interact, something that is below the surface of our awareness. This is why one person feels like the underdog carrying a heavy load and feeling burdened.

Action Step

Look at your financial activities and notice where you are doing more than your share and where you experience doing less. Are these familiar patterns around money? What thoughts or emotions surround these actions?

Become aware of your environment. Are there things in your space that support you doing and paying for more than your equal share? Or for doing and paying for less than your share? Would you be willing to release them? If yes, by when?

Does your pattern of spending more or less than your share emerge only in certain circumstances? Notice and give yourself some breathing room.

CELEBRATING RESPONSIBILITY What if we looked from another perspective, such as from up above? Let's assume that people in this experiment who step up are whole and willing to participate. Then what? Well, if I'm whole, then 100 percent is my percentage. Then I can take care of myself and step into the place of equality, rather than assuming I am a lesser percentage. So I begin to celebrate my 100 percent, and I am responsible for all of the situation and the actions that follow. I freely pay my 100 percent, no more and no less. I contribute my whole self rather than a smaller percentage. I step into place, rather than being corraled or cajoled. If I step into responsibility, then responsibility is my ability to respond. Feel the change in your body. Would you rather step forward and celebrate, . . . or step under a heavy burden? You get to choose. Me? I like the celebration energy.

So what about other people? They begin to take care of themselves, and they step into the energy field of equality, celebrating their wholeness, their 100 percent, and bringing their 100 percent to whatever is afoot. So of two people, each assumes 100 percent, and each is a whole person, not a lesser percentage. While the old numbers added up, the new numbers have a different feel and vibration and seem like a whole lot more, like an abundance of responsibility and fun—like a celebration!

So what happens when "they" don't pick up their share? Interesting question. It seems like you stepped back to the old vibration. You have 100 percent and they have 100 percent and you interact. If one of you doesn't step into the place of dancing with your 100 percent, then can celebrating responsibility even happen? It seems silly, but once you realize they are coming from the perspective of assuming a burden and looking from underneath a heavy load, you have to stop dancing with them. Remove yourself from the situation. The goal is to get off the River of Shame and travel on the River of Gold.

A classic challenge is contributing to the financial support of aging parents. One child is wealthier than another and contributes more money, while the other(s) have less wealth and contribute less money. The situation requires that you participate; you can't walk away; and it seems as if there is no other way than the way it is being done. You also have lots of thoughts and emotions from the past that pile up upon the present situation. Help! The truth is the contribution of money is not equal and cannot be, especially when everyone knows it and keeps silent.

What to do? Step into the energy of celebrating. Call the game on yourself! Fully acknowledge your own thoughts and emotions *to yourself*. Separate the past from what is happening right now. Deal with your past issues with the appropriate people, whether it's your siblings or your parents. Here is the bigger challenge: They may not want to or be willing to hear you. First, listen to yourself. Then write out everything that you are experiencing—all of it. Read it through, then, ideally, destroy your writing and send it out to be healed on the breath of the wind. Let go of trying to fix your past. Sometimes in feng shui, when the challenges with one space are just too much to cure despite many attempts, we finally suggest that you move. In this case you move on. You go with the flow and allow the river to carry you to another place where the energy is more harmonious.

The shift begins with you. Really listen to yourself about the current situation, all of it. No holding back or hiding something from *yourself.* You cannot get away from or give away what you do not have within your own experience. Really feel your whole experience, what it is like when you avoid, lie to yourself and others, and when you visit with your parents and your siblings. How are you with any other caregivers? If you hold back to yourself about your experience, then you cannot shift the energy and the sense of "burden" and inequality.

Now, what do you really want? What would you be willing to do? Are you willing to talk with your siblings and your parents about your *own* feelings? If you feel something, they feel something too. However, they may not be able to articulate their feelings and thoughts—or they may. Do you love these people? Underneath this situation, is there a flow of love from your heart? If so, then send them love several times before you actually talk with them. And use the Open-hearted Love Process.

Finally, tell yourself the truth. Is the issue about how much money you contribute or some other issue, such as your own sense of worth, or your old position in the family, or a relationship with your sibling(s) that is calling for a shift? Do the Forgiveness Process. When your emotions are no longer so intense, when your mind is clear and your thoughts are orderly, then go and talk with your family with an open heart. And share your deepest heart longings for your own wealth and abundance. See what is waiting for you around the bend. It could be something wonderful!

Are you ready to step into celebrating responsibility in more areas of your life—like creating abundance?

Action Step

Stand up, breathe, then ask yourself if you are willing to step into the energy flow of celebrating responsibility. When you are ready, step to a new place in the room. Allow your body sensations to signal to you how it feels, and ask your thoughts to embrace the idea of celebrating responsibility. Shift and go back to your old place in the room, experience that, and then shift again and step into celebrating responsibility.

Wonder how you can create a celebration of responsibility in the flow of your life. Say "Hmmm? I wonder how I can be a vibrating, celebrating, energy field of responsibility on behalf of my own wealth and abundance." Something will come to mind. Take one small step into your new field of energy and do something positive about that idea.

If you want to be known for celebrating responsibility, keep taking small steps on the ideas and financial challenges that show up when you ponder this concept.

ACCOUNTABILITY Accountability is another one of "those" words. Few of us check our intentions when we use either responsibility or accountability. And we also ignore our own attempts to shove someone onto the River of Shame. So accountability is about how you keep track, how you keep your agreements with yourself. I keep my agreements with myself, or I don't. I'm accountable, and here is the clincher, *to me.*

If I didn't do what I said I would do, there are several alternatives. It is a given that I will experience whatever emotions and body sensations show up. The options are

- keep the same action and agree to change the time frame

- change the action and the time frame

- agree to drop the action

- be more careful in making agreements with this person in the future

- decide to not make future agreements with this person

No shame, no blame, no excuses, and no reasons. How successful are these actions? Well, I have changed my life again and again when I realize I have slipped in any of these areas. I hear story after story about other people's lives smoothing out and moving forward when they look at these options and make a clear choice of action. And yes, it may seem as if you've hit rough waters when you first start out. Some people are even thrown out of their vessel for a while. But they get back on board and adjust themselves and their tangled ropes and head out for the ocean of abundance once again.

Action Step

Notice how you keep your agreements with yourself. Notice how you keep other people's agreements with you . . . and your agreements with them. Become aware of any differences, especially of other people's facial expressions and comments around your actions as you interact with them.

To step up into another vibration, acknowledge when you have kept or are about to not keep your agreement. For example, if you agree to meet at 3 P.M., then being one minute late is still late. If you said around 3 P.M., then agree to the time range, five minutes or fifteen, before you finish making your agreement. Being honest to the penny adds to the smooth flow in your own energy field. Be honest with yourself about your responses, the emotions, thoughts, and judgments you heap on yourself. Ride the waves of energy and come to a peaceful conclusion. Become a celebration of responsibility and accountability for yourself.

Entanglements

Mentioning the tangled ropes in the accountability section reminds me of entanglements. Entanglements are a wonderful can of worms! We entangle ourselves as we go about our lives. The people, places, and things we avoid interacting with actually have a connection to us, like a piece of rope or cord that we tie between ourself and others. Everywhere we go we take them and the connection with us. Are you getting a picture of how bound up your life can be? The love and focus of energy draw us back to one another, either in physical form or through our energy. The avoidance cords both whip us around and act as a barrier so we can avoid confrontation. Entanglements tend to strangle us, guaranteeing that we will never make the move to straighten things out. (Yes, I purposely wrote this paragraph this way to create some entangling energy.)

You can become untangled by focusing on one cord or rope at a time. Engage your breath and spend a moment with your Creative Current imagining yourself free. And with that imaging, you have set an intention. Now what is the first thing that you can do to become free? An action step that you can take will come into focus, then another. Now start taking action steps to face and complete whatever is incomplete, to untangle yourself, so you can freely flow with the River of Gold.

I was touring Robert's company with him and noticed his jaw was tight. He had the same complaints in each area, pointing out how lazy and disorganized his partner was. After the tour, we went back to his office and I again mentioned his tight jaw. Seeing the neat piles on top of his desk prompted me to ask him to open his credenza and desk drawers. I didn't know what I was looking for, but I did have a sense there were relationship issues hidden somewhere.

Later Robert said, "I was resisting noticing the tightness of my jaw. It was only when we went back to my office and Suzan asked me to open my desk and credenza that I was willing to acknowledge my part in any of this. I was hiding several things from my partner. One item was a birthday gift for him that I had forgotten about and discovered months later because I had so many things stashed away. I was too embarrassed to admit my error, and there was no way I would ever actually give the gift to him.

"Rather than make a big deal about my own lack of integrity, Suzan began playing with the forgotten gift. After talking for a while she said she would like to have it, since I was never going to give it to him. That broke the dam. I was playing quite a deadly game with my anger and self-righteousness, and paying a consultant good money to boot. She later helped facilitate a challenging series of exchanges between my partner and me. For a while it was like a pile of tangled ropes. When we gently pulled on one section, everything shifted and gradually began to untangle itself."

The two made several feng shui adjustments, and along with other changes, Robert and his partner cleared up many misunderstandings, releasing much energy that allowed the company to reach its sales goals for that year. They also enjoyed a newfound flow of positive energy between themselves.

Now let's get back and see what's happening on the River of Gold.

PART III

ROUGH WATERS

Getting Control of Your Finances

The journey on the River of Gold includes many types of rough waters where your focus, abundance, and vessel can be at risk.

9

Water Hazards: Navigating through Financial Difficulties

There are troubled waters in every life. The greatest skill we can learn is how to navigate them. Everyone has had some challenges around creating a positive inflow of abundance. The goal is to recognize these challenges and your own responses to them and to glean the gifts. Rough waters are full-body experiences involving all five currents that show up as recognizable patterns of energy flow, like canyons, rapids, waterfalls, swamps, portage paths, and deserts. With each challenge some things are out of balance. Creating harmony begins with recognizing and resonating with the various frequencies that are present.

Rough waters involve both wind and water. Remember, water symbolizes money, emotions, body sensations, tangible physical objects, and the flow of energy. Wind is symbolized by breath, inspiration, the Divine Spirit, movement, intuition, your mind, and intangible things. Rough waters also separate the dross from the gold in your finances and your life. They occur when what you think you want comes face to face with the deep longings of your heart, and suddenly you must make a choice. Then you discover whether you will be true to your own sense of self or whether you will follow someone else's heart longings out into the world.

The first thing to do when you realize you are in rough waters is to take a deep full breath and begin to resonate with the experience. The second thing is to check out your intention and inquire of all of your currents whether you are committed to being on the journey to the ocean of abundance. The third thing is to laugh at yourself and the situation and take a time-out so your head can clear and you can get your bearings again.

The order of the challenges in this section may have nothing to do with their sequence in your own life. Feel free to read them in whatever order seems right to you, and reread them from time to time to gain a deeper understanding of the energies involved. Use this "map" to give you a broader view of the possibilities and to see things from a different perspective. Continue to do the Penny Dance and keep your Travel Log close at hand to record your personal observations and insights. Even in the midst of rough waters you can tap into the larger flow of the River of Gold and the depths of the ocean of abundance.

The Canyon

★

A canyon experience occurs when the financial walls are close together and tower high above you. Canyons may have water flowing through them all, part, or none of the year. There is always a subtle sense of pressure from the walls, from the water coming up behind you, and from the possibility of danger lurking up ahead or around the next bend. Allowing an arm or leg to dangle overboard invites an injury when you quickly pass through the canyon. When the river is flowing smoothly and quietly, you can drift along peacefully, enjoying the interesting view. However, when the flow speeds up, your level of anxiety increases with each incremental increase in the speed. In a canyon,

★The artwork above and on pp. 179, 202, 218, 226, 244, and 274, courtesy of the artist, Master I-Hong Chou.

your options seem very limited, and you can see only as far ahead as the next bend. And once you have lost your ability to navigate your vessel as it careens downstream, you may become terrified—your focus narrows and the walls seems to move closer. Looked at from a larger perspective, canyon experiences are like coming through a tight space and time that eventually proceeds to a huge opening.

From a feng shui view, a canyon might be a staircase or a dimly lit narrow hallway that you try to navigate quickly while carrying two heavy bags. Anything in your way will add to your level of anxiety and your difficulty moving through this space. Add to this scene a ringing telephone that you desperately want to answer and notice your breathing, body sensations, thoughts, and emotions. You seem to have very few options as you try to accomplish several things in a narrow physical space and time frame. You may experience confusion, and your level of anger may increase the faster you try to move. A feng shui canyon can be a very narrow entrance into any room or a small work space where tall things tower over you, such as bookcases, furniture, walls, people, or tight deadlines.

Canyons are the narrow places in your life where your financial resources appear to be very thin. There seem to be barriers to a larger view, and you wonder if you have enough money for today and the rest of the month or year. Your money seems to flow out very quickly. Moving through a narrow canyon at a fast pace implies a very small margin for error, maybe a hair's breath. Financial canyons include the sudden loss of a job or a major client, or having a major order or sale canceled. Talk of a recession while you are currently employed is another canyon. Are you trying to carry too much debt or holding on to too much of your old spending style as your options seem to narrow? Would lightening your financial load and pulling your "arms and legs" inside your vessel, perhaps slimming down your cultural and vacation expenses, enhance your movement forward?

A financial canyon is also where you seem to need to make quick financial decisions with very limited information and a narrow view of the long-term implications of your actions. You wonder if there is more money coming up behind you or more waiting just around the corner. Can you count on any financial support, or is there some disaster waiting for you—something that appears without warning? Does anyone know where you are, and is help coming or not? And underneath all of this you wonder whether your vessel and your money will last until you come through this challenging tight experience.

In a canyon, your thoughts come quickly and have a narrow focus, often a let's-get-through-this-in-one-piece focus. While moving quickly through a canyon with turbulent waters, you're rarely able to seriously consider the many options from your Rational Current. Your Creative Current quickly narrows to visions of impending disaster instead of opening up to some wonderful new approach to creating abundance. Taking even a five-minute time-out to calm your various currents may not seem to be possible in a canyon experience—yet it is necessary to shift your experience and navigate with some ease and grace. For example, rumors flow at your workplace and you suspect you'll be laid off, or the huge new client did not sign up with your company and you've already gone out and bought that new vehicle you've wanted. It's time to shift focus and pull yourself and your financial resources in a bit—or a lot. Time to let go of your previous living style—to spend less on the luxuries and even some apparent necessities, so you can create some flexibility with your spending options or some savings.

The biggest challenge in a canyon is to be honest with yourself about all of your currents. Acknowledge to yourself and allow yourself to experience your own body sensations and emotions even as you participate with whatever is happening. In the West, our stories and mythology often require you to "be brave" and discount your internal experience to yourself. Remember, emotions that are not experienced become a wave of energy caught in midcycle waiting for completion. Do you freeze your own emotional flow and then remain stuck in your frozen Emotional Current? When you notice repetitive canyon experiences in your life, it's time to pay attention. Cycles of energy held tightly in check reduce and impair your ability to move with ease.

When the river flows too fast for you and you must move or shift suddenly, some sort of injury—to your body, your environment, or your finances—may ensue. Allow yourself to experience your earlier cycles of emotional challenges, and check your intentions and the feng shui challenges in your environment for rapidly moving energy.

Wrecking your vessel with trapped, pent-up energy as you career through a narrow canyon is always an option—and a necessary part of some people's reality—but it is not a pretty scene to watch. Many hearts, bones, and financial agreements may be broken in the process. Being shipwrecked in a canyon adds to the drama of a good adventure story, but it will not aid in your movement toward the ocean of abundance. Right now take some deep breaths and name and claim your prior experiences in the financial canyons. Notice that they did come to an end and that you are still here and in fact becoming much wiser. Now you can move ahead and work on avoiding future canyon experiences.

THE COUNTING DANCE. Counting is done to keep track of the flow of money in and out of your life. Carry a small notebook with you to record when and how you spend or receive money. Remember to record every penny. Let go of any judgments, just record your emotions and body sensations along with the rest of the transaction, date, description of the item, and amount. Later you'll use this information to create your spending plan. In the meantime, doing the Counting Dance gives you time to check in and be honest with yourself as you spend money—cash, check, or debit or credit card. With these actions you literally count all of yourself in the money flow of your life, paying attention to some of the details you have been overlooking.

Engage your Creative Current and write with your favorite color of ink. Create some fun abbreviations for what you are experiencing, and consider giving yourself a gold star every time you remember to tune in before you hand over your money or credit card.

With the Counting Dance, your awareness of your patterns in dealing with a canyon experience or any other financial challenge can gently surface. Once you see these patterns, you can decide where to put your money with new clarity. You may realize that you are purchasing an item for some emotional or self-worth reason rather than as a necessity for your current life or your long-term financial well-being. Use this information in future decisions on spending money.

Rapids

Moving water in the midst of rocks and large boulders creates rapids. Rapids can appear in a canyon or in open spaces. They represent fast-moving energy flowing in the midst of stuck energy that has hardened into solid physical objects, impeding the larger flow and creating turbulence and chaos. The faster the flow, the more interesting the whitewater and the bigger the danger—and excitement! With rapids there is not enough empty or available space in the river for things to flow with ease. Things are too dense, and some "pruning" is necessary to open up space and induce a gentle flow.

Picture a room with awkwardly placed furniture that impedes your movement and flow from one area to another, or emotions that have congealed and hardened and are stuck in your body. Consider the thoughts that you rigidly hold on to that impair forward movement in your career and life, the rigidly held thoughts of scarcity and your unworthiness to receive abundance. All of these represent blockages in a flowing river of energy. In rapids the river does flow and the whitewater is exciting, yet past a certain point of excitement you realize that you are terrified and unable to move with ease. These rapids represent physical, emotional, and financial chaos that eventually frightens even the bravest among us.

Rapids and the chaos they create are feng shui nightmares. Lots of interesting and potentially dangerous things in your physical space, and even in your Wealth Area, are creating turbulent energy. None of them contributes to moving you safely through your space. Opening up the flow means removing clutter, moving furniture around to create a gentle path through your space, and moving out and releasing the furniture that holds old stuck energy that impedes your movement toward abundance. For example, a broken or beat-up couch or something that cannot be repaired can be a large obstacle. Holding on to it blocks your energy since every time you look at or think about it, the message of lack, broken, or beaten down rises to the surface. Abundance and wealth cannot harmoniously exist with such symbols of dissonance. Slowing down any fast-moving energy is also part of the process of addressing the rapids in your environment.

Your Rational Current flows like rapids when you keep encountering a repeating thought that holds you in check or prevents you from moving forward with ease. For example, thoughts like "I can't have a better job and more abundance," or "I'll never perform that task with ease or be financially free" are the hard rocks that create rapids in the flow of your Rational Current. These thoughts emerge whenever you begin to experience the flow of abundance, whenever the river begins to bring you your heart's longing. These thoughts actually create turbulence and drama, and may even lead to a serious "accident" that prevents you from enjoying your abundance with ease and joy. Other thoughts that create rapids are "I've never been successful before," or "I don't know how," or "I can't learn this stuff." Worry thoughts are classic boulders that show up in the midst of flowing thoughts. Rather than focus on blasting them to smithereens, just let your worry thoughts flow on by and focus on the more creative ideas and rational thoughts that will move you forward.

Your Creative Current encounters rapids when you imagine and continue to focus on the terrible things that will come from taking some positive and expansive financial action. As you hold on to an image of impending doom that hangs like a cloud over your life, you send this energy out into the universe, and it acts like a large boulder blocking the flow of your heart's desires to you.

Rapids include holding on to emotional energy until it has congealed and hardened. For example, anger held too long turns into bitterness and revenge, sadness congeals into a heart that becomes armored and closes off, and fear congeals into frozen movements where you eventually retreat into a protective cave. Eventually this stuck emotional energy will add to the blockages in the other flowing energy in your body and your physical space.

Your Body Sensations Current also experiences rapids. Pay attention to your tightly held muscles from old physical or emotional injuries. Imagine blood clots lodged in your blood vessels or heart. Consider, for example, the other stuck body fluids found in your various organs, such as bile stones in your gall bladder and kidney stones in your urinary track. The blocked energy that has congealed creates turbulence in each of these systems and impedes the free flow of fluid. Each of these blockages and the resulting rapids say "pay attention, there may be more blockages in other systems."

Money flow becomes blocked when it is held so tightly that its energy slows down, congeals, and eventually stops. Any money that does flow by, or goes out, does so with a lot of turbulence surrounding it. For example, picture some money buried in the ground or kept under a mattress. This money is stuck; it earns no interest while it is being held there and it is not available to grow in other ways. It is also surrounded with the energy of fear, literally the fear of its being lost or stolen by other people. This money is not placed in banks to earn more money for the fear that the bank may collapse or fail to return the funds to the rightful owner. All of this blockage and fear flows from an earlier loss or stories of earlier losses. If your flowing money once encountered some rapids, crashed, or was lost, now your pattern may be to hold it in place to prevent being shipwrecked on the challenges of life. This behavior pattern happens with people with hundreds of thousands of dollars and with people who have much less money.

Action Step

Now notice whether you are holding your breath or breathing shallowly, and begin to refresh yourself with a few deep breaths. Allow your own wind to blow away any cobwebs from looking at this stuck energy. What emotions are you experiencing? What thoughts are circulating through your Rational Current? Did any images show up on the screen of your Creative Current?

Do you have any money that is stuck? Would you be willing to release it into the flow and allow it to increase? On what day will you gather yourself and your money together and take action so it can begin to grow? What about your own Emotional Current? Is it free to go with the flow—or do you need a time-out to experience your full cycle?

Do you now see a feng shui challenge in a new way? Are you ready to take action and shift some furniture and belongings? By what day will you have made the changes?

You remove the rocks and the stuck energy in your flow one step at a time. Now consider where you and your other currents are blocked and whether you are willing to release the stuck energy. Something as simple as cleaning out your sock or makeup drawer or your entryway begins the process.

"Rapids was a new concept for me," Terry told me after a workshop on creating abundance. "I had assumed there was something wrong with me, the usual make-myself-wrong approach whenever I experienced a challenge in meeting a goal, especially financial ones. Once I began to inquire into my family's actions and beliefs, I began to see a pattern emerge. Someone had always pulled the rug out from under me just as I got going on a cherished goal. I had never let myself recognize any of my emotions around these crashes. Eventually the emotions and thoughts around them had congealed, and now I was cocreating that pattern for myself. It was very obvious in my environment. So I decided to change it. I began rearranging furniture, opening up new pathways. I even felt a shift in my body with the new arrangement. Then I allowed myself to feel, just a little, my stuck emotions and body sensations of tension. I began to move my body, allowing myself to dance before I started my chores at home. In a few days one project that had been sitting for months was finished. By the end of the month I'd even opened a savings account!"

Action Step

Gently expose and begin to dissolve the hard rocks that are lodged in your thinking patterns. Begin to work with the affirmations found in Appendix A. Choose one and use it for a day or a week. Allow it to free you from the pattern of rapids. Then choose another. Enjoy your new freedom!

Crosscurrents and Undertows

Unlike canyons and rapids, crosscurrents and undertows are difficult to spot from the shore. They show up once you are actually in the River of Gold and wondering why you are not progressing as planned. Crosscurrents require lots of extra work for you to even stay in place, so life becomes a struggle to maintain your position, let alone move forward. Undertows actually take you backward, away from your dreams and goals. Both represent values, belongings, thoughts, emotions, and actions that are out of alignment for each of the five currents. These dilemmas are calling out to be faced with a full-body approach. They can be accepted, embraced, and loved, and put in their proper place like all feng shui alignment challenges.

Classic monetary crosscurrents would be a missing feng shui Wealth Area in your office or home when you say you want to create more abundance. You have been living with it outside of your space. Without your awareness, you have been telling yourself that financial abundance is not important in your life. Your unconscious intention has been to be without wealth and abundance since it is missing from your space. Spend some time in quiet meditation considering what your heart's desires are and what actual feng shui cures would work for you and your space. Remember that one feng shui cure placed with intention is more powerful than several different cures placed quickly and haphazardly.

You may realize that nothing in your work space is set up so you can actually work with ease or keep track of multiple projects. The tension in your body increases as you work due to the nonergonomic placement of your desk, chair, telephone, computer, and body. Another crosscurrent is when you lose things, forcing you to spend your precious time hunting for something rather than creating a more positive flow. You are there at work, so on the surface you appear to be working and creating more flow toward abundance, but in reality you are unable to complete work-related tasks, such as finished projects, quick solutions to a challenge, answers for a customer, and billable hours. Instead, you spend your time in the energy of a crosscurrent heading off to another destination.

Action Step

First, look around for what is missing or out of alignment in your space and life. Engage your Creative Current and really explore your work area. Picture yourself explaining to a foreigner the functions of the equipment and the layout of your work activities. Perhaps sketch your work area and with a colored pencil, trace the flow of papers, your activities, and interactions with other people through your space. Use one color for things coming in and another color for things going out. Do you now see some possible improvements? When will you take action? Have you put off enhancing your Wealth Area? Review the Wealth Area cures. Then tune in to your heart and notice what calls out to you. Put it in place before a week passes.

Your awareness of a crosscurrent often surfaces when you tune in to your Body Sensations Current. Perhaps your pattern is to scatter your cash in multiple pockets in various outfits, then forget to empty them. You have money or think you do; you just can't seem to get to it. Or perhaps you may scatter your money in the various compartments of your wallet and/or purse, or in multiple accounts whose statements you seem to lose. At any point in time you cannot count your money and know what you have available to spend, to save and earn interest, or to purchase an asset that grows in value. Heads up! This is a classic crosscurrent stalling energy toward creating abundance.

Action Step

Let's look for things that are out of alignment. Take a few minutes and go through your pockets, wallet, briefcase, and purse. Release old papers and odd bits of things that are there, gather and arrange the paper money, and reduce the number of coins that you carry. Do the same for your vehicle.

Locate your checkbook and any bank statements. Reconcile your accounts. Put on some music, create a lovely atmosphere with a pleasant aroma, and shift into enjoying this process.

As you consider crosscurrents and engage your Creative, Body Sensations, and Rational currents, you may recognize other areas where you are not reaching your destination. Each of these reveals a series of flows where you are unaware of what is really happening, where the flow that appears on the surface is not what really happens in your life. You will find yourself reconsidering your intentions about creating financial abundance.

Underwater Intentions

Your intentions are always engaged and working, even if you have never paid any attention to them. Your below-the-surface, underwater, or unconscious intentions are always flowing. You become aware of them by taking a look at the results in your life. Your current results reveal your underwater intentions, and you can begin to change your results by setting new intentions. It's okay to be shocked and disagree with me! I did that too when I first encountered this information. If you have not paid much attention to your prior intentions, then just let go of any ideas or judgments about your past. Embrace it—it happened just the way it did. In fact, call it good and consider it as water under the bridge. From today forward, include setting an intention as part of your daily life.

Here is an interesting underwater intention that I watched surface. One woman, I'll call her Leslie, was complaining to the seminar facilitator about her employees. "I'm sure they're stealing from me and I want to know what to do about it! My customers love me, my products, and service, but I am not making any money with this business. What am I going to do about my employees stealing from me?" As I looked around while the facilitator gave Leslie her full attention, many people appeared sympathetic to Leslie's troubles. Then after several questions and answers, Leslie said, "Well, I never intended to make money with this business!" Several people's mouths fell open. I took a deep breath and relaxed and realized that I was glad I wasn't the facilitator. There in plain view was the source of her challenges—her underwater intention.

From the comments that followed, it quickly became evident to the facilitator and to me that Leslie didn't understand what she had just said. Without her realizing it, Leslie had "once upon a time" set a firm intention, probably even silently, and forgotten about it. She was very successful in meeting her below-the-surface intention, and her results confirmed that: not making money even though her products were great, her customers were happy, and her income seemed to be more than her expenses. Now, in order to meet her unconscious or below-the-surface intention successfully, someone or something had to fall in line with that intention—and her employees were the ones who complied. Probably they did not even realize or understand their part. Leslie had attracted the very people who would help her out—in this case out of money and products and being profitable. Leslie seemed quite confused since she only wanted to know what to do about her employees and was not open to considering her part in the problem. She ended up leaving the meeting looking as if she hadn't gotten any worthwhile information.

You, like Leslie, may be confused as you consider your underwater intentions and the results you are currently experiencing. Just begin with setting clear, spoken intentions and continue on with this journey. Eventually clarity about your prior underwater intentions will emerge as you go with the flow of the river.

Action Step

When you engage your Feng Shui Current, set an intention before you take action. When you decide to place a cure in a Ba-gua area, set an intention for the cure before you place it. Consider putting the item for your cure on your altar, or taking it to a very spiritual place, to absorb your energy and intentions for abundance with an open heart.

Now spend some time focusing on what you really want before you enter in to each upcoming experience. What kind of day would you like to have? How would you like to experience creating abundance? Look around your own home and work space with your Rational and Creative currents and consider your intentions for abundance and ease in your creative flow. Bring to the surface and release the thoughts and things that have not served you, and set some new intentions.

Commitment to Struggle

Heading upstream without a paddle is a common phrase for a good reason. It is a very real experience for many people and is often revealed in very public statements, repeated with a lot of energy and a sense of satisfaction or even righteousness. Commitment is simply bringing together and sending off, so being committed to the struggle means you've made a decision, a gathering of yourself and your resources, to continue struggling as you move through your life. Here in the West, there is a very general and widespread commitment to struggle seen in statements like "No pain, no gain," "I can't . . ." and "Life is a constant struggle." The difference between a commitment to struggle, which is publicly acknowledged, and underwater intentions is that the latter are silent and we are unaware that they exist. Commitments to struggle are proudly displayed. They are part of the culture in the West. Proudly and fiercely independent and committed to struggle, the hero triumphs over repeated battles with rough waters as he journeys onward—rather than being committed to ease and flow.

A commitment to struggle shows up in your Rational Current's repeated comments of "That will be very hard to do" or "Impossible!" "Life is hard and I have to struggle" or "No one has ever done that so why do you think that I can?" Whenever you say or think "This will take a lot of time and effort," you're restating your commitment to struggle. Saying "I can't keep track of money or my statements" also restates your commitment to struggle. All of these indicate that the erroneous thinking is flowing freely. This type of thinking actually invites more struggle into your life as you are vibrating in harmony with the frequency of struggle. Pay attention to your thoughts that indicate something is impossible or very challenging. Your life does not have to continue with the energy of struggle and conflict.

If you are willing to release your grip on and your commitment to struggle, you can choose to experience more flow and ease. Begin by checking with your various currents, your body and mind, and release any tension. Smile as you exhale, inspire yourself with a deep breath, and state a new commitment out loud saying, "I am willing to experience more ease in my life. I am willing to go with the flow." You also shift into a new flow when you change the sentence to say "In the past I believed that my life required pain and struggle. Now I am experiencing more ease," or "Today begins a new day where I am . . ." Omit following any of those phrases with "but now . . ." The vibration and the word "but" negates whatever thoughts precede it. It may seem like a small detail, yet these details matter to the flow of both your Rational and Creative currents. Use the word "yet," "except," or "however," and keep watch on your Rational Current, as it may still focus on repeating an old pattern. Simply smile, let go, and state out loud your new commitment. Bless yourself as you turn your vessel around and go with the flow.

Saying "I can't visualize or do artistic or creative things" is also a commitment to struggle against your Creative Current. "I can't visualize more abundance. It's too hard" is another one. Most people have experienced a challenging event early in life that led them to shut down this flow. The Emotional Current surrounding the event is also blocked. Pay attention to what you say and think about with both of these currents. And commit to taking a small step to open up the flow. Buy a tape or book, or attend a seminar where visualization is used or taught. Sign up for a creative activity. Turning your vessel around happens degree by degree and one step at a time.

Action Step

Examine the Feng Shui Current in your work and living spaces for commitments to struggle. Look for areas that are blocked, where you must struggle to get what you want or where you must detour or struggle to move from one area to another. Look at your closets and cupboards and your garage. Can you easily retrieve things, or do you experience another struggle? Are there doorways or areas where you must move things out of the way to just walk through? By when will you have cleared these areas?

Also look for a Five Element Regenerative (Destructive) Cycle, where one element is out of balance and another element continues to contribute to that imbalance. A destructive cycle is also a commitment to struggle, although a very subtle commitment, one that you may not yet be aware that you have. Schedule thirty minutes to focus on this information. Reread the section on the Five Elements and walk around your living space noting which elements are present and which are missing in each Ba-gua area. Keep track in your Travel Log. The solution may be as simple as moving some objects yourself, or it may require a full feng shui consultation.

Roger, a management consultant, said, "Over the last two years I had experienced several unpleasant and expensive surprises in dealing with my clients. I often said that life is a series of challenges and you must struggle to surmount them. A feng shui look at my office revealed that my back was to the door. People and situations could sneak up and challenge me, and they did. I had to rise from my position to address them. Turning my desk was not an option, so we placed a mirror on top of my computer monitor and on the wall in front of my workspace. Now whichever way I sit, I can see the doorway in my peripheral vision and am immediately aware when someone approaches. Amazingly, the surprises with my clients stopped as well." Roger shared with me that in his home he realized there were things stored behind many of the doors, reducing the opening space. As a result he struggled to move through some doorways and always struggled while bringing in groceries or other packages. Roger realized that both his verbal comments and having no other options in the arrangement of his office revealed his commitment to struggling in his work and his life. Opening up these doorways, expanding his awareness, and releasing his old commitment literally opened up the flow. Two years later his lack of expensive challenges and his improved finances revealed the inflow of abundance into his life.

Whirlpools

Whirlpools are spinning energy, where challenges arrive demanding your attention before you have recognized and addressed the prior situation. Such spinning energy throws you off balance, forcing you to take some sort of action when you are literally standing on one foot, in a contracted state, and being "bumped" by someone or something else. The consequences of a whirlpool appear life-threatening, and you may contract or clamp down on all of your currents to avoid them. You are overloaded with information and demands from various sources regarding which way to turn, where to invest your savings, which important client to contact first, what asset to buy, how to go about reducing your debt load, which demand of your boss's to work on first, and many more. A whirlpool of information eventually leads to inaction and missed financial opportunities.

Any time you are spinning, unable to make a decision or move forward, you are experiencing a whirlpool of energy. Sometimes it is just your own energy, sometimes not. Your basic response to uprising energy—your Four F Preference—comes into play here. You may not realize that someone or something else, perhaps from long ago, has influenced your natural ability to slow down, lean into your emotions, and breathe through the experience as you calmly analyze the situation. Literally you are spinning out of control with all of the energy.

From a feng shui focus, spiral staircases at home or work can create a whirlpool of energy, causing energy and money to quickly circle down from one level to another. If you have a whirlpool in one area, notice whether you also have another somewhere else in your space. Remember that the outer mirrors the inner. Thinking that such a staircase does not matter may indicate your insensitivity to whirlpools that are draining energy and money from your life.

In a financial whirlpool, many things are demanding your attention at the same time. All of them seem urgent and may result in dire consequences, such as huge financial penalties for missing a deadline. It is as if you are spinning around, listening to lots of financial ideas and moving from person to person, each one giving you advice and demanding that you take action. Too much data can be paralyzing. You literally drown as your overwhelmed circuits quickly try to switch from one thing to another while nothing creative or life-enhancing happens.

Multitasking—trying to attend to many activities all at once—is another type of whirlpool. You are requiring your Body Sensations Current to handle lots of quick actions. Your head swims as you try to focus on each item as it flies by. You barely have enough time to focus on one, let alone to look deeply and consider the consequences of your actions with your Rational and Creative currents. Important things that are buried in the wealth of information and frenzy of activity will slip by your notice. Things will come back later—perhaps as a lawsuit over some "missed detail" that impacts many people's lives. You look busy yet you are not really moving forward toward your deep heartfelt longings. The ocean of abundance remains outside your ability to focus when you experience a whirlpool of energy.

In a whirlpool of water, you hold your breath as you are sucked down. Here, dealing with such a challenging situation requires that you breathe and engage your Body Sensations and Emotional currents. Otherwise your emotions and adrenaline will flood over you and keep you spinning. Using the deep, abundant breath technique, even when you fear you will drown, stops the downward spin.

Whirlpools are revealed when you realize that the most important issue for your financial abundance is not the one associated with the loudest presentation. Or there may be demands on you that will not benefit you—just others. Investments and buying assets that drop in value may show up here. You can realize this only when you look at the "whole deal" for a few minutes and understand that taking this action was not your first choice and that any further participation indicates that you agree with the project or premise of spinning energy when in fact you do not.

Action Step

When you are experiencing a financial whirlpool of energy, take a time-out, breathe deeply and fully, and center yourself. Take a short walk. Begin some creative movement where you don't have to get anywhere or make any decisions. Doing this gives you time and space to access and assess your own currents. Take this time and space to identify what it is you are really dealing with and what you really want as you encounter this whirlpool of energy. Once you have slowed down and your mind has cleared, then ask yourself: What is really important and what do I really want? Once you have addressed these issues, consider what would be the best possible outcome for you and everyone else in this situation. An outcome that creates more financial abundance for you will begin to move you toward the Crystal Lake where your money can grow to even more.

Financial whirlpools often last for a while, so remember to take it slowly. Do the "aah" and the "om" Creative Meditations as part of your daily practice. They provide a significant time-out from the spinning energy and allow clarity to surface with ease.

Portage Path

When the river and your extra financial resources seem to disappear into very dangerous waters, and you find that you are carrying your own vessel rather than its carrying you, welcome to a Portage Path experience. It is different from a desert experience since there is still enough money and flow to support this part of your life. Your environment is still "green" and life-sustaining. Clearly, you have agreed to carry your vessel as you know that the river will appear safe again, and fairly soon. And carrying it is a necessary action to keep moving forward.

Acknowledging the heavy load may be all that your various currents need to shift you into enjoying an inner experience of abundance as you head toward where the river again flows smoothly and freely. Or you may realize that some other shifting is necessary for you to reexperience abundance. The question to ponder is whether you are carrying more than what you will really need or even want when you resume your journey. Many of us carry financial responsibilities that are quite large. We seem to support them when things flow nicely, yet when the extra money disappears into dangerous-looking waters, we become aware of how heavy these loads really are. These financial loads can be a very large house, two or more houses, several vehicles, many pets, or hosting numerous parties. They include serving on various nonprofit committees (with their hidden financial commitments to contribute), to supporting the hobbies of various family members, or even supporting your extended family.

Some people can carry their vessel easily for a short distance or time; for other people, it is the thing that tips them over and causes them to let go of their load. Checking in with all of your currents, especially your Emotional and Body Sensations currents, will give you a clearer understanding of how much of a load you can really carry.

Action Step

Suspend all judgment and gather up all of your credit card statements. Really look at how much debt you are carrying. Regardless of the individual balances or the total, stop adding to your debt load. Buy nothing on credit for one day, then one week, and then one month. Allow your load to stabilize. Begin the Penny Dance and Counting Dance if you have let those activities lapse. Feel free to say no to any new requests for your time, money, or support. Treat yourself very kindly, and attend some activity or event that is free and speaks to your heart. Remember to feel grateful several times a day.

Floodwaters

Most people long for sudden appearances of wealth or a flood of money, yet few people truly are prepared for a sudden large inflow of money. Few of us wish the challenges of actual floodwaters on anyone. Too many things can go wrong when the waters flood over their banks and spread far and wide. You wonder if you can trust your footing as you move through the surging waters. The losses can be enormous: homes, furniture, businesses, vehicles, animals, and even one's life.

So it is with sudden wealth; you may lose your old life in coping with the flood of abundance. At the very least you will need many more advisors—investment, legal, and tax—than you had before the inflow. When a lot of money suddenly appears—for example, if you receive an inheritance or win the lottery—it spills over all of your boundaries and impacts all your day-to-day activities and relationships. A flood of abundance and the stress that follows can ruin many relationships. Whom can you trust to give you good advice regarding where to spend, lend, and invest all that money? Are you ready for all of the calls from people and organizations that suddenly want you to share your abundance with them? Some friendships will grow deeper, yet with sudden wealth, people's hidden expectations surface. Many relationships are ruined by all of the sudden financial requests. You can avoid much of this by preparing for floodwater situations ahead of time.

Action Step

Whether you've experienced a flood of wealth or not, spend some time with your Creative Current imagining all of the things you would do with a large influx of money. Note your dreams in your Travel Log. Now spend some time listening to your Rational and Emotional currents and log those responses. Consider which advisors you already know and how you would interact with them. What long-cherished dreams would you engage and bring to life? From this information there may emerge some urge to readjust your life. Even small changes can lead to an experience of more wealth and abundance. Pay attention to your Rational and Creative currents for several days after you do this exercise; other information and heart longings may surface. These activities can prepare you for floodwaters that otherwise could be very destructive. Use your findings to turn floodwater situations into positive, constructive experiences to increase your wealth and sense of abundance.

Detours

John, a friend of mine, was enjoying his life, moving with ease and seeing his heart's longing coming into view. He called me to share his joy and his experiences and both of us saw his heart's desire moving toward him. Excitement vibrated through him; he was almost there! Then within a couple of days his focus suddenly shifted. He blinked and realized he was looking at a totally different scene. What had happened?

John took a detour just as he was readying himself to expand to a level of abundance unfamiliar to him. Often we resist the energy of "more" and its uncomfortable levels of intensity, commitment, and abundance. Many people detour into distractions just as they close in on their heart's desire. Detours show up in many forms, such as going on a spending spree, suddenly having to clean and straighten rather than working on a moneymaking project, creating an argument and then buying a gift to redeem yourself, focusing on a hobby, playing a game that lasts for hours or days, or eating and drinking to excess. With each of these actions we are unaware of what is going on around and in ourselves. Instead we arm ourselves against any wisdom our currents may share, and we create a detour to utilize this "excess" energy. We simply do not know how to enjoy, use, and focus this much energy. Instead of seeing an invitation to dance and resonate with the energy of "more," we perceive enormous danger in the unknown. We engage our familiar patterns to keep us safe and protect us—rarely admitting we "don't know" how to enjoy and move with the excess energy that is so close to us.

Each of our currents engages in our detour. The huge uprising energy overwhelmed each current in some way as we moved close to our dream of more. When we experience too much uprising energy, we stop in the middle of projects and activities that we love and take a detour. Right now notice whether you are still breathing—or did you take a detour? Fung shui hints of too much uprising energy in your past that led to a detour show up with unfinished projects lying around or hidden away and as a blocked area where you have trouble moving forward.

Detours result from imagining something uncomfortable and unknown—something that is not in a familiar area of your map. Ancient maps showed dragons in the areas beyond what was already known. Dragons are used here in the Eastern sense; they guard what is most valuable and possess great wisdom. In Chinese mythology, dragons are capable of growing to miles in length and shrinking to the size of a dragonfly. Dragons simply represent more energy than we have danced with comfortably—until now. Out beyond our limits of what we already know and experience, dragons are also there to guard dreams, heart longings, and levels of abundance. Anything beyond these limits is more energy than we commonly resonate with and allow to flow through us. Accepting and flowing with new energy is a challenge.

We begin moving all of that intangible energy by honoring our detour pattern, imaginings, and emotions. All you did with your detour was imagine and shift away from your destination. Now you can imagine shifting back and dancing with your dragon.

Action Step

Your dragon dance toward abundance begins with enjoying several deep abundant breaths as you embrace yourself and your experience. Get up and gently begin to move creatively. Play music that you love and step outside your holding pattern. Remember to breathe into any places in your body that seem tight or frozen. Allow the fiery energy of your dragon to gently thaw you. Then admit to yourself that you don't know how to move forward with that much energy. A simple "I don't know" allows you to resonate with your detour. You didn't know how. Instead you took a detour. Now tell yourself all the things that you imagine will happen out there. By moving around and speaking out loud, you release some of the pent-up energy so it can dissipate and flow on by.

Once you have released some energy and imaginings, then step into the flowing energy of the wonder move, using the "Hmmm? I wonder" energy. Here are several wonder questions:

"Hmmm? I wonder how I have been holding myself
   back and creating a detour."

"Hmmm? I wonder how I can embrace this
   new energy."

"Hmmm? I wonder how I can enjoy this experience."

"Hmmm? I wonder how I can create a sense of safety as
I begin to take the first steps toward my edge."

"Hmmm? I wonder how I will know what steps to take
next."

Using "Hmmm? I wonder" allows both halves of your brain to
work together as you face your unknown. Moving your body allows
you to thaw your frozen pattern. Fire-breathing dragons are only trying to warm the frozen energy they encounter. Their approach is just a
little too exciting for many people. As you breathe more, your fire-
breathing dragon will calm down and invite you back from your detour. Then both of you can continue on your journey on the River of
Gold.

Action Step

Begin today to spend even a few minutes on a long-ignored and partly
finished project. Take note of what you have to do that would allow
you to finish this project. Can you move forward without buying anything new? What small step can you take today? What step could you
take tomorrow, and later this week? Keep taking small steps, one at a
time, utilizing the warmth of your dragon's breath to warm your heart.

When you are finished with the first project, look at another partly
finished project. Do you still want to complete this project, or do you
want to let it go and open up space for something new? If you do want
to complete it, by when will you have begun to take action?

Noticing our detours and the dragon's energy dancing in front of
us is the very place where we can turn away from or experience some
very uncomfortable emotions, body sensations, and thoughts. Few of
us have been taught to turn, face, and lean into our emotions, to embrace and experience the very thing we run from. Instead we hope
such uncomfortable sensations and emotions will wither and die.

Dancing with your dragon is just that, moving with your body sensations and emotions, especially your fear. Your Creative Current is already flowing. Now see and experience the dragon's energy. Enjoy all of that flowing creativity!

Action Step

Look around your work and living space for the things that consume your time and energy and assist you in creating a detour experience. Do you really love these things? Do they assist you in moving forward toward your heart's longings? Are there any things around that you use to arm yourself against experiencing your emotions and body sensations? Do you love them? Do they represent creating abundance with an open heart? Would you be willing to streamline your life and space, release any of them, and create more alignment with your heart's desires for abundance?

Both dragon and detour energy are very powerful. You can feel and sense both when you are willing to look at the symbols and metaphors in your life and environment. Inviting your own dragons out to dance and play releases your own energy to go after and obtain the treasure you are seeking in the unknown. When you experience a detour, you're right at the edge of immense creative energy. Lean into and embrace that flow. Allow yourself to vibrate at a new level of intensity and enjoy the dance!

To summarize, water hazards on the River of Gold represent moving energy and issues regarding money and creating abundance when things are moving. There are also challenges on the journey when energy comes to a standstill or in standing waters. Let's see what adventures await us there.

10

The Doldrums: Overcoming Personal and Professional Obstacles

We play two major games in our everyday life as we go about creating abundance. These games rob us of energy and money, and most of all they detour us from our cherished dreams and goals. With these games we are very successful at distracting ourselves from the main flow of the River of Gold—sometimes for months or even years. Playing these games results in the doldrums where energy comes to a standstill. These games, and their slow or stuck vibrations, are so common that we forget that we are playing them. They become natural to us, and we think that this is real life. Most of us, me included, are stunned as the rules are explained. Once we begin to realize our part in creating the game and how it serves as detour, we can open up to how to get back into the flow.

The first game is Preserving Old Money Dramas, a game that represents our part in the common money dramas found in every family and business. The other major game is called Waltzing on the Sticky Triangle of Life, or playing the role of the victim, rescuer, or persecutor—or all three! How do these games impact your abundance? Let's take a look.

THE SEA OF SALT

The first game, Preserving Old Money Dramas, is located in the Sea of Salt. Why do I call it the Sea of Salt? Salt is used to preserve and enhance the flavor of food. What this game does is preserve and flavor the whole drama of our life, our own masks, and our own money scripts in which we are playing a role. Bodies of water become full of salt when there is significant evaporation and nothing flows out. The Dead Sea and the Salton Sea, in California, are two examples. They do not sustain much life, and if you are actually in them, they will draw the water and moisture out of your body. Remember, water is a symbol for money. The Sea of Salt allows people to float along on the surface and to appear to move from one place to another, but going deep into the water is a challenge. Your money script remains hidden from full view while the salt is drawing out the moisture and money from your life. The Sea of Salt receives the flow from the River of Gold but diverts and collects it. Getting out of the sea and back into the larger flow means stepping out of your old view of how things work in your life.

Feng Shui and the Sea of Salt

In the Sea of Salt, there is no movement forward and what accumulates is not really what you want when you take a deeper look. From a feng shui perspective, you may have an abundance of something that is out of balance, say too much metal energy in your Wealth Area. Look again at the diagram of your living and work space, your Wealth Area, and the Five Elements. Many imbalances in your physical space are direct reflections of the various masks you wear, the personas in your life. Once you have begun to tease out your roles in the various dramas, you can see the specific ways you and your varying personas impact your environment. Walk around your own space looking for things that are out of alignment with the various Ba-gua energies and with your deep heart longings. For example, perhaps you have symbols of money and abundance in your Relationships Area, travel symbols in your Wealth Area, a missing Wealth Area at your work, or too much wood energy and a feeling of stuckness. Review the cures and Five Elements sections. Put the various cures in place only after you have "sat" with them for a few days to know that they fit your challenges and that your intentions are clear.

Looking at someone else's life may clarify the issue. Penny shared with me that she is beginning to enjoy her main drama of waiting for permission. As a child she was admonished many times to wait and to be good and do the right thing, which in her family meant not giving her mother any trouble. To receive love and approval for who she was, she went along. As a child and, as a teenager, she became "a good girl." She continued to wait for permission and approval, which resulted in going along with her parents' choice for college and a major. She also waited for them to indicate their preference for a husband. And for years she allowed her husband's preferences to take precedence over hers. Her home had a stuck feeling. There was too much wood energy in many areas and no red, fire, or passion energy. When she turned fifty, she found herself wondering who she really was. Penny began to find herself when she started to focus on her main complaint: "No one ever listens to me!" Now she listens to herself first, without waiting for permission from anyone. Just yesterday she said "no, thank you" to a volunteer organization that had assumed that she was waiting for them to call and would just go along with their request. She also told me "no, thank you" when I asked her to join me for lunch; she had already made other plans. Penny was now able to recognize and enjoy her main drama—waiting for permission to speak—and step out of her role of being a good girl. Her money drama also fit her main drama. She kept track of all of the financial details while someone else made the big decisions. And yes, she kept beautiful and orderly financial records that just waited for someone to notice how nice they were. Now she has taken control of her own financial decisions and doesn't wait for anyone.

Looking at your life as a drama may be a stretch. And considering your money script may start your head spinning. Begin to listen to your complaints and consider your old stories—the ones that you have heard about your family and told about yourself. Few people actually listen for their story and the family's financial drama—the old stories of people who had, made, spent, saved, and lost money. These stories are important; they create our own attitudes toward abundance. Listening with an open heart to the old stories reveals the details of your own patterns, the life you are living from your script, including your money script. Only by paying attention to what was so ingrained and discovering what parts we want to keep and what we want to release overboard do we become free from the past and able to create a new life and script. A drama can be a comedy or a tragedy, and your interactions with money probably have been both.

Preservation

A *drama* begins with a theme and various characters. You may already have some idea of the ongoing drama in your life and your work and the roles you play. Let's assume that you don't and go back into the dramas to discover the themes from the various masks that show up and the roles you step into.

Life appears to go along and we seem happy, and then some challenge occurs and we, as actors in this drama, fundamentally adjust ourselves and how we behave to keep afloat in our current environment. This situation marks the beginning of the drama of preservation. One adjustment calls forth another and another, and the various cycles of energy flow are short-circuited by the heavy masks and costumes. Some body sensations and emotions are sent underground while others step out into the spotlight. This process begins very early in our life. We desire to remain in good graces with the other major players in our life so we put a mask over our true face, our true self, and turn down the volume inside that says we are capable and our dreams are important. Instead we begin to focus on preserving the drama and money script of the major players—our family, tribe, and religious community— while we step into a minor role.

We stay afloat and weather the challenge, but one day we might experience something that causes us to question who we really are, where we are headed, and what we really want. We suddenly realize we are not going anywhere; rather we're stuck in the Sea of Salt, maintaining ourselves based on life as we lived it long ago.

Persona

When we encounter a challenging situation, or a series of them, often we try to deal with it by creating a "persona," which comes from the Latin word for mask.

With a persona, there is dissonance between who we really are and the face and energy flow that we present to the world. Under the mask are the thoughts, emotions, and body sensations that we hide from the world and from ourselves, the very ones that were part of the overwhelmed feeling of the initial experience(s) that called forth our mask. These energies are stuck. We continue to add to those denied energies as we live our lives and play our part in the ongoing dramas. Much less energy flows through us. Yet here is the key: Over time we become our persona. We spend energy preserving it and forget who we really are under the mask. Years later we may begin to question and to recognize our persona whenever we notice that we are feeling "a bit off," as if there is something going on within us. There is! Our mask has slid into place, to preserve our role in the ongoing drama.

Each persona has a costume of outward markings—the clothes we wear, the classic body postures, the range of movements, and the preferred emotions—that are scripted into the given role. In order to remain safe in the environment where the challenge initially happened, we adjust our breathing, our movement style, and our thoughts. We also change our dreams, usually reducing the goals that we reach for or setting them up way beyond our reach. All the while we are wondering why accumulating and enjoying our abundance is such a struggle. We have literally forgotten ourselves. We are lost inside our persona and our role in the larger dramas.

The postures and movements of your persona reveal how your Body Sensations, Rational, Emotional, Feng Shui, and Creative currents are frozen and held in check. Notice your own breathing patterns and those of the people around you. Are they breathing deep, full, and relaxed, or shallow and life-threatening? Just changing your breathing is enough to cause a shift in your sense of well-being—and doing so begins to release your grip on your scripted role and persona.

Your persona impacts your methods, dreams, and actions toward creating abundance. You cannot experience the full range of your peripheral vision through your mask. So you begin to miss opportunities. Seeing any more than your role requires you to turn your head and sometimes your whole body, so you also take your eyes off your goals and the flow of the River of Gold. Doing this takes time and energy that you could use to move forward if you were not wearing your mask or engaged in preserving your persona.

Life jacket ready? Let's go! By the way, what style and color of jacket did you just picture? Serious orange, military fatigue green, high tech, or a fashion-forward model? Each one represents a preference of your preferred persona. The roles we play, with their corresponding costumes, say a great deal about how easy and fun our journey to the ocean of abundance will be.

CLASSIC PERSONAS Each of these personas shows up in an identifiable costume and moves into the body in recognizable patterns. They also engage with other people and their personas in classic ways. Why am I bringing all this up? Each persona interacts with money, making attracting wealth and abundance much more challenging than it needs to be. With your persona engaged you'll find yourself lost, floating in the midst of the Sea of Salt rather than off enjoying the flow of the River of Gold and creating abundance. To make it easier to locate yours, here are a few of the classic personas:

Space Case/Cadet	Con Man/Woman	Bumbling Fool
Sickly Child/Adult	Stud	Flirt
Superman/woman	Mighty Mouse	Martyr
Helper	Host/Hostess	Caregiver
Hypochondriac	Geek	Mr./Ms./Mrs. Fix-it
Rebel	Tough Guy	Misunderstood Genius
Cop	Jock	
Robber	Big Man on Campus	Know-It-All
Wishy-Washy	Underdog	Beauty Queen
Sex Kitten	Good Girl	Class Clown
Hussy	Miss Perfect	Inquisitor

Loner	Careless Idiot	Crusader
Saint	Worrier	Suffering Artist
Rogue	Dreamer	Warrior
Doormat	Spoiler	Clumsy
Harried Businessperson	True Believer	Show-off

And yes, there are more. In fact, your favorites may not be listed, or you may have some more interesting names for them.

Action Step

As you review the list of Classic Personas, jot down in your Travel Log some of the ways each familiar persona dresses, moves, and speaks; the persona's theme song; what emotions the persona would favor and avoid; and how the persona would interact with challenges and with money. Somewhere your own persona preferences will come to light. Spend some time feeling love for your own persona. Thank it for working so hard to keep you safe all of these years. Embrace your own persona and the person you were when it first showed up.

FINANCIAL PERSONAS It's time to recognize your own financial personas—the masks you wear when you focus on creating abundance—and how they drive you. Maintaining your persona costs you both energy and money. Many people remain frozen in time, locked in an old persona and drama. These same personas prevent you from pursuing true abundance and instead throw you on the rocks of ruin or require repeated passages through rough waters.

Each of us has at least one financial persona, and most of us have two or more. Feel free to add to this small list:

This Is a Big Deal	Money Is Evil	Easy Come, Easy Go
High-Stakes Gambler	Tightwad	Spend, Spend, Spend
	Nothing Works	I Can't Understand Money
It Ain't No Use	I Can't Afford It	
Poor Me	It's Only Money	The Rules Don't Apply
Let Met Help You	Clueless	
Penny Wise/Pound Foolish	Wannabe Rich	There Will Always Be Enough
Bargain Shopper	Happy Idiot	Sharp Pencil

Action Step

Which ones call out to you? Which ones seem most distasteful? What other phrases and names would you use? Note all of this in your Travel Log. Notice what costume you put on when you slip into your persona, what money/financial activities you prefer to engage in and which ones you avoid. Consider what they do to create or consume abundance. What kinds of situations or dramas drive these personas? How can you change these situations to encourage more abundance? What might your larger drama and money drama look like?

Spend some time sending love and gratitude to your financial persona(s). They have been working very hard to safeguard you and your abundance based on the money drama they are engaged in.

To identify the presence of your financial persona, pay attention to all of your currents and sensations as you interact with the flow of money in your life. Notice your energy flow while paying your bills, buying a special treat for yourself or someone else, accepting a compliment or gift or money, or covering the tab for a friend or relative on an outing.

Noticing your currents as you deal with your boss or colleagues will be especially interesting since that is where you spend hours of time and lots of energy. Also notice whether you are preserving an old script, playing variations, creating a new script, or flowing and creating abundance as you recognize your own personas.

Action Step

Before you realize it, you have put on your costume and are engaged in protecting your persona and your place in the play. Once you realize you are engaged, spend some time noticing what was happening just before you engaged. Were you experiencing flow, contractions, and blockage, or being overwhelmed?

What emotions were you resisting? What body sensations were you trying to ignore or control? What thoughts were racing through your mind? What were you imagining would happen?

Whose voice was talking or shouting at you—inside your head or not? What scene were you about to replay? How old were you when this scene first occurred? Who else was involved? What or who were you trying to protect? Who got injured? Who was rescued? What triggered it? How often did this happen? How do you feel about it now? What else is triggered by remembering these things? All of these questions are worthy of some time and space in your Travel Log.

Remember, you are floating on the Sea of Salt and preserving someone's script as long as you resist owning your part in the money dramas that are central in your life. What we resist persists; what we face and embrace will lose its grip on us and our life.

Let's look at Les's story. Les made good money working in sales for a high-tech company, and his clients loved him. He was always pleasant with the accounting people, yet he couldn't understand why anyone would spend their time crunching numbers like that. So he didn't. He always had some sort of receipt somewhere; he just didn't pay any attention to keeping them together. Classic for I Can't Understand Money personas. Sometimes Les found receipts days or weeks later, stashed in a pocket or folder. This drove his assistant nuts. "It's only money," he would say. His assistant occupied the Sharp Pencil and Let

Me Help You personas, and together they managed to keep Les's income flowing. His wife played the same role at home with their investments. It turns out that Les's dad had been obsessed with making money and keeping track of details, recording amounts down to the penny, including Les's earnings and spending as a child. Very early on Les had vowed that he wouldn't be like his father. And he was not; now he focused his energy on quietly rebelling, resisting and pushing against his dad. His financial personas fit nicely with his subtle rebellion against his dad's "obsessive" focus on money.

As an adult, Les learned that his dad had had a partner who had been too easy with money and details. They nearly lost the business and their shirts. His dad had taken charge and turned things around, however, he didn't understand that his unresolved anger and fears were running and ruining his life. Both Les and his dad were focused on creating abundance; yet, their perspectives on the story, personalities, personas, and techniques were very different. Soon Les decided to adjust his manner of keeping receipts. His deeper appreciation for details and the people who handled them well shifted those relationships, and his money flowed with more ease. Les's eventual reconciliation with his father—from whom he had angrily distanced himself many years earlier—was an answer to his mother's prayers. Now Les is included in the flow of love and abundance from his family.

Enough

So, you may be saying, what do these personas and stories have to do with creating abundance? Everything! They are at the very core of not getting or creating what you really want. Each of us has a Number-One and a Number-Two Persona who engage when we feel afraid and think that there is not enough of something—not enough money now or for the future, or the fear that we will be left short of money when we need it the most. Many of us also conceal some unresolved anger about someone else having more—more than enough money, food, a bigger nicer home, better jobs and clothes than we do. The classic statement "It's not fair!" brings with it feelings of fear, anger, and sadness.

For each of us the "Not fair!" events in life are played out under the weight of our costume and money script, rather than simply facing and experiencing the full cycle of our emotions, imaginings, body sensations, and thoughts. Again, any energy held in midcycle will keep repeating until the full cycle is experienced and allowed to flow on and dissipate.

Your own Number-One and Number-Two Personas come into play as you go about creating abundance. Number One shows up as you seem to be successful, and Number Two emerges when you come up against some obstacle. Your banker, boss, and colleagues also have their own Number-One and Number-Two Personas. Add these up and there are enough people to create an event! We parade our personas around in a persona promenade as part of a larger event, the grand masked dramas that many of us mistake for real life.

Now imagine one person changing her lines and her place on the stage of the grand money drama. Picture the many adjustments and reactions that the rest of the actors on a stage would make to keep an old play going. For a while many actors would be confused, ad-libbing as they tried to get back on track, to a known place in the drama. This is what happens when you step out of your persona. Wonder where all of these money scripts come from? I thought so.

Money Scripts

Your particular money script is lifted from the larger drama of your family of origin. Although this should come as no surprise, it does for most people. No one ever admits to this, but your great-grandfathers and great-grandmothers initialed your particular script when they birthed your grandparents.

Your great-grandparents did not know that they were writing a script for you when they birthed your grandparents and started telling the old stories. Your grandparents did not know that they were writing and adding to your parents' scripts, and yours, when they gave birth to and named your parents and continued to pass on the old stories.

Nevertheless, your script was written, signed, sealed, and delivered. Let's look at the script before your parents' scripts. Begin to notice where and how you are living out the story that people put into motion long ago. Your family gave you a role in its financial drama by virtue of your relationship; however, you can change that role or how you play it. Now exit stage left for a costume change, gather up your Travel Log, and put on some music you love.

Action Step

Whom are you named after? Whom do you look like or take after? What are the old stories about the person who had your name? Who plays the villain in your family? How much do you resemble them? Who plays the hero? Who makes or has a lot of money? In what way do you take after this person? Who plays the victim and does without? Who loses money? How do you resemble them? Who rushes in and saves the money and the day? Are you expected to follow suit in any way?

Which classic and financial personas are already claimed in your family? Which ones are still available? Which ones are off limits? What careers are acceptable in your family and which ones are not? What part do you want to play, and whom do you want to be in the family story? Notice your reactions to identifying and releasing your personas and changing your roles. Give yourself some time to integrate this information and allow all of your currents to go through a full energy cycle. Get up and move around to some music as you experience all of this energy.

You keep your family's money drama going whether you realize it or not. You simply continue to play your part until you become aware of the drama. Once you are aware, you can review your prior choices to play along or to resist. Only then can you make a new choice, think new thoughts, and take new actions as you release the backlog of emotions and energy you have held close to your heart and dragged along like excess baggage.

Action Step

Write a short outline of your family money drama, your initial choices, and how old you were when you made them. Consider whether you are still enjoying your prior choice(s) and whether they are moving you toward the abundance you desire.

Business Action Step

Now change the focus of the last two exercises to business to see what roles you are playing there. Remember to insert your nickname and who you align with or are mentored by. Which personas do you assume and recognize while at work? In your relationships with your boss and colleagues, which personas do you parade about? As you go about creating abundance, which personas do you prefer to interact with? Which personas do you avoid? Which ones do you dislike? Loathe?

The results of the money drama in any group indicate a lot of people working at cross-purposes rather than the presence of a cohesive goal. Recognizing which money scripts are present at work is the first step toward effective teamwork and increased abundance.

Action Step

Is your organization making money and becoming abundant or not? How about the feng shui of the offices; does it support the goals? Are you making money while playing your role in this organization and its drama? What about the feng shui of your office and your living space; do they support your financial goals? How well preserved is your role in this drama? Each person influences the play. Over time, the theme of the act and the whole drama can change and influence an organization's overall abundance. Would you be willing to embrace your personas and your emotions?

Projections

Projection Acts are part of the larger drama. Taking their name from the film industry what you see "out there" on the screen comes from what is "inside" the projector. Projection Acts happen when a person becomes the projector. The person who is seeing something outside of himself calls attention to it and forgets that it is a reflection of what is going on inside of himself. Everyone engages in this little act, and almost no one recognizes it for the first hundred times the scenes are rolled out for other people to see. Projections surrounding money are numerous. Here is an example:

Several years ago Betty noticed that everyone at her firm was suddenly spending more time at lunch than they had in the past six months. One day she blew up at her lunch partner about the issue, accusing her partner and everyone else of being slackers. It turns out that she had missed a memo officially extending the lunch break another fifteen minutes because, for the prior year, all of the salaried staff had been working through lunch or staying late to accomplish a firm-wide goal. In essence, the message was for everyone to get out of the office for a few minutes every day. However, Betty had never allowed herself this extra time, claiming she worked hard enough without needing it. When she looked back through her memo file, she couldn't find her copy, so two colleagues handed her their copies. Both had handwritten on them "You deserve this!" She never did find her copy of the memo. She did, however, decide to put herself on a projectionless regime, and she gave up using the word "slacker."

PROJECTIONS AND MONEY How do projections apply to money and creating abundance? Any time you are talking about someone else, ask yourself how you are like that person. If you realize you are complaining, take a deep breath and look at your body sensations. Notice what emotion you are feeling or avoiding, and scan your life to see if you are doing the very thing you are complaining about. Seeing other people as thieves, scoundrels, tightwads, or spendthrifts invites an inquiry into whether you can be considered in the same way. Once you realize your place in the Projection Act, then open your arms and welcome that persona and energy into your awareness and feel love for both of you.

For example, several years ago I listened to a man who worked in the fraud detection division of a state agency. Over several months I noticed that nearly every observation he made about other people or organizations implied fraud was being perpetrated on someone. I was even told how stupid I was to patronize my usual mechanic, gas station, car wash, and on and on, because they were clearly defrauding me. I got to where I had to stifle a smile whenever I spoke with or heard this man speak. I quickly learned that he was not interested in any other information when I tried sharing my own emotions, feelings, imaginings, and observations. Even my sharing was tainted with fraud, according to his view. We verbally sparred back and forth until an ugly scene ensued. Then one day I learned the man had three cats that his landlord did not know about, nor had he paid the extra pet deposit when he moved in. Oops! His projections of fraud had been in full flower.

Action Step

From a financial perspective, think about how you engage in the Projection Act at home. Now consider how it might play out at work. Or in your religious community. What are your favorite scenes to project onto another player? Which ones do you seem to have projected onto you? How does all of this impact your abundance? Write about what you are imagining in your Travel Log.

Let's consider one last drama.

Ralph loved big deals. He played life large and was always chasing after the next big thing. He also liked to say that the rules didn't apply when big money was involved. He had some great winners, and he lived like it—until the bottom dropped out of his life. In one year he went from being a multimillionaire to losing his company and filing bankruptcy, going through a divorce, and foreclosure on his home. A classic Grand Fall. It turns out that his former home was missing its Wealth Area, and he didn't know about feng shui at the time. In the Career Area of his yard was a very fast-moving waterfall without a collecting pond.

His former personas—"this is a big deal," "the rules don't apply here," and "harried businessman"—were running his life. They flowed from his childhood, when he saw his mother pinch pennies and work really hard. His dad had left them behind as he sailed off into a new life. Stories of an inheritance and lots of wealth floated back but no money. There had not been enough of anything during his parents' marriage and his youth. Ralph was driven by never having enough—money, love, things, ideas, or time. As a result, he was always doing something to get more. Even when he was at the top there was never enough, and he could never do enough. After he crashed, he began to build his life rather than react to his past. He shifted his focus to inside and learned to love and forgive himself. Then he experienced enough for the first time in his life from a firm foundation of an inner sense of abundance.

Your classic and financial personas work together to protect you from old views of financial challenges and ruin. Your projections show up on someone else so you can see them, integrate them, and let them go. All of your dramas and personas are old patterns of protection when the world seemed dangerous and there was not enough. They will continue to limit you until you recognize them and appreciate them for all that they have done for you. You can loosen their grip on you when you send them love and reach out and embrace them. They will continue to be a part of your life and may show up whenever a financial challenge appears. Love them and play with them. They are a part of you. Laugh when they show up as just another indicator that you are at the edge of moving forward into a larger flow of energy and abundance.

Each persona has classic ways of engaging, playing its role, and creating abundance. Now you have a sense of your family drama and your money drama. You realize that sometimes the money flows and there really is abundance, and sometimes there is just noise about how it doesn't show up. Stand up and stretch. Are you ready for something new?

STANDING WATERS

Another major game people play is called Waltzing on the Sticky Triangle, the Flypaper of Life. We play this game in the Standing Waters, in the swamplands of our lives. Waltzing on the Sticky Triangle actually prevents you from engaging your creativity and enlivening your own dreams. Instead, you focus on playing the game and participating in the activities, thoughts, and relationships that create a stuck and foul living environment—in other words, a swamp. Nothing happens in this swamp that would move you closer to your heart's desire. Each persona adds its own flavor and unique flair to this game, and each persona can show up and play any of the positions in this game.

Swamps are like debt. The more you have and the more it increases, the less able you are to move forward. At some point your debt can swamp your vessel and take you down. Swamps are bodies of murky, cloudy water where you cannot see the bottom. There is no clarity in your thinking or your emotions—or your heart's desires. Swamps are also great places to hide things from yourself and other people, such as your personal debt load, whether you have paid your share of the expenses, or how much you spent on your hobby last week. Moving forward in a swamp is like waltzing on the flypaper of the Sticky Triangle, where you are the fly that is caught and stuck.

Waltzing on the Sticky Triangle

The Sticky Triangle was first described in the 1950s. Originally it was outlined as the victim-persecutor-rescuer triangle (V-P-R triangle), and people appeared to take up residence on one of the positions, from which they viewed life. Now we realize that a person can move from position to position. Personas from your classic and financial dramas are also quite welcome to participate in this waltz. In fact, they add to the murkiness that hides below the surface of this game.

The game begins when someone is financially wronged (or thinks she has been), and believes she can do nothing to set things right. She begins to tell other people about the financial injury and the impossibility of the situation. Someone else hears the story and is deeply moved to solve the problem, to rescue the wronged victim, who is obviously helpless to do anything about the situation. The rescuer, of course, is the only one to take action and solve the financial dilemma. The rescuer demands in his own way that the persecutor stop whatever she is doing that keeps the dispute going. The persecutor believes that she is just exercising her right to demand the money or take from the victim what is hers, by right, of course, and she will not stop. So to recap, you have three positions: the Wronged Victim, the Rescuer, and the Persecutor. Any or all can be wearing the favorite mask of their persona.

For the game to be played one party must have the presence of the other two parties. However, all of the positions can be occupied by three, two, or even as few as one real persona. The glue that holds the game together is that none of the three players is aware of the layers of emotion that hide under the complaints and accusations. You can begin to see why most of us don't recognize this game. The underlying theme that keeps the game going is that each party believes him- or herself to be right and the other party(s) to be wrong and thinks everyone else can see the truth in his or her position. So the Sticky Triangle game also includes playing "I'm Right, You're Wrong," along with "Aha! Gotcha!" and "Waiting for Change." Getting anywhere while standing on the Sticky Triangle is nearly impossible. The players are stuck glued to their position.

VICTIMS' ROLL CALL You can hear victims stepping onto the triangle even before a move is made. They have been wronged. Things did not turn out for them, and they don't know how to turn anything around. Notice their body posture and the tone of their voice. They need help and money, and they are the first to tell you so. Just listen to the vibration of helplessness that resonates through their voice box like a whine. Helpless whines have a certain quality in common regardless of what persona is engaged. Learn to recognize the various whines in your life: "I can't afford this." "I don't have any money to give you." "I really need the money." "My money just disappears." "They just came in and just took it." "How come I have to do all this work?" "I never make enough money." "I got laid off again." "Where did I go wrong? How did this happen to me?" Victims play the game "I lose and you win."

Action Step

Consider the complaints you voice. Now think about the ones you don't speak out loud. You spend your energy and step into the victim position with both actions. Allow yourself to recognize when you have moved into position. Take time really to experience your Emotional Current, all the hurt feelings that come out through your voice that are looking for a place to resonate. Remember, no judgment. Everyone steps into the victim position from time to time. Eventually five min-utes will become enough for you to hear your own call, the one that says "I feel hurt."

RESCUERS FRONT AND CENTER! Irresistible urges call rescuers. They just keep responding and responding. A classic rescuer is the knight in shining armor. Often the rescuer has a romantic appeal, for the victim or for the persecutor. Rescuers' hearts are engaged and their wallets are wide open, ready to help at a moment's notice. Knights need maidens in distress, or businesses that need to be bailed out, so they can put on their suit of armor, mount their trusty steed, and whip out their checkbook, or call their investment banker or their accountant, and send money flowing.

Rescuers are the glue that holds the game together. They care and feel, with their heart pumping full out, that they have to keep every-one going. They also think that the victim cannot take action without them. Rescuers engulf rather than empower, and they are committed to helping until the bitter end. Sometimes they become bitter before they get engaged in their own dreams. The solution that dissolves the glue is empowering a rescuer as well as the victim.

The costs to rescuers can be very high. Their generosity can lead to their own perpetual debt, lost income, and poor money management. Despite rescuers' charitable efforts, victims rarely thank overly quick and generous rescuers, especially when they do not feel empowered. Rather the victim is glued to the Sticky Triangle and committed to the game of being rescued and making the persecutor wrong. Few people who occupy the rescuer position want to admit that they were badly used—and that they took a misstep and engulfed rather than empow-ered. The sting is too close to their heart. Rescuers play the game "I lose and you lose."

Action Step

Spend some time considering when and how you volunteer your time or money to help those with whom you live and work. Do you feel tired and drained afterward? Does your money seem to evaporate among various other complaints? What personas show up when you step into the rescuer position? What emotions are you avoiding? And please, don't add up the money you have already spent. It's gone, so forgive and love yourself. Now, what dreams have you been postponing? By when will you begin to take action on your own dreams?

PERSECUTORS Persecutors elevate their own standing by taking advantage of someone else. They see a weakness and move in to take advantage of some fairly easy pickings. Bullies are a classic example, as are shady characters, whether they are landlords, shop owners, drug dealers, or anyone else. I've even seen this position played in religious communities behind a large façade of denial. Persecutors lurk behind doors, alleyways, smiles, and business plans, looking for an opening. Unfortunately, persecutors rarely open their hearts to their own old "hurts." Persecutors play "I win and you lose."

Action Step

This step takes courage. Right now, only you need to know that you step onto the persecutor position. You do. I do. Everyone does from time to time. No judgment, just awareness and compassion. To shift your perception, consider some classic persecutor comments: "How could you spend that much?" "Why did you do that?" "Who made this mess?" "I'm going to get you to pay for this no matter what!" "You just wait until _____ gets here! Then you'll really pay!" "I'm going to give you something to really worry about!" "I'll throw the book at you!" "Do that and you're going to be sorry." "How stupid could anyone be?" This is classic I'm-right-and-you're-wrong energy. Take a moment and shake all of this energy off yourself.

Which of your persona(s) slip into the persecutor position? What happens just before you make that move? What goes on just after you take up residence on the Sticky Triangle? Awareness can allow you to take a time-out, breathe, and catch yourself so you don't go there. This is where your belief that there is "enough" in the universe is severely challenged. Be kind to yourself, then offer that kindness to someone else.

Stepping off the persecutor position can have some amazing results. By letting go of your demands and shifting your focus to creating your own abundance, you allow the universe to send money and abundance to you from other sources. Haggling over a drawn-out divorce and child support are classic examples of the oscillation between the persecutor and victim positions on the Sticky Triangle. I have heard numerous stories from both men and women of letting go their demands for more money or visitation rights, then turning and loving themselves and their children, and focusing on creating their own abundance. Within a year or two they have twice the money and abundance as the disputed amount. It came from a different source from their original focus. They now experience more love with their money. I've also heard a couple of stories where years later the person who was resisting has a huge change of heart and everyone benefits from the increased love and money flow. The former resistor now pays for everyone to come and enjoy time together and covers all the costs. It all began when the person occupying the persecutor position let go, began to refocus energy, and forgive . . . everything. Money talks. Forgiveness speaks even louder. Give it a try.

Stepping Off the Triangle

You begin to dissolve the stickiness of your position on the Sticky Triangle just by realizing you are playing the game. Take some deep breaths. Give yourself some space to realize and resonate with your position on the triangle. Experience the emotions underneath your persona and role and part in this game. Notice which of your personas steps into which position. Now wonder about how you are contributing to your complaint and how you are keeping the game going.

Any of a number of steps can be the first one that begins to dissolve the glue:

- Exhale and take a deep full breath.

- Listen for the sound of a whine in your own voice.

- Notice what emotion you are not experiencing.

- Pay attention to how you are holding your body and where you experience tension.

- Notice any repetitive motion, such as twirling or stroking your hair, rubbing your arm or face.

- Wonder what you did to create this situation.

- Admit, first to yourself, your emotions and imaginings.

- Share that you realize that you are playing one of the positions on the triangle.

- Share the experience you are having, the body sensations that have surfaced, and your emotions.

Once you have realized you are on the Sticky Triangle, you then are able to move to the space outside the triangle. From this place you can release your body holding patterns and your grip on the complaints or challenges.

Only after you have let go of the game can you move creatively and spend some time in addressing new solutions to the situation at hand. Now it's possible to approach a financial challenge from a new angle. Maybe you'll focus on altering your spending habits, pursuing a more favorable loan or mortgage rate, creating more income flow, or just setting up a schedule to reduce your debt load. You begin to move forward only when you focus your own energy on the things you can do to shift the challenge into a gift. For many people this is a totally new thought, and the territory may seem to be fraught with dangers. In the middle of a new idea, some people race back to their former position on the Sticky Triangle. If this happens to you, simply reengage the list of steps to get off the triangle once again. Treat it like a game.

At some point in playing with these ideas and steps, you may call the game on yourself. Then you can laugh and realize that everyone gets caught waltzing on the Sticky Triangle several times a month. How long you spend waltzing around is up to you: It may be only a few minutes, or it may be days or months. Expand your willingness and your abundance, and allow your good friends, your partner, and colleagues to laugh and play as well.

Action Step

In a swamp, the flow of energy and money is stuck. Here's what to watch out for: jammed closets, attics, and basements; your own constant complaining and blaming of other people for what happens; your lack of focus on and movement toward your heart's longings. The body movements in a swamp like this are low, heavy, slow, and jerky. A few deep breaths can start your movement out of the swamp and begin some inspirational ideas and actions. Do the Cross Crawl in Appendix A. Add creative movement as a regular part of your day. Check your intentions around getting unstuck. Be easy and gentle with yourself as you work with experiencing more flow and abundance.

"I realized that for over two weeks, I had just 'stood and looked' at my closet and then my garage each time I opened the door," Leslie, a mortgage broker, told me. "I was frozen and needed some help in moving forward. It turned out that my best friend had decided to clean out her attic. We partnered and helped each other. She wanted a taskmaster or a persecutor, so I got really good at saying 'Now tell me why the hell you are holding on to this after all these years?' After I helped her, I needed less and less help in deciding to release my own clutter. I also realized I was stuck in, and just complaining about, several areas of my business life. Clearing out the clutter in one area released my energy, and I took care of the backlog in my business. And several new clients appeared the next month."

Now you know some new information and are gaining some new tools and techniques. The journey continues whenever you are ready to step off the Sticky Triangle. Welcome back to the River of Gold!

The Grand Fall

Here we are going along the river in our vessel, enjoying the view, when all of a sudden everything drops out from underneath us, just as if we were going over a huge waterfall. What happened? Shocked, we become aware of a basic game in our lives: that of "Being Right at All Costs" and making other people and ourselves wrong. Our Grand Fall allows us to realize that our ideas of what was right have shattered and come apart. The right-wrong positions we take consume time and energy and prevent us from enlivening our dreams and creating lasting abundance for ourselves.

For example, a financial Grand Fall happens when the stock market takes and enormous nosedive. The conventional wisdom before the nosedive was that many things were worth a lot of money, raising the value higher and higher, until eventually the bottom dropped out. Then people began to realize that they had agreed on the inflated value without any practical support underneath it, such as the price/earnings ratios or other financial indicators of continuing value. For a while everyone had been right; then reality set in and the conventional wisdom took a nosedive along with the stock prices.

Another Grand Fall happens when you assume that something will continue to increase in value at its current rate. You buy or join in assuming that someone else will come along and that you will sell it before the bottom drops out. Some people call this the greater fool theory; others refer to it as a Ponzi scheme. It eventually results in a Grand Fall where there is no continuing foundation for you or the next person.

A financial Grand Fall happens when you buy a good investment, planning to sell it after a reasonable time, and then the market turns and the buyers disappear. Or you suddenly lose ownership of an asset when you thought you had clear title. You think you're in a financially stable situation and discover your partner has enormous gambling debts—and they impact you. Or you're unable to take any reasonable action as the value of your asset is declining so fast that no one else is in the buying stage—until it hits bottom. People gather to watch a Grand Fall, amazed by the enormous energy, the whole spectacular scene, and the impossibility of doing anything to shift the process once the energy and investments begin to fall. The various stock market "adjustments" are just another name for a Grand Fall.

A feng shui Grand Fall happens when you literally fall down as you move through your environment. Besides the bruised emotions of a fall, you often have a bruise on your body where some blood vessels broke, or you really rearrange yourself and break a bone. You have come apart and crashed in some manner. Your Emotional, Rational, Creative, and Body Sensations currents were flowing and encountered something that altered the course and they separated. After this crash landing, you realize that only you can really collect and rearrange yourself and resume your journey.

Action Step

Financial Grand Falls are opportunities to review what you value and where you think you are going financially. If you have recently experienced a fall, look at your Wealth Area and your entire physical environment for pathways where you end up out of balance as you maneuver through. Shift the furniture or the energy to create more support and balance while you pay more attention to your body sensations. Look at your support systems in all areas of your life and in those places where you know that you are right. Spend some time each day in meditation and creative movement. Reset yourself with the abundant breathing process by actually lying on the floor.

Review your values. Are your investments in alignment? Notice what else in your life might be at risk for a Grand Fall. Are Grand Falls typically part of your money drama? Are you willing to experience more ease and abundance?

Looking Back

Often the very things you have been or are complaining about are, when we look back, a gift.

What if you turned your dramas and money script on their ear? What would they look like to someone seeing them for the first time? Would they look funny, even to you? Can you imagine, even for a few minutes, that there is something wonderful trying to emerge from the challenging things in your life? What do you now know that you learned through responding to the challenges? What now might look like a gift in disguise? Now appreciate yourself and your journey so far.

As you have seen, various water games stop the flow of abundance. Your money supply comes to a standstill, stagnating or shriveling. The doldrums are quite different from the rough waters where money flows on by very quickly. Here you are stuck in an old pattern, one that is connected with your early life. Love it and let it go. Forgive your prior persecutors and the victims you have tried to rescue, including yourself. Look for the silver lining in the challenges that have stopped you. You are now much wiser and more compassionate. Reconnect with your dreams, get back in your vessel, and go with the flow of increasing love, money, and abundance on the River of Gold.

11

Emerging from the Desert: Rebuilding Your Wealth from the Ground Up

even in a prosperous and peaceful life there are times of drought, when the inner flow of ideas and creativity dries up, when you lose your sense of self and your dreams fade. The desert is a real experience where the flow of money evaporates, even if only for a time. Most people deny their desert experiences and those feelings of despair and anger that surface. Desert experiences are similar to hitting bottom or hitting the wall, and many people feel a sense of shame about these constricted financial situations. I know that in my younger years I added to that pile of shame with my critical thoughts and judgments. I used to ask myself, "Why didn't they see it coming and change course?" In America it seems there is a whole body of shame heaped on these dry riverbed experiences. Now that I have walked through my own desert I know the treasure that is to be found there and the deep channel of compassion that can flow out of the winds of a desert experience.

What is the desert exactly? The desert is a place of abundance— but of a different sort. Here the waters have become so rough as to disappear into thin air, leaving behind a dry riverbed. There is an abundance of sand, literally the small gritty particles of life, and an abundance of wind, and great expanses of open space. In the desert there also can be an abundance of loneliness, terror, and confusion. Water and money seem to be lacking, yet when I contemplate the great deserts of this place we call earth, I am reminded of some great treasures, things of immense value buried there. Oil, diamonds, and uranium have been found in or near deserts by people willing to look beyond the apparent lack. A desert experience also can lead to wisdom of another sort, a kind of initiation into the abundance of one's truest values and deepest companions. Let's take another look at the lack of water and money.

Desert Ch'i

Deserts have a lot of wind and little water. Things are out of balance. According to the Chinese, in deserts the ch'i has withdrawn and gone underground, like a big intake of breath that is held and never released. There is no flow. Drawing the breath out from the earth, literally exhaling, gets things moving again. With our abundance, most of us instead focus on holding on, clutching our money, belongings, and our careers as if they are a very small vessel of water we hold close to us.

With a desert experience, at least one area of the Ba-gua is out of balance, perhaps more. Looking at the Five Elements, noticing what element is most prominent and the cycle that is occurring, will indicate what to enhance and what to reduce in that area. Look closely at the Five Element cycles in your space, since the flow has stopped and money has evaporated. Since fire can boil water to the point it evaporates, look at both the wood and water elements and notice if they are also out of balance. Do this for both your work and your living environments. One element of the five must be added to your Wealth Area and the out-of-balance element so that the flow can begin again and the desert flowers can blossom. Really balancing the whole cycle may require enhancing two or three elements so the cycle gently and steadily flows.

Financial Desert Energy

The financial desert begins when there is too little money coming in to sustain the river. Your money has ceased to flow in and has flowed out to the point there is almost nothing left, as if it has evaporated into hot air. Some people recognize these early signs and busy themselves by running around trying to tend to their vessel. They may try to create more money by changing jobs or careers. Other people focus on lightening their own load as the river seems to evaporate and dump various things and people overboard, such as spouses and children that they have been supporting. Everyone then experiences a lot of turbulence worrying themselves silly, disturbing their sleep and their lives, and creating more financial challenges.

The desert presents a range of financial experiences, from buying an asset that then leads to more expenses than you had planned, to an investment that precipitously drops in value just before you were ready to sell it and use the money for living expenses, to losing your job just after you purchased another asset. It also includes becoming sick and missing a lot of work with your bills mounting, or drowning in a mountain of debt and declaring bankruptcy. In all of these experiences you lose your own footing, your ease in creating abundance dries up, and your options for creating future abundance decline precipitously.

Desert experiences where your source and support seems to dry up are often not discussed before they occur. Most people are afraid even to acknowledge that such experiences exist until after they have experienced one for themselves. Here is the place where your money shrinks and your source dries up. People experience their emotions at levels of intensity that often shock and scare them. Often your coping resources are stretched beyond your ability to name and recognize what is happening. Being unaware of your own emotional intensity and having little experience of going with the flow often lead to both you and other people wandering away very quickly.

The classic experience of losing your job leaves many friends and family tongue-tied. They may be feeling very sad, afraid, and angry, yet they have no way to express this to themselves and to comfort you. Recognizing their emotions and communicating clearly comes with experience, from going through the desert themselves so they know the territory and can spot the signs and signals. Few people realize that an underlying current of fear surfaces when one's money flow dries up. Many people scatter when they see the empty riverbed for a friend or relative. Few people have a grasp on the source of their own abundance and flow, and they fear any drought. Helping someone in trouble in the desert is a minor challenge for people who have already been there and know the territory.

I still remember not knowing what to say to a colleague I respected and admired who was let go the day before a major reorganization. I was shocked, sad, confused, and unable to say much of anything. Even months later I stumbled over my words. Then we lost track of each other. Later, when I was released from that same company, many people reacted the same way with me. And for quite a while I wandered around in the desert.

How to Get Through?

When your currents dry up, it is time to treat yourself very tenderly and do a thorough review. If you are frantically searching for water, for the flow of abundance that has evaporated, pay attention to all of your currents.

A desert experience is a good time and place to review your physical environment for any feng shui blockages. Things will be out of balance. There is probably a Five Element Regenerative (Destructive) Cycle that calls out to be halted and energy channeled into a new flow. Look again at cycles of the Five Elements. What did you not see before? Are you willing to move some items to a more harmonious area? Did you ever contact a fung shui consultant? Did you do a follow-up consultation? This may be an excellent time for a follow-up appointment.

Take some time to streamline your belongings once again, looking at where you accumulate clutter. Do you have a lot of incomplete projects lying around? Choose one and begin to finish it. Ask yourself again what you love and what really suits you. Now take some small steps to enhance your Wealth Area. Have you stopped your Penny Dance? Take a deep abundant breath and begin anew. You also may see some old feng shui challenge in a new light. Now is the time really to look at anything you thought would be "easy" to overcome.

Tune into your Body Sensations Current again. Walk around your office or living space. Are there any signals you have overlooked? Do you feel a contraction in your body as you walk around? Take some time to integrate the subtle messages. Too many feng shui challenges in your present space may be more than you can cure. It may even be time to consider moving to a new location.

Desert experiences also can lead to physical dehydration, where people are in a very fragile state of health, needing help with food, water, and medical care. In the midst of a financial desert, you also need very tender care. Pay attention to your Emotional and Body Sensations currents, and honor all your feelings. At some point you need to lie low, experience the dark time, and take a few days to do very little but grieve. Walk by yourself, stare at the sky or a river, and realize you have let go of many things, both physical objects and relationships. A sense of losing yourself is very common. You have left a part of your identity behind. You are not who you used to be, and your new awareness of yourself has not yet flowered. Remember to interact with appropriate medical professionals for any health issues. Not only did money or a job or career go away, so did part of your sense of self, part of who you thought you were. This is very true for the experience of bankruptcy. To regain a sense of being supported, do the abundant breathing lying down on the ground. Allow your connection to the earth give you a new footing so you can begin to travel again. Practice the Openhearted Love Process at least once a day.

ENGAGING NEW FLOW Desert experiences actually can be the contraction before a time of immense growth. The phrase "The night is darkest just before the dawn" has proven true for many people. Many people experience a challenge before they move to a higher level of living. The image of a butterfly emerging from the cocoon after the caterpillar has totally dissolved comes to mind. What emerges is so much better than what was there before that the challenge and transformation is more than worth the cost—after a time of adjustment. And yes, you know this only down the road, once you have been through the process of a desert experience. Before and especially during the drought, these can seem like empty words. I know this myself; I have despaired and lost my way during my own desert experiences.

Once you have begun the cycle of grieving, it is time to play with your Creative Current and ask what you now want to create with your new life. Often the first two to three times you engage this current, it will not be active. That is okay; let go and try again in a few days. Just tuning in will make a difference. Spend some time on a regular basis with the creative movement exercises in Chapter 4.

Attend a play, visit a museum, go to the zoo, take a walk, watch moving water, walk through an art gallery, read a novel or mystery, try your hand at a new recipe, and listen to your favorite music. Keep coming back to your creative flow. Your dreams will resurface as you continue to engage your Creative Current.

Creating a collage, doing visualizations, and practicing the "aah" and "om" meditations will restart the flow of your Creative Current. With them you will begin to shift your vibration to the higher end of the emotional and rational vibrational ranges. You also will begin to lift yourself out of whatever emotional or creative pit you have fallen into.

Your Rational Current probably has been flowing with lots of critical thoughts during your time in the desert. Turning this current around so you maintain a positive outlook is very important and very challenging. Here you may remember any judgmental or critical thoughts that will diminish you and your abilities. Anything anyone ever said to squash you and your dreams can and will surface. You can pick over those old bones many times and feel even more diminished— or you can leave them to dry in the sun, deteriorate, and blow away. The choice is yours. I recommend vigilance and walking on by and letting those old thoughts—those old bones—go. Spending time focusing on what is positive will move you forward. Restart using the affirmations found in Appendix A.

The Penny Dance is very important to get you restarted on creating your own river and taking the first steps toward the Crystal Lake and your ocean of abundance. The smallest step is still a step. Take it one day at a time. More than once you will wonder if you will ever make it; just keep moving ahead one step at a time.

Focus on what is free in your community—the things you can enjoy without an obvious exchange of money, such as parks, outdoor music festivals, libraries, art galleries, bookstores, shopping malls, street musicians, flowers at sidewalk stands, and churches. Attend various services, especially those with beliefs that are totally foreign to you. This is a time for a positive expansion in other ways for your mind and sense of self. Volunteer once a week. Help other people learn to read. The time and attention that you give away will come back to you in amazing ways.

Yes, you will wonder if you will ever feel secure again. And you will feel secure again only when you are down the road and able to look back. How long will that take? To be honest, I don't know. I do know that the time will come sooner the more steps you take and the more gratitude you create. Feeling gratitude for even the smallest thing, for what you have on your plate today, sends out a new energy field that lifts the negative, low level of frequencies you have been experiencing. Every morning and evening allow the earth and ground to suport you by doing the abundant breathing exercise lying on your back. Reset yourself upon the earth so you can move forward with an inner sense of support. Add the Cross Crawl exercises in Appendix A to your daily activities.

Spending some time reviewing your life patterns around money will be profitable once you can see the end of your desert experience. Doing a review in the early stages or in the midst of your desert experience may keep you stuck rather than moving you forward.

The Gifts of Letting Go

Desert experiences can be times of immense personal growth. With the feng shui view that the breath, the ch'i, of a desert has gone underground, this is a time of intense inner work where you can focus and review your deepest values and draw them out to create a new life. Once you have begun to separate the dross from the gold, to recognize the lack of compassion and wisdom in any of your prior actions and thoughts, you can open up to understanding at a much deeper level.

The sense of grayness in your everyday activities that seems so distressing during your time in the desert is actually the generous sandpaper of life, softening and smoothing the rough characteristics we all have and experience. You can let go of old patterns and ways of being that no longer serve you. Your authentic self can emerge, the self that is connected to and flows from your heart.

IDENTIFYING YOUR CORE VALUES Most people rarely view heading off into the desert by themselves as a positive experience. Why else would a desert be called Death Valley? However, a solitary experience, one in which every aspect of your actions, beliefs, and values is challenged, can be enlightening. You become aware of your core values and what is truly important to you. In the desert, the sun is intense and the rivers dry up. Most people avoid applying the heat of the desert to their lives, forgetting that gold is purified with increasing temperatures. The impurities rise to the top to be skimmed off and dumped. So it is when money dries up—what is essential remains.

Asking yourself what and whom you truly love in the midst of a desert experience is a way of drawing the energy out of the earth and bringing it back to the surface to move and flow again. You may start to wonder what calls to you at a level so deep and profound that you feel the impulse to move forward. Look at the reasons for and the results of your earlier life, since who you are now follows from that information. You become what you do with those insights. From a desert experience you can flower into a person who is truly wise.

Action Step

Open your Travel Log and answer these questions:

- What do you value?

- Where do you give your heart away?

- Is it really worth your while? Or do you sell yourself cheaply?

- Have you looked at your options, the ones in your life in general, to see if they reflect the values that you now hold dear?

- Is there some deep inner longing calling out to you? Something that you have been ignoring all the while it calls your name?

Desert experiences can be mystical times. In losing so much, you gain everything. Nothing rational can explain such an experience. No one in their right mind will call forth such an experience, yet all that is left at the end of a desert experience is what is most important to truly living and experiencing abundance. There is no logic to such an experience, and yet one's mind can become totally whole after such a trial. This is a mystery . . . and its result leads to a deep inner experience of abundance and wisdom beyond words when the larger flow resumes and money is in hand.

Keeping going, taking a step-by-step, I'm-going-to-get-there persistent approach requires hope. You have to dig down deep inside to find your own source of hope when everything seems to dry up. Hope is also something we can inspire in one another. It's being there for another person, as he wanders in the desert, and following the flow that issues from an open heart.

Many times people see mirages in deserts, often false visions of water and shade. Vision, that ability to see even farther than your immediate personal desires, goes beyond the illusory image. Regaining your vision will allow you to see where the gifts of the desert can become the great treasures of your life, a quantum leap where the deeper meaning suddenly comes onto focus, a type of epiphany. More treasures and even more activities that will lift you out of a desert experience can be found at the Crystal Lake. Let's go there next.

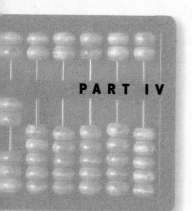

PART IV

SMOOTH SAILING

Securing Financial Stability

The sun is shining, the river is flowing smoothly, and your destination is just around the bend. Feel the wind lift your spirits and fill your sails.

12

Finding True Abundance

I t is peaceful and quiet at the Crystal Lake. The water is deep and clear, and the surface is calm. There is a vibration of peaceful energy and a deep inner silence that can be accessed here. More water enters a lake than leaves so it grows steadily, just as the Crystal Lake represents your money quietly growing every day. This money grows, similar to the "dull" investments that you add to on a regular basis that gradually increase. The Crystal Lake is both a place to visit and a wellspring of energy that you can draw from to maintain yourself in the midst of storms and challenging experiences. You come here to access your own sense of inner peace when your life is in a state of upheaval from rough waters, such as a change in job responsibilities, a new addition to your family, a financial challenge with your work, or a divorce.

Crystal Lake

What flows into your Crystal Lake is as important as the growth that happens there. Your river has been flowing with the vibration of your Five Currents since your earliest days. Your feng shui enhancements directly influence your Crystal Lake experience. Your lake includes the energy and accumulations that flow from doing the Penny Dance and the gratitude you expressed as you began to save in a new way. Unbeknownst to you, you have been enhancing your Crystal Lake with the information you've gleaned from doing the Counting Dance, the peace you experience from the Quieting Mind Chatter meditations, plus the clarity from your daily "aah" and "om" meditations.

You indirectly add to your Crystal Lake when you stop adding to your debt load. And you directly add to its growth and your wealth when you begin to save money and start to reduce your load of debt. Enhancing your feng shui Wealth Areas at work and home, correcting any feng shui challenges, and creating a collage that focuses on the wealth and abundance you desire have opened you up to even more powerful energies. Moving in creative ways on a regular basis also has presented you with new ideas, experiences, and levels of energy. If you have stopped doing any of these activities during your week, simply begin anew. No judgments will be pronounced, no look of condemnation will come your way. Each of us starts and stops various activities that truly benefit us, and then we start again. The reasons are just water under the bridge. Allow them to flow on by in peace.

You can experience even more peace at the lake every day with the tools and techniques presented in this chapter. Here the pace is slow, and your body posture low and wide, like lying on a hammock in the sun, at rest at last. The sunrises and sunsets are glorious, and all is well with the world. All currents eventually flow to this place, on their way to the ocean of open-hearted abundance.

First, appreciate yourself and everyone else throughout each day. Toss a small pebble of appreciation into the lake and see it ripple and touch things far and wide. Then, while gazing at the clarity of the Crystal Lake, ponder who you are, and spend time both meditating and moving in new ways. You offer to others and enjoy for yourself so much more with an open heart and mind. You also can notice more nuances, those little things that slip by in a busy life, and correct your course and interactions based on subtle events. The Crystal Lake allows you to experience a deeper sense of abundance, where peace and calm is possible even in the midst of your life's greatest challenge.

Ripples

Come and sit by the lake for a few minutes. Enjoy the peace and quiet. Nothing to do, just watch the water. As a fish emerges from the waters, notice how the ripples first appear from that one event and continue out to the edges of the water. Think about how everything is connected and touched by the energy of that wave. Your earlier feng shui enhancements and your wealth and abundance collage will take on a whole new meaning. Later you watch a bird land on the surface while new waves appear and spread out. Here both wind and water have interacted. Pondering this connection, perhaps you commit to a more regular practice of your "aah" and "om" meditations as a way of incorporating more wind into your energy. There is flow everywhere, and now you can see this flow and work with it in your everyday world. After a while you will sense that it is time to move on to the next thing. No alarm rang, no one showed up for an appointment, and you didn't even look at your watch. Instead you tuned in to your own flow.

Leading with Appreciation

What leads your vessel is what gets you to the lake and the ocean of abundance on time. In the old days a very beautiful woman, a figurehead, was at the prow of a vessel. She led the way with a smiling gracious face, a face you could appreciate. Leading with appreciation, adopting the practice of looking for things your mind and body can appreciate, regardless of your circumstances, shifts your energy and tunes you in to the higher frequencies of abundance so you can resonate with them as you go about your life.

Appreciation is a fine art, one that is beyond flattery. It is not about getting something in return, which is the subtle current flowing beneath flattery. It is about resonating in harmony, really seeing another person, object, or event and communicating that special essence to them. *Webster's* defines the word *appreciate,* as "to value, to esteem, to be conscious of the significance, desirability or worth of; to be fully or sensitively aware of; to note distinction in." *Appreciation* is defined as "the means to accurately estimate; recognition of good points."

Leading with appreciation means you shift your focus from finding out what is wrong or at fault to what delights your eye, your mind, and your other senses as you look around you. Pay attention to what can you communicate, verbally or nonverbally, to indicate your appreciation. Whenever you think about a person, consider what can you focus on and communicate that you appreciate. Then share what you notice, verbally or in writing. And begin to lead your life with appreciation.

Action Step

Every day choose to appreciate five things about yourself, then five things about your living space. Then appreciate another five things about your work, and still another five about each of your colleagues. Actually communicate at least one appreciation every day. Appreciating five things a day for your partner, your children, and colleagues will transform your life and theirs. Doing this as a regular practice aligns you with the energy of the Crystal Lake, where things grow in value. Wonder what would happen with your savings and investments if you appreciated them? Consider sending the energy of appreciation toward your financial advisors.

Leading with appreciation is an energy vibration that is very powerful. Adding a layer of gratitude on top of it and feeling it with great intensity sets up a very powerful energy field around you. You will attract amazing results, so give it a try.

Action Step

Here's a more radical step, one that you may not understand right now. When you hand money to someone, give it to them with a blessing from your heart. When you pay for anything, whether it's with cash, check, or credit card, send a blessing with the money. When you pay your expenses, actually write "thank you" on your checks; hold the checks in your hands and infuse them with your vibration and feeling of gratitude before you send them off. Use the "hmmm" sound as you experience gratitude. Add a message of gratitude to your electronic payments as well. Open your heart as you open your wallet and checkbook, feel gratitude and add the tone of gratitude, the "hmmm" sound.

Try it for a month. Notice and log your body sensations, your emotions, your rational and creative thoughts, and the experiences you have with money and your sense of abundance. Notice any patterns that show up. This is a tangible activity that connects you to the intangible flow of the universe. Over time you may choose to spend your abundance in different places than you do now.

Accumulation

Lakes both give and receive. This is a basic part of the cycle. How do you honor the receiving aspect of flow? Are you in tune with and do you allow yourself to receive? Or did you learn that it is better to give than receive? Here is one person's thoughts and energy about receiving and accumulation.

At one of my workshops, Ruth told us that she was taught to never accumulate money. Accumulating was evil, she thought, and would lead to really bad things. So she either gave her money away or spent it. I noticed her appearance and asked if she enjoyed any abundance. Yes, she admitted that her closets were bulging with clothes.

As my heart fluttered and my skin tingled, I just stood there amazed, then took a deep breath. I took another breath, relaxed, and opened my body up to what might be next. The verse "I wish you to have life and to have it abundantly" popped into my mind. I shared it, paused, and asked her how she integrated that with what she had been taught. Ruth held her breath and sat very still as her eyes opened very wide. To me, it looked as if her whole being and her sense of self quickly fell apart, shifted, and then gathered back together. It only took a couple of minutes of silence. She then wondered, out loud, if all that was connected to the major fights she had with her husband. And what did they fight about? "Money." "Yes, and what about money?" I asked. "Well, he wants to save and I don't, and I don't think we should," she answered. I smiled and paused, and in that open space she seemed to have an "Aha!" experience.

Ruth had been fighting with herself and her husband about saving money. Yet she had been attracted to him because he actually had money and seemed to know how to manage it. Underneath her outward actions was a desire to save and accumulate. Overlaid were some old beliefs that no longer harmonized with the person she had become. She desired more abundance and was still fighting against actually receiving more. You may be floating on the River of Gold in a similar vessel, fighting against your desire for true abundance.

Action Step

Consider the following questions. Move and dance with them and record your responses in your Travel Log. What thoughts do you hold and believe about giving and receiving? Can you accept a compliment and just say "thank you"? Do you give compliments without expecting something in return? How much and how often are you supposed to give? Receive? Presents, parties, invitations to hang out together, money? How much money are you allowed to have in a savings or investment account, given your present thoughts about abundance?

The Penny Dance began your steps toward creating a Crystal Lake. The small accumulations have added up over time and are filled with the energy of gratitude. Soon you can send that small amount out to begin earning its own way in the world. Having money create more money, even while you sleep, is a calm Crystal Lake experience. This is the money that is safe and secure, protected so that it is there when you decide to draw upon it. Now, as you consider where to place it, ask yourself if it's safe. Is there any risk of decline during the time it continues growing? Two places that are volatile are places where inflation will cause it to decline in purchasing power over time, such as under your mattress or in a savings account that pays less than the current rate of inflation, and in the daily fluctuations of the stock markets. For long-term investment, money in stocks can be very beneficial when you have good advice and clear intentions. Commenting on commodities is done best by expert traders and investors—people whose abundance over time has actually increased in this arena.

There are very few guarantees on this journey, so when you move your money, place it in a positive environment with gratitude.

Accumulating enough money to flow easily through a six-month drought begins with the little increases added to a small pond, like beginning the Penny Dance. Eventually a pond can grow to a lake and then a large Crystal Lake. When you have safely accumulated more than enough to float past a six-month drought, then your next accumulation of money can handle bigger fluctuations, such as a higher rate of interest. First accumulate a small pond, and then focus on a larger one. Eventually it will become a Crystal Lake, step by step creating a pattern of steady growth.

Doing the "aah" and the "om" meditations every day will connect you to the larger flow. From this connection you will also find yourself attracted to the financial opportunities and other investments that will enlarge your Crystal Lake. Trust that they will show up at the right time. Remember to do the financial analysis with your Rational Current before you invest. There will be times when you realize that it is time to shift out of an investment, to let it go. Pay attention to and honor these realizations.

Growth

Accumulating money is one way for your Crystal Lake to grow. Investing it so it can grow and earn more money is another. Acquiring assets that grow in value is another form of adding to your Crystal Lake. If those assets do not create an income stream, then they may be doing something else. Many people were taught to buy the largest house they could afford because it would "always increase in value." That advice may have been accompanied with the phrase "They aren't making any more land, you know." Many people can tell you that their house did increase in value over time, yet there were also times when its value seemed to be less than the mortgage on it. If you talk with them, they probably will be thankful that they didn't have to sell their home then. And they may know of someone who had to take a huge loss when they had to sell unexpectedly.

The house that you live in is an asset that costs you real money to own and maintain. During the time you live in it, it is not creating a flow of cash that increases your Crystal Lake. Instead expenses drain your cash flow. Yes, houses appreciate in value, but only on paper until you actually sell them. In the meantime, they cost you money and drain your lake. Think about whether this is the right time to carry such large assets, and be cautious about acquiring assets that appreciate in value but do not create an income stream; this includes things like vintage vehicles, antiques, coins, or collectible items. Remember to engage your Rational Current to do the calculations, and check into your Body Sensations and Emotional currents when the numbers say this is not a positive increase in your lake. Even at the Crystal Lake, some water evaporates. It also turns to mist and goes away when there is the turbulence of a windstorm.

Action Step

Consider where your money has evaporated in the past and where it might now be at risk. Do you have investment assets that are not increasing in value? What action steps can you take to change this so your money and wealth will grow? By when will you begin to take action?

Self-Worth

As your Crystal Lake grows and you enjoy more abundance, you may suddenly detour out of the lake and later wonder what happened. The Crystal Lake is more energy than any you've experienced before, and locating it allows your feelings about self-worth and your willingness to receive to surface. What if you're suddenly afraid of this newfound energy and abundance? Common responses like "Stop! I don't deserve this!" or "No one should have this much," or "I don't know how to deal with all of this" issue from your mouth. This is simply your sense of self-worth bumping up against your outer edges of acceptable abundance. You may feel that you don't deserve this much, thoughts that can ultimately diminish your self and your value. All of this is simply too much energy for you to enjoy with comfort. And you exit the Crystal Lake—detouring back to somewhere more comfortable—with less abundance.

Abundance—or its lack—is often connected to diminishments that frequently surface in the Crystal Lake. Your past experiences of not feeling worthy, not feeling like you do enough, and not valuing yourself flow from earlier events in your life, those times when you were not valued by others. What to do?

Action Step

When you find yourself on a detour out of the Crystal Lake, think about expanding your awareness of your own worth. Dance with all that energy and bring your hidden issues to the surface. And release them with gratitude. Open your arms, heart, and hands and become more willing to receive love from yourself and others. Abundance is always flowing to and filling the Crystal Lake, and it will always be guarded by your own sense of worth. Expand your self-worth into the experience of abundance and enjoy the Crystal Lake once again. Here is something that might help guide you.

FLOATING A QUESTION. Floating a question is about considering a really big question, allowing it to move you to your depths, and opening up to all of its possible ramifications. Such a question is much more significant than stepping into the wondering move, which is about solving a challenge or issue. Floating a question about your own sense of self-worth requires seeing yourself from another perspective, where you envision the question floating like a feather above you, watch it gently landing on the lake, and you just allow yourself to float on its energy. Take no outward action. Instead, just take the question with you into your heart, your sense of self, and your everyday life and allow it to touch and move you. The awareness you're seeking will gradually settle into your heart. Are you ready?

Here are several questions. Take one and be with it, float it out, let it go as it settles on the quiet waters of your life. Just observe what surfaces in your life and your awareness over the next few days or weeks. Then take another question and float it out. Notice what shows up in your awareness.

How do you live knowing that money is just energy?

How do you live knowing that money is just another form of love?

Who are you when you become the source of abundance?

What is the sound of a hand contributing money?

What is the sound of your heart opening?

Who are you without money?

Who are you without your longing for wealth?

Who are you when you laugh and play with your sense of self-worth?

Daily Practices

You can come back to and experience the Crystal Lake on a daily basis. It is a place on the River of Gold that represents a multitude of experiences of abundance during your everyday activities. Meditation is a classic daily practice for many people and something that will help you locate and draw from your Crystal Lake. However, many meditation practices require you to sit very still or in ways that are a challenge to maintaining the flow of your body movements, or they require you to ignore body sensations that signal you are in discomfort. Here is a quiet set of movements that will connect you to the larger flow of energy both in your body and the world. These movements are also designed to open up your mental pathways so you can see new possibilities. They will allow you to see new solutions to challenges at work, in your relationships, and in how you create abundance.

FLOWING MOVEMENTS MEDITATION Focusing on the flow of your body during your meditation activities connects you to the River of Gold and leads to a Crystal Lake experience. Spend a few minutes sitting and doing abundant breathing with your hands open and resting in your lap. Then add the movement of your hands gently turning outward as you inhale and inward as you exhale. A very small movement is still movement. Once you are flowing with your hand movements in harmony with your breath, enlarge the movement to include your arms. Raise them up off your lap as you inhale and gracefully let them down as you exhale. First move them in front of you, up and down, then out at your sides like the wings of a bird. Keep the movements gentle and fluid. If you feel any discomfort, reduce the size of your movements.

Another variation is to stand, with your feet about hip-width apart, moving your entire arms in harmony with your breath. Inhale and gently raise your arms, exhale and let them down, then again and lower them like the wings of a bird. Keep the movements gentle and flowing. Thank your Rational Current for whatever comments it offers. Laughing at yourself is a good thing. So is creating a peaceful energy field.

Next alternate arms, extending one arm up while the other goes down. Stretch your torso and rise up on your toes on the side where your arm is opening to more flow. Then alternate sides, all the while coordinating your breathing.

Continuing to stand, shift your arms to a horizontal pattern and gently hug yourself as you exhale. Then open your arms to the world as you inhale. Remember to be comfortable with your movements. Then bend down toward the ground and hug yourself, contracting your energy. Then flow and open up and reach for the sky. Think of alternating between withdrawing to yourself and going out into the world.

With these practices you will develop more flexibility in your body and your life, and your breath will be able to expand into all areas of your lungs as you gently stretch your body. Your mind will quietly slow down and stop its normal chatter. Feel free to laugh at and with yourself as you do these practices. Enjoy the smile that may form on your face, and take it with you as you go about your day creating open-hearted abundance.

MOVING IN NEW WAYS Spending time, as little as five minutes, every day moving in new ways takes you back to the Crystal Lake. Here you are making interesting connections between and among your various body parts so you can return to the gentle and peaceful stance of the Crystal Lake experience. This activity enhances your ability to be continuously innovative.

Shift your attention to nonrational patterns of movement so you can open up your range of experiences without spending any money. Focus on your elbow and move it in a way that is new to you, and then concentrate on your knee, your hip, or your ear, moving in a new way. Continue to change your movement pattern when you realize you are engaged in a repetitive one. Play some music you enjoy as you create new connections in your body. The goal is to keep moving, discovering, and creating new patterns. Once you realize you are moving in a predictable pattern, shift to something new. Feel free to hum as you do these movements.

When Russell, a gardener, lost a major client, he panicked but quickly regained the sense of peace he had learned by listening to himself, noticing all of his body sensations, and doing the moving meditations daily. "One day," he said, "it seemed like the flowers on several azalea bushes sang to me. I had ten dollars in my wallet and I felt like a millionaire! I kept doing the Penny Dance and in a month I had a bigger client."

WORKING WITH AFFIRMATIONS Gently growing in your own awareness and experience of wealth and abundance includes allowing affirmations to work with and for you. Using them will assist your Rational Current's ability to release old blockages and focus on more wealth and ease. Consistently working with an affirmation for a day or a week will reveal interesting shifts. In Appendix A you'll find some common affirmations. Use these and then feel free to create your own.

SPACIOUS LISTENING How many of us listen—*really* listen—to ourselves? Very few. Listening to yourself is often the last thing that people do. When I ask people what they truly desire, there is usually a long pause and then the response: "I don't know." Coming to know your own heart's desires as well as what you really want in your day-to-day activities is the goal of spacious listening. There is space to listen for your own desires, space to hear the people you live and work with, space for abundance for yourself and everyone else who wants to create open-hearted abundance. With spacious listening, you can connect with people and discover that they have things and connections to other people beyond what you thought was possible. Carl Jung coined the term "synchronicity" to refer to connections appearing that astound you. Spacious listening taps into the flow of this energy.

We commonly listen to one another to gain information, to rebut, to put forth our own point of view, to overpower someone else, or to make them wrong and prove ourselves right. All of these intentions have an agenda, and listening with an agenda is what most people do in life and in business. We are not open to just listening, to truly hearing someone else's point of view or their deep longings. Usually we listen standing or sitting opposite the speaker so we can interject our own agenda and comments before the person has even stopped speaking. Rarely do we move alongside and see the world from the other person's perspective. Spacious listening is where there is space for your heart and mine to resonate, to create abundance for everyone who wants to play in this vast field of energy.

In developing the ability to listen without an agenda, we go through various stages. The first is to realize we have an agenda. We realize we are ready to jump in with our point even before the speaker has stopped to take a breath and long before she is done with sharing. Many people deny this style of listening and often feel angry with the person who calls it to their attention. Sometimes this goes on for months. Imagine what happens to the abundance of people who deny their agendas during this time.

How does spacious listening work? First, realize you have an agenda as you listen. Take a deep abundant breath as you resonate with this information. You will move from occupying the energy of your agenda when you can listen to someone talk, take a couple of deep breaths after the person finishes, and then say "Tell me more" and mean it. Here you have interrupted your pattern of jumping in and presenting your own point of view. Most people have trouble listening for even two minutes!

Now notice whether you already jumped in to disagree with me. For a newcomer, listening for five minutes can seem like an eternity. In seminars we use a timer, sitting people opposite each other with a designated speaker and listener. The speaker talks and the listener just listens—for two minutes. The exercise works best if the people do not already know each other and the topic is something that is really bugging the speaker, something that engages the Emotional Current.

Moving to the next stage, listening for content, means you just repeat back to the speaker what was said and remain open to being corrected by the speaker if your reply is not what was said. Do not put forth your own agenda until the first speaker is satisfied that you have repeated what was said accurately. This exchange really shakes loose your full agenda style, especially if you focus on listening for content for several months.

Listening for resonance is quite a shift. You listen, repeat back the content of what was said, and include your sense of the emotional communication. Here is where things get interesting! You don't know what the other is experiencing. You may have some clues, but you don't know until you are told. So, preface your gentle reply with "I am imagining you feel . . ." or "I suspect you feel . . ." The purpose is not to argue or to put forth your agenda, your opinion, it is rather to come into harmony with both content and emotional flavor, to resonate with the message and the speaker. Mastering this one takes concentration, energy, and a willingness to just let go. Expect a couple of years to pass before you get this one, even if you are quite disciplined and put forth a lot of effort. Then remember you will slip up—often!

Spacious, no-agenda listening is where you are open to resonate.

Here you become an open space where you receive what is said with open arms. You even invite more sharing with your intention and your words. This is the place where the "Tell me more" response shows up, becoming an open space when the speaker pauses. Tuning into your breath and other body sensations aids your awareness of the open space, or lack of it, in your body.

Feeling an urge to speak or a contraction in your body or some other sensation or urge to jump in signals you are moving back into full-agenda listening. Few people can maintain an open space and just listen, yet it is worth the effort and the letting go it requires. The results, resonating at a profound level with another person, are worth the effort!

Come back to and enjoy your Crystal Lake as a daily practice, knowing you are flowing toward the ocean of abundance. Now it's time to shift perspectives and look at a map and create a plan for enjoying more abundance.

13

Creating a Spending Plan

most people avoid taking the steps to create a spending plan, and for good reason. Spending plans don't seem to be fun. For many people they are connected to pain, constriction, budgets, and the River of Shame. The usual approach is to create a budget and engage the Rational Current, plow ahead, and ignore the other four currents. But creating an environment that is pleasant and inviting, especially to your Creative and Emotional currents, allows your Rational Current to focus and engage with fun and harmony. Now put on your Chancellor of the Exchequer costume, hat and all. You do have a funny hat stored somewhere, don't you?

CREATING A SPENDING PLAN

Creating a spending plan can be fun. What and whom do you really love? What if the way you sent money out into the world really honored what you long for and who and what you love? What if you wrote checks with gratitude? For all of us, some things are out of alignment. Creating more balance leads to more flexibility and, ultimately, more peace, harmony, and financial abundance. Knowing when you will have major cash flow challenges, the celebrations and yearly expenses in your life, and being prepared for them leads to more inner peace. With a sense of inner peace you can experience more gratitude and joy in your life. And that connects you to the vibration of wealth and abundance.

CREATING. Since the first word is *creating*, let's engage your Creative Current. Get out a colored pencil or special pen and some fun paper. Turn on your favorite music and move around a bit. Do a little silly dance, something creative with your body, before you sit down and focus. Now write on one sheet of paper the names of people you love. Take a moment and send love to each person. Take a couple of deep breaths, see the person in your mind's eye, surround each with a bubble of pink light, open your heart energy, and send your love.

Take another sheet of paper and do the same for organizations. It doesn't matter whether you belong to them right now or not. Let's say you love trees. What organizations also love trees and focus that love on nurturing or preserving them? Write those names down. Take another sheet of paper and creatively note the places you love to visit or would like to visit in the future. And another sheet of paper for the objects you love, whether you have them in your possession or not. And another sheet of paper for the things you want to create, your deep heart longings. This could be a house you want to buy or build, or a vehicle, or starting or finishing your education, or a career change. Don't worry if many of the things on your lists are just longings. We are creating a spending plan that will include these things.

Take a few deep breaths and spread out these papers so you can see all of them at once. Put the date on them. Here are your creative urges and heart's desires. These are the reasons you will refer to, as you realign your current life. Your heart's desires will then come into full flower. Spend some time every day—it can be as little as five minutes—for several weeks reviewing these things. Send love and gratitude to the things on your lists and to yourself for taking the time to be honest with your own heart. During your morning "aah" meditation, use your mind's eye to see yourself actually experiencing each one of your heart's desires. Once a week see yourself touching them, sitting in, or using them while you feel your emotions of love and gratitude. Know that you're attracting these things into your life and send out gratitude to wherever they are on their journey to you.

SPENDING. The next word is *spending*. A whole series of questions come up in my mind with this word:

How are you currently spending your money? Do you even know how much money you spend on food, clothes, entertainment, transportation, and your living environment? Are you joyful and grateful as you write checks and exchange cash for things? Do you have any hidden expenses, ones that suddenly show up once or a few times a year? Are you enjoying the work you do, the way you are trading your life energy for money?

Some green paper might be useful here. Again we are in the creative mode, so get out your favorite writing implement. Take some time to limber up. Stand up and move around a little. Now go locate your check registers, or gather your computer sheets that tally your expenses for the past twelve months. Do a little dance with those papers just as they are. Embrace them. No judgment here. They simply contain numbers that signify flow, what has already happened in your recent past. They are not who you are, just what you have done.

Have you been playing with the energy of a sharp pencil and already listed and categorized these numbers? Or have you been playing the part of a happy idiot, just haphazardly writing them down anywhere? Neither is good or bad. Both allow you to see the extremes of a pattern in how you handle your money. Right now the goal is to know how much money you currently are spending on living your life. You may dread putting numbers in row after row of columns. That is okay. Take a couple of deep breaths and realize that there is another simple way to separate out the information. You can write out each category on separate sheets of paper. Colored paper works just fine if you already have it close by.

Action Step

Begin with pondering the following questions. In some way, you already know some of this information, you just can't always see it in front of you in a form that allows you to make decisions that support your creative dreams.

Where does your money go? How much of it goes there and how often? Do you enjoy this category? Do you wish it to continue? Is it necessary for your career or your lifestyle? What if you played with releasing some spending patterns? What if you shifted how and where you sent money out into the universe? Would you be willing to experience gratitude and be in alignment with your heart's longings?

Set a timer for fifty minutes and go through your check register, credit card statements, and Counting Dance notes, noting your inflow and the money spent on food; clothing; insurance; household maintenance such as utilities; transportation; education; career enhancement; entertainment; and other miscellaneous things. Some categories will be easy. If your rent or mortgage is the same each month, then that dollar amount times twelve could go on one sheet. The goal is to know what your monthly averages are and the yearly total. Utilities will vary, so note each month, add them up for the yearly total, and then divide that amount by twelve for the average for the year that has past. You will have some categories that are not listed here. Just keep track of where you actually spend money.

The ideal is to accumulate the totals and the monthly average on one sheet of paper so you can see the overall pattern. List the categories in a preset order, with the largest amounts first, the smaller amounts first, or the ones you do not want to change first. It is up to you.

What to do when the timer goes off? Set it for ten minutes, get up and stretch, go to the bathroom, get yourself some water or tea. All the while do a little dance. Then put on some more music, set your timer for another fifty minutes, and continue on. If three hours pass and you are not done collecting information, decide if you want to continue for another hour or set the project aside and refocus later that day, the next day, or next weekend. For the best results, complete this project as a unit. Yes, you may feel overwhelmed, or angry or afraid. Just breathe into all aspects of your experience and lightly ride your emotional wave. And let go of judging yourself! We are creating a new plan, and it may be a little messy in the beginning.

PLAN. The final word is *plan,* as in a spending plan. First, you created a list of your heart's connections and longings; then you gathered the information on where and how you spent your money. However you do not have a plan on how to integrate the two—yet.

Whatever emotions and body sensations you have right now are real. Experience them without judgment. Acknowledge the judgmental thoughts of your Rational Current, the ones that may sound like "Well, you have never been able to do this before; who thinks you can do it now?" or "What a stupid exercise, everyone knows that it won't work for you!" Thank your thoughts for showing up and release them with love. These are patterns to be loved and released as you move forward on the River of Gold. Choose a new expansive and uplifting thought and hold it in place. Infuse that new thought with your love and gratitude. Remember to log in your Travel Log whatever flow challenges arise from your various currents.

Creating a spending plan for the future begins with looking at what you are doing now. Right now I don't care why you spent the money, and I hope you will give up asking the "why" question for now. The deeper reasons will surface on their own as you continue to look at your life script and patterns. Instead, focus on whether you want to continue your life and your spending patterns without including your creative dreams. Take some time to notice how your body and emotions respond to giving up your dreams. Remember to enter your responses in your Travel Log. I ask you to consider living without your dreams so you can become aware of all of your body's responses. Now you realize how important your dreams really are to you! Don't leave home without them.

Now you can include dreams in your new spending plan—and the streamlining of your money patterns will flow from focusing on what you love. Here are some interesting questions to ponder as you review your prior spending patterns:

Does buying a particular item serve you? Does it move you toward your dreams? Who are you if you no longer spend your money on this item? Do you love this person? Do you love your vehicle? Do you get up every day willing to attend to this career? Do you enjoy this expense more than you want your creative dreams? What if you let go of keeping up your persona, its costume and the other gadgets that go along with it? Can you spend this money with gratitude?

If you have always done something, then now is the time to wonder whether doing it makes your heart sing and moves you toward your dreams. Does doing it less or in a different way still move you toward your dream or maybe open you up to new dreams?

Review your first pages and the information from your prior spending. Somewhere in all of these dollar amounts will be things you now want less or have wanted less than your dreams. That is the place to streamline. Either reduce or stop spending your money on these items, whether it's takeout food, beverages, household items, entertainment, transportation, or clothing items. Maybe your living space no longer calls to your heart or serves your life. Notice where you feel gratitude and where you constrict as you review these items.

Debt

You may realize that your debts are out of hand and are calling out to you to address them. And until you do face and address your debts, it's challenging to incorporate something new into your life, like a spending plan. There is no space—yet. The first step to take is to give yourself the gift of inner space. Here is where you begin to focus more energy on money so your debts will diminish.

For example, let's focus on the money you owe to others, commonly called debt. Debt has two costs: the amount you owe, the principal, and the interest that is added on each month. Many people, without realizing it, are only paying down some of the interest that is added each month while the balance grows from new charges and new interest.

Remember the swamp? Debt is like a swamp—it sucks you in and makes it seem impossible to move or escape. Eventually things will get unbearable if you stay in the swamp. Let's begin to get out. Pay attention to the interest rates. Some interest rates are set, while others, especially credit card debt, can be had at a lower interest. Knowing the rate is not set in stone means asking for the rate to be lowered, and asking more than once and of the right person. You also can move your debt to another lender where the rate is lower. Experience gratitude, remember the Open-hearted Love Process, and do it before you make the first call to request a lower interest rate.

Getting out of a swamp also means not adding to your debt either directly or indirectly. Giving up the practice of living with and on more debt is the first step. Are you willing to step out of the swamp, willing to release your pattern of increasing debt? You accomplish this by putting away your credit cards, by cutting them up, or by closing accounts with a zero balance. Yes, you can keep one card for emergencies. Just remember, you are still in the swamp and your vessel can be upset at any time by the appearance of the alligator of more debt. You move forward by paying off the debt with the highest interest rate while keeping current on your other debts. Why the highest interest rate? It's like snapping jaws, eating up your money faster than you realize. You are now draining a swamp. It *is* a big job and may take some time. Allow your emotions to surface and to flow through you with your breath. Give yourself the gift of focus and persistence. Your rewards will be beyond what you can see from this vantage point. You may feel all kinds of emotions and body sensations and hear your Rational Current say all kinds of unkind things. Stay with the program. The end is in sight. Soon the swamp will be drained and the alligators will no longer be snapping at you.

What if your fears about your debt load are more than you can manage? You have been juggling your debt payments, and it seems as if you are about to fall over into the swamp. First just be with your emotions and your body sensations. Allow their energy to pass through you. Now feel some compassion come your way. Many people have been where you are and experienced just what you're experiencing. No judgment, no blame, and no shame. In fact, many people will feel compassion for you—they know what you're going through. Ask yourself: Can I freely move forward by myself and take steps to stop adding to my debt and drain my swamp? Or do I instead want some help? If you do, then contact a debt counseling service. The service can work with you to contact your creditors, negotiate a repayment plan, and make a difference in your sense of inner peace. Regardless, continue with the various other practices as you drain your swamp.

Plan Ahead

Now we're going to step forward into the future and begin to fund your dreams. It begins with collecting money for a six-months-I-can-live-with-ease fund and a dream fund. Both of these start with your deep heart longings and probably a zero balance. Now, this may seem radical, yet it will make sense once you have turned your vessel around. Up to now you have been living without your dreams, yet today begins a new phase where you put money into your six-month and dream funds—first! When you receive money and before you pay your expenses, you place money here first, literally funding your safety and dreams. What you focus on grows. It doesn't matter how much money goes into the account or the envelope; what matters is that it's done first and with gratitude. Have you ever heard the phrase "Pay yourself first"? This is where you do that. Attend to your sense of self before you attend to anyone or anything else. It is like meditating before you start your day. You then live your life from a deep reservoir of abundance and peace. Remember the Penny Dance? You began with the smallest coin, too small to hand over to a banker or to put in a savings account, but it's a step in the right direction. Getting started, acknowledging and stating your dreams, and taking the first small step toward realizing them moves energy and invites the support of the Divine Spirit. Begin with a penny or a dollar. Just begin.

Does your current income allow you to fund your current style of living? Can you pay your monthly expenses every month as long as you do not increase your expenses? If yes, then congratulations! Simply add up what you consider necessary, notice when things are due, pay them, and feel grateful. Now make it a fun game to create some money that is available for you and begin to pay yourself first, putting money into your dream fund and in your six-months-I-can-live-with-ease fund. Begin with a dollar, or ten dollars. Just begin. A good goal to work toward is using 10 percent of your inflow to pay yourself first. This may seem odd if you are just getting by, but soon you will realize that the streamlining you do in other areas allows you to play the game with more options. Just feel how wonderful this would be and feel gratitude.

Now let's create your spending plan. List a category for your dreams and your six-months-I-can-live-with-ease fund, then list your monthly expenses. Add a category for your annual expenses. The goal is to set aside some money every time money flows in toward your dreams, your six-month-ease fund, and your annual expenses. One twelfth of the annual amount is reasonable. Remember, if you are less than twelve months away from writing a check for an annual expense, then for a while you will have to realign the balance in one area with money from another. This is the classic borrowing from Peter to pay

Paul. Right now, you have just begun, and things are out of balance. Within a few months you will see a major shift. Congratulations! Steady at the helm is the watchword. Yes, you may feel afraid or angry and may think this will take forever. You may feel overwhelmed for a while. Just breathe into and through all of your experiences. And keep a steady course, feeling grateful for the ups, downs, and the bends in the river. Remember to keep your spending plan in a place of honor.

You may want to adjust your spending plan after the first month or two. Really look at how you are spending and where. Consider whether your discomfort is short term and will dissipate as you stay with your new plan, or if you missed something and really need to shift your pattern of spending. In the beginning, all people experience some discomfort as they shift into new ways of living. And then things smooth out and ease returns. The longer you are steady at the helm, the more ease you will experience. Eventually you will have money left over at the end of the month. Then you can gradually increase your contributions to your dream and ease funds.

Long-term Abundance

Everyone wants to take a vacation eventually. It's also very important to plan ahead and look at what you desire your long-term future to be like. Having abundance for your future, both short- and long-term, and taking steps in alignment with your deepest longings, is the focus of this section. Here your basic patterns, your financial persona, and your stance on the Sticky Triangle come into play. Creating abundance for your future actually can be a fun game rather than some awful task. What if you realized you could make a major shift in your sense of abundance by enjoying this process?

"As a young accountant," Larry shared, "I just wanted to get on with the task of creating a cash flow projection for my own family and prepare for retirement. I knew it was an important thing to do. I had tried several times to include my wife, but our young children's imme-diate needs always interrupted any time I set aside for this. Making the process fun and beginning with our deepest heart longings was a new concept. I suddenly realized that we could take a weekend holiday without our children and have some fun and some focused time. The suggestion of talking *after* we had taken a walk or gone skiing was what did the trick for me. After some fun it was easy for my heart to open and hear what my partner desired. I then realized we were already a team with the same big goal, so the plan flowed together very quickly that weekend."

For many people, the future is so far away that they never focus on it until it looms up in front of them. Yet you can begin creating a future of abundance with an open heart today. Now take a deep breath and step forward in time. What do you really want in the year to come? What are the dreams that seem impossible because they're so far in the future? Write them down in your Travel Log! Say them out loud every day so the universe can hear you, so you can hear yourself and feel the energy of your desires. The goal is to vibrate in harmony with positive emotion so the two realities can begin to move toward each other. Add "vacation" to your spending plan. Begin contributing a dollar to that fund. Feel grateful that the energy is moving.

Now, what options for creating an abundant future do you have at your place of work? Do any of them include matching funds? That is like free money. Begin to claim your share! Adding to your Crystal Lake experience includes anyone who wants to match money with you. Even if your money seems to be fully occupied with draining your swamp, take a small risk and step into the wonder move. Wonder how you can contribute a small amount toward the matching money your employer will contribute, commonly called 401(k) plans. If it is not possible this week or month, determine when you can begin to contribute. Mark that day in gold letters and take action! Right now feel grateful that you are draining your swamp. Doing so is also creating a bright future for you, one that you will be enjoying sooner than you now realize.

As your swamp drains and your streamlining opens up other options, begin to contribute to your future in new ways. After you start contributing to the 401(k) plan, eventually you can increase your contributions to the maximum your employer contributes. Do you qualify for some other retirement option? If so, begin to contribute money there. Once you are at that point, with your swamp drained, your pattern of increasing debt a thing of the past, and your six-month fund growing nicely, then ask yourself: What's next?

Do you want to manage your money and focus on your investing activities, or do you want to turn them over to someone else? Both require some thought, an awareness of your emotions, some education, and an assessment of your level of risk avoidance. Are you breathing or feeling afraid? Or did you freeze, faint, or run away? If you are a "fighter," more than likely you have already begun taking steps to learn about and begin investing. If you don't want to manage your own investments, or if you are less sure of your own ability to invest, then open up to connecting with a financial advisor to guide you and/or manage a small portfolio for you. Use your "aah" meditations to draw to you just the right advisor, and see who shows up and when. Either way, you are on your way to the ocean of abundance. Now it is time to check all of your settings as you move forward. Begin today to review your spending plan and allocate some amount of money to these things. Growth is based on regular additions and allowing something to increase over time. The sooner you begin, the more time things will have to grow.

From your small Counting Dance notebooks, your credit card statements, and your check register have flowed the pattern of your previous spending pattern. With some creative movement and music you have created a new spending plan that focuses on your sense of safety and your dreams and includes your current life. You are reducing your debt and draining your swamp. All the while you're experiencing more inner peace and sending your money out with gratitude. Place your spending plan in a place of honor and use it as a new pattern to guide your day-to-day spending choices.

When you have reached your current financial goals, enjoy your abundance. Then refocus on your dreams and deepest heart longings. What dreams are still hidden? Begin to focus on those new goals and honor them as they begin to surface. Continue to contribute to your short-term and long-term abundance as they grow and move you along the river out toward the ocean of abundance. Be at peace.

14

The Ocean of Abundance

Come and stand with me at the ocean's edge. Take a deep breath, smell the ocean's scent as it enters your nose, feel the breeze caressing your face, taste the salt on your lips, and feel the water's spray on your exposed skin. Close your eyes and listen to the ocean waves as they break upon the shore. Do you feel the pull of the waves deep inside your body? This is the dance of the wind and the water, the basics of feng shui, the interplay of yin and yang and the Five Elements. Feel the energy of the ocean waters and the wind as they dance with each other, creating flow.

Using feng shui principles, you now understand why and how to realign the energies in the Wealth Areas in your home and work space to

The Ocean of Abundance

harmonize with the vibration of abundance. You know how to be honest to the penny and flow with whatever emotions you are experiencing in the moment. With your own deep abundant breath you inspire your body, your mind, and your spirit. You've learned to refocus your rational mind to look for abundance and appreciate what works and what is harmonious. Setting clear intentions is now a way of life, and you're more aware of your underwater intentions. Your imaginative mind has created and set forth visions of your heart's desires and energized them with your actions and your most positive emotions. You have taken steps to create a collage, actually work through the various action steps, and create an amazing Travel Log of your inner journey. Your spending plan now sits in a place of honor and actively guides your daily spending choices, creating a new pattern that includes a sense of safety while enlivening and funding your dreams. Step-by-step you have become the source of your own ocean of abundance.

The ocean of abundance is a symbol of the source and flow of water and of money in our lives. The ocean is beyond our full comprehension, yet we can come into harmony with its patterns of flow through feng shui. It accepts the waters that come to it and integrates them, and together they become the waves and the tides that come in, go out, and create flow. The ocean flows freely and freely gives of its abundance. This is the source of true abundance. When you look out upon the ocean, you can see, smell, taste, and feel its abundance. And when you come into harmony with its patterns of flow, you come into harmony with the vibration of abundance. Tune in, harmonize, and float with the ocean of flow. Fighting against it creates scarcity, fear, contraction, and perhaps disaster. Now you can see the Ba-gua in a new way and realize that money flow is connected to all that we are and experience.

Connecting with the ocean of abundance means you have money whenever you need it—money to buy and do whatever is necessary to live your life; more money to use to create your dreams; and even more money growing for your future. This experience occurs when your heart is engaged, your values are fully honored, and you're breathing in an atmosphere of love as you enjoy your wealth. The ocean of abundance is such a different place, a quantum leap of energy from where most of us live our lives. Quantum leaps are levels of living significantly different from a small step or change. Your old way of living changes in the process of increasing the flow of abundance into your life. Ready for another leap?

As you stand at the edge of the ocean watching the dance of the winds and the waters, you will realize that this water is connected to all of the other oceans and touches every landmass and ultimately all other peoples on our earth. And so it is with the flow of money. Our individual dollars touch and flow with all of the money around the world. When we are connected, there is abundance; and once we understand the patterns of flow and how to encourage them, we can gently open up to more flow and more abundance.

SOUND OF GRATITUDE The ocean waves make a particular sound—one that has a familiar feel. It is part of the sound of abundance. You can connect with this sound when you express gratitude. Gratitude can be expressed out into the world with words, such as "Thank you, I love it," and sometimes with sounds, such as "Mmm . . . that is wonderful."

Say your own words of gratitude silently, and resonate with the feelings and the sound. Listen to this sound of gratitude for five minutes five times a day and see what happens in your life. Just go about your life sounding your gratitude. Hmmm. You can do this while walking, driving, at the airport, and even silently as you sit in meetings.

Give thanks for everything just as it is and as it has been. Look for the gift that every experience has given you. Remember, all of your challenges have at their core a gift. Unwrap the gifts, put your arms around them, and embrace them and yourself. Let go of your past and let the ocean waves shape your money script. Step into your creative energy and begin writing a new money drama. Claim your connection to the Divine Spirit. Today begins a new cycle of energy, a new experience. Feel gratitude. Hmmm.

The ocean moves and flows and the tides come in and shift while something else is always changing. Water flows to the ocean and changes from liquid to spray, moisture or vapor, and rises to the heavens. There is balance and the cycle begins anew. May fortunate blessings be upon you as you begin a new cycle of creating abundance with an open heart flowing with peace and joy.

You may ask, "Is there more?" Yes, with abundance there is always more.

> *May many fortunate blessings*
> *flow to you as you gaze out on the ocean*
> *seeing the creation of harmony and balance*
> *from the eternal dance of the wind upon the waters*
> *the sound of gratitude flowing from your heart*
> *and wealth and abundance in your life.*

Appendix A: Affirmations and Cross Crawl

AFFIRMATIONS

affirmations do several things. They assist in setting up a vibrational energy field around you; they reveal the blocks in your belief system and the hard rocks that help create an experience of rapids in your flow; they focus your attention; they open you up to new ideas and ways of living; and they highlight areas where you could refocus your thoughts and energy toward a more positive experience. Most important, they remind you of who you are, your truest self.

Affirmations are something you work with. They also work on and with you, your thoughts, emotions, and consciousness. Take one phrase and write it out longhand, ten to twenty times, and notice the comments that show up in your Rational and Creative currents. Write your affirmation on one side of a page and the "fallout" on the other side, or use two facing pages in your Travel Log.

As you write an affirmation, you may experience a contraction in your body and your Rational Current may raise an objection. Simply write down the objection, getting it out in the open. You can then clearly see how your Rational Current is blocking your flow. Thank it for showing up and choose to entertain the more positive and expansive thought. Soon you will develop a new flow and be comfortable with a new vibration.

You also can write your affirmations out on cards and carry them with you to refer to during the day. Here are some powerful affirmations for you to work with:

I pay my expenses on time and with ease.

I have all the money I need right here and right now.

I live in an abundant universe that supplies all of my needs.

I easily receive more money and abundance and freely express my gratitude.

The right thing shows up at just the right time and I experience more abundance.

I spend my money in loving and healthy ways.

I buy wisely.

I save money with ease.

I enjoy work that rewards me financially.

I charge for my services an amount that reflects my true worth.

My money supply is constantly growing.

I have a six-month rainy-day fund that is invested wisely.

I accept the good that flows to me.

I am clear-headed about my finances.

I spend money wisely according to my spending plan.

I am open to guidance from wise advisors.

I shop carefully for major purchases.

I know and write down the essence of something before I begin shopping.

My abundance allows others to prosper.

I open myself up to receiving more money.

I value myself. I am worthy of more wealth and abundance.

Money is energy. I am comfortable with more energy in my life.

I easily attract my heart's deepest desires.

I am wise in my investments and they grow in value.

I enjoy saving my money.

I enjoy an abundance of love and money.

I easily and wisely control my own money.

My dreams deserve my own financial backing.

I accept more ease into my life.

Today I am enough and I have enough.

CROSS CRAWL

Here the focus is to create a new pattern or reinforce an old one that has fallen out of use. The Cross Crawl is useful for when you are missing connections, when life seems out of sorts and you don't know what else to do. Connecting your Rational and your Creative currents is enhanced when you play the piano, walk, or touch yourself across the midline of your body.

With one hand touch your opposite elbow, shoulder, knee, or toes. Then do the same thing with the other hand, shifting from one side to the other for five or six cycles.

For a wild experience and one that will "reset" your cycle of flow, get down on your hands and knees and crawl. Make sure the opposite arm and leg actually work together—that your left arm moves at the same time as your right leg, so that you are working across opposite sides of your body's midline. Do this slowly so you allow your mind to integrate the actions and any new connections can begin to flow.

Humming also connects the opposite sides of your brain. You can do this alone or add it to the Cross Crawl exercise. Silently humming also works to connect the opposite sides of your brain and your body—creating more flexibility and harmony.

Appendix B

THE BA-GUA

the Chinese view humans as the connection, and touchpoint, between heaven and earth. This concept flows through as a foundation for feng shui, ikebana, the martial arts, as well as other art forms, business, and the way the Chinese live their lives—when they are in balance. The Ba-gua indicates a pattern for creating balance in your own home and life.

The Ba-gua also has layers of information, some of it mystical, some not. It is made up of eight outside lines, each corresponding to an idea and space, and an inner space at the center called the tai ch'i. The nine areas are referred to as guas

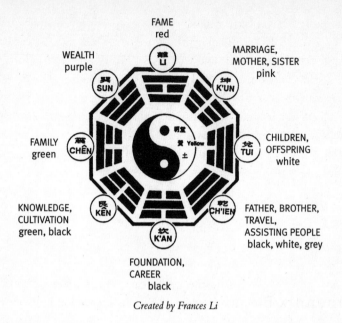

Created by Frances Li

and represent the nine areas of physical space and your life, both inner and outer. The area of the tai ch'i is where the yin-yang symbol is located.

Three patterns emerge from this Ba-gua. The outer octagonal shape represents the progression from one area of your space and your life to another. The middle symbolizes the progression of colors, seasons, and life according to the eight primary trigrams from the Chinese *Book of Changes,* the *I Ching.* You stand on the round circles and look to the center, reading the trigrams from this position. This is an approach unique to Professor Lin Yun's teachings, looking towards the center and the earth in all situations. Finally, the inner section is the circle of unity that surrounds and holds the constant movement of the opposites, the dance of yin and yang, yielding and being still, or taking action and remaining firm, which are the polarities of life. When you look at the *Book of Changes* you will see that the trigrams have Chinese names and characters, and those names are also the Chinese names for the eight areas of the Ba-gua. Unity and harmony flow throughout.

Book of Changes was written by Chinese sages to reveal and explain the ancient and mysterious information about the Tao, the Way, pointing out how humans can live wisely and in balance with all of the changes and the flow of life and spirit, one with another. The *Book of Changes* assists us in developing and strengthening one characteristic that is too weak or small, softens another that is too strong, and perhaps reduces still a third that is too prominent, while remaining balanced and flexible during all of these changes. To the Chinese, everything moves, even when things appear to be at rest, hence the meaning of the yin and yang at the center of the Ba-gua. Yet behind this movement and change, there is a point of reference that does not change, the idea that all of life is governed by an ultimately harmonious system rather than chaos. Einstein presents the Western approach with his view—and I'm loosely paraphrasing—that our life is determined by whether we see the universe as friendly or as hostile. We live and move in very different ways when we see friendship and unity than we would if all of life appeared to us to be chaotic and dangerous. One's view of going with the flow often leads to imagining oneself as a cocreator with the prime mover. With the opposite view, that there is great danger, the automatic response is to withdraw or to fight.

The Ba-gua reveals layers of patterns in your living and work space, and in your life, indicating a more harmonious pattern to create balance, move with the flow, and achieve results—your deepest heart's desires.

Appendix C

RED ENVELOPES

You might be wondering what this book's cover design refers to. In China there is an ancient custom associated with good luck, the exchange of new Red Envelopes with money in them. They are given for auspicious occasions, such as New Year's, a wedding, a birthday or anniversary celebration, a holiday, and to honor wisdom. Every time we in the Black Sect Tantric Buddhist tradition share information with someone, the Grand Master of this tradition, Professor Lin Yun, has asked us to exchange Red Envelopes, usually nine new ones.

Here are the thoughts of two of Professor Lin Yun's disciples:

The following excerpt was written by Lynn Ho Tu, reprinted with permission from Yun Lin Temple News, Vol. III, No. 11, pages 19 and 20.

Why the "Red Envelope Ritual"? In the Chinese folk culture and custom, the color red signifies positive power, courageous strength, and auspicious good luck. All of these qualities when combined provide a strong power to drive away negative and evil forces. Besides, the shape of the red envelope resembles an ancient shield that protects the body of a soldier from being harmed. When you receive transcendental knowledge and regardless of the form of receipt, whether it is feng shui advice, mystical, holistic healing or transcendental solutions, or divination, physiognomy, palmistry, meditation, and any other additional teachings of the Black Sect Tantric Buddhism lineage, you should give the person who transmitted such knowledge directly to you a number of red envelopes with some money within each. This offering of the red envelope symbolizes our respectful intention towards the sacred esoteric information. On the other hand, when you are giving away any transcendental information, you must clearly explain the red envelope ritual and request that the person you are helping to comply with the ritual. This process shows your deepest commitment in safe guarding the sacred knowledge you have with greatest caution.

Dr. Chang Chiu offers his own interpretation of Red Envelopes and feng shui.

From an earthy point of view, you pay lawyers, accountants, and doctors who provided services to help you solve your problems. Similarly, you should also compensate a feng shui consultant who employed his or her knowledge, precious experiences, time, and effort to answer your perplexing questions, whether they are related to health, career, or wealth. You do this by offering the consultant red envelopes with offerings in them. The purpose of the feng shui advice is to assist you, not because the feng shui consultant wants to get money out of you.

Transcendentally speaking, offering red envelopes symbolizes your sincerity. Secret cures are sacred, and not to be disbursed at random. Otherwise, the teachers of the secret cures will be condemned by heaven. So by giving your teacher the red envelopes, he or she can thus be protected. You may wonder, helping others is a good deed. Why should the teacher be punished for performing a good deed?

I once was aboard a bus, and I saw the thief pickpocket another passenger. Out of good heart, I immediately called the attention of that passenger to what was going on. The thief left empty-handed, but after I got off the bus, the thief ran after me and beat me. Wasn't I doing a good deed? So why was I punished?

Secret cures are also "secretful." The saying goes, "A cure should never pass through six ears." In other words, those cures are for your ears only. Once you receive a cure, tell no one unless you also receive red envelopes in return.

Dr. Chang Chiu says to keep the feng shui cures secret. Why would you do this? One reason is to honor an ancient custom associated with feng shui and to preserve and honor the shared sacred information for the current and future recipients. It's as if the energy and blessings of the Grand Master flow through to his students and then on to you. And the Grand Master's blessings include those of *all* of his teachers, both human and divine. In the East the number 10,000 is often associated with the blessings of the Buddha. Consider yourself blessed by 10,000 times 10,000 divine beings from all spiritual traditions, including Christian and Jewish. Information is energy, and receiving it calls for an honoring and exchange of energy. The color red is associated with vitality and the life force. The square or rectangular shape is like a shield. This tradition is very old and vital, and has many layers to shield and protect you so what is received is just what you need and can integrate in a harmonious, balanced way. I am also protected and guided so I present the "right amount" of information to you. Nine envelopes are used because nine represents the energy of completion. Sending them out is similar to saying "It is done," "So be it," or perhaps "Amen." Including money in the Red Envelopes represents the energy and reality of any exchange when we buy or sell something. Doing this aligns our body's physical action and gives the message to our other currents that this information is real and powerful.

So what to do? Please send out nine Red Envelopes to your favorite charities, *where your heart is open and your spirit nourished*. They can be Chinese Red Envelopes or Western-style ones as long as they are new. You decide how much money to place in each one and which charities receive how many envelopes. Do it with gratitude and love, and visualize many blessings pouring out on the recipient as you place your money in each Red Envelope. Then everyone involved will be blessed with good health, protection, and abundance. Many blessings!

Appendix D

THREE BLESSINGS: CALLIGRAPHY AND EXPLANATIONS

these three calligraphies are a special blessing for you from Grand Master Professor Lin Yun. A description follows. Feel free to photocopy them and hang them in your Wealth Area.

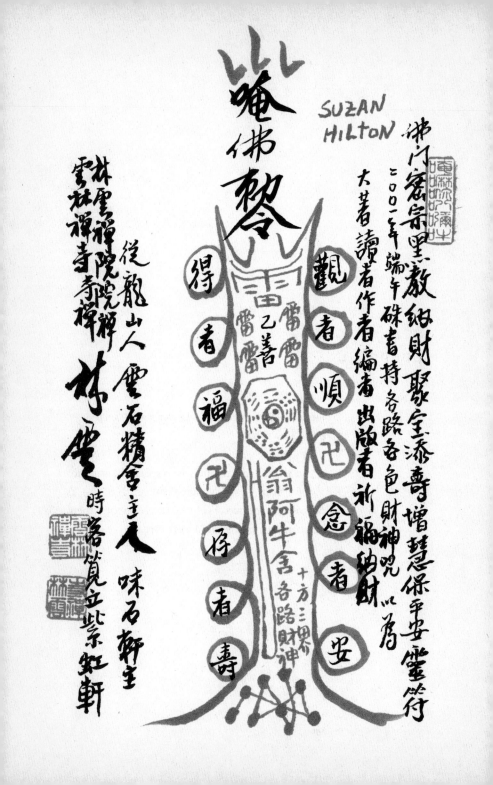

SUZAN
HILTON

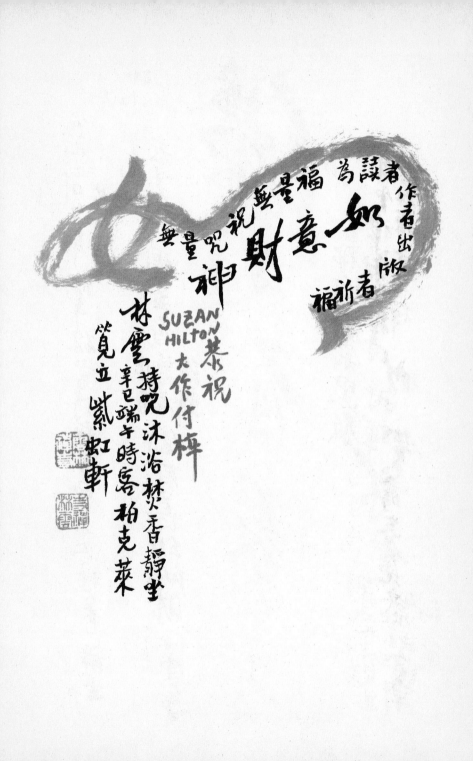

佛渡有緣

SUZAN
HILTON

公元二〇〇一年端午硃書持無量咒沐浴梵香靜坐

謹為

宏著祈福並為讀者編輯

作者

盧府長幼納財保康寧

雲林禪寺 寺禪林雲

佛門臨濟宗黑教

時菩薩立

貳虹軒

CALLIGRAPHY 1: BLACK SECT TANTRIC BUDDHIST TALISMAN

The Blessings (the first three rows on the right part of p. 290)

As a blessing for this book, Professor Lin Yun prepared this Black Sect Tantric Buddhist Talisman on the auspicious date of the Duan Wu Festival, 2001, to bestow the blessings of wealth and treasure accumulation, extended longevity, enhanced wisdom, and personal safety to the readers, author, editorial staff, and publisher of the book. While he was preparing this calligraphy, Professor Lin Yun bestowed the aforementioned blessings by holding the expelling mudra (esoteric hand gestures) while chanting the mantras of the Zhambalas (wealth deities) of the different colors, from all directions and the three realms, and visualized that all those for whom he prepared this calligraphy, as well as all those who see this calligraphy, will receive the aforementioned blessings.

The Talisman (center part of p. 290)

When preparing this talisman, Professor Lin Yun used both black ink and a red ink containing cinnabar powder, which has the effect of expelling evil. The first set of Chinese characters underneath the three ticks signifies that this is a buddhist talisman and literally means, "By the order of Buddha. . . ." Immediately beneath these characters is the character "thunder" followed by four smaller "thunder" characters (two on each side). These "Five Thunders" represent five protectors that have been called upon to protect those receiving the blessings. Below the "Five Thunders" are two black characters that combine to mean "a single benevolent deed." This reminds us that in order to receive good rewards, we should first plant seeds of benevolence, reinforcing Professor Lin Yun's teaching that "a good deed each day will keep evil away." This is followed by the Eight Trigram, or "Bagua," which encompasses all sentient beings and elements in the universe, in the six realms, from past, present, and future. After the Eight Trigram, there are four large characters which correspond to four key tantric Buddhist syllables, respectively, OM, AH, HUM, and SHA. The inclusion of these syllables, with their sound and mystical powers, is meant to ensure the blessings of the talisman will be realized. Following the four syllables are the characters that mean "All the Zhambalas (deities of wealth) from all ten directions and the three realms," the power of which Professor Lin Yun visualizes as being incorporated into the talisman. At the bottom of the talisman is a pattern with nine dots connected by lines, representing "Tracing the Nine-Star Path," the purpose of which is twofold. First, it represents Professor Lin Yun's sincere prayers to invite the myriad of buddhas, boddhisattvas and other deities to be present in the talisman and to incorporate their powerful blessings into the talisman. Second, when tracing the Nine-Star Path, the Professor visualizes that the entire universe is included and that all of mankind's wishes, buddha's power, taoist's and other esoteric methods and solutions are incorporated for the benefits of the entire universe and this talisman.

On either side of the talisman are loops (in this case seven) within which Professor Lin Yun has added additional blessings. The characters in the first three loops on the right and left, respectively, mean "Success to he who sees the talisman" and "Blessings to he who receives the talisman." Characters in the last three loops on the right and left, respectively, mean "Tranquility to he who reads the talisman" and "Longevity to he who keeps the talisman." In the fourth loop on either side is the character (the Bon Swastika) which is a very powerful sign signifying the Dharma Wheel and Indestructible Truth.

Professor Lin Yun's signature (left side of the calligraphy)

Professor Lin Yun signed this calligraphy with his name and his various poetic names, and completed the calligraphy with red chops. The two below his signature on the lower left of the calligraphy says "Yun Lin Temple" and one of the Professor's poetic names; the one on the top right is the Six Syllable Mantra, OM MANI PADME HUM. Professor Lin Yun completed the calligraphy by performing the Three Secret Reinforcements. Professor Lin Yun wrote this calligraphy at Zi Hong

Sun (or Purple Rainbow Study—the private study of Ms. Crystal Chu, CEO of Yun Lin Temple and Lin Yun Monastery), Berkeley, California.

Grandmaster Professor Lin Yun carefully designed this calligraphy by combining Buddhism, Taoism, and Chinese folklore with Black Sect Tantric Buddhist transcendental elements. This calligraphy is not only a unique folk art, but also a religious artifact that embodies the teachings of the Third and Fourth stages of Black Sect Tantric Buddhism and provides powerful blessings and protection.

Translated by Jonathan Chau with input from Ms. Crystal Chu

CALLIGRAPHY 2: *RU-YI* GOD OF WEALTH

Literally, the phrase *Ru-Yi* means "as one wishes" or "according to one's heart." Written with red ink containing cinnabar powder, the single stroke "Ru," the first character in *Ru-Yi*, embodies the entire meaning of the phrase and Professor Lin Yun's blessing that "one will get what one wishes for." Inside the "Ru," Professor Lin Yun has added two sets of blessings. First, the four characters written from right to left—"Ru-Yi" Wealth Gods. The second blessing, "Infinite mantras, boundless blessing," contains seven characters and traces the loop of the "Ru" from left to right. With these, Professor Lin Yun enhanced the blessings of the "Ru" by visualizing the blessings and power of the Wealth Gods. An infinite number of mantras have also been incorporated in the calligraphy.

Professor Lin Yun also sends his congratulations in this calligraphy to Suzan Hilton for this great book and offers the combined blessings of the "Ru", the "Ru-Yi" Wealth Gods and an "infinite number of mantras" to the author and the publisher.

Strengthened with the blessings of Professor Lin Yun and the Three Secret Reinforcements, the single stroke "Ru" is one of Professor Lin Yun's most sought after blessing calligraphies. As a gesture of sincerity, Professor Lin Yun cleansed himself, offered incense, and meditated before he composed this calligraphy at Zi Hong Sun on the auspicious day of the Duan We Festival.

Translated by Jonathan Chau with input from Ms. Crystal Chu

CALLIGRAPHY 3: "HE WHO IS KARMICLY LINKED TO DHARMA WILL RECEIVE BUDDHA'S GUIDANCE AND REACH ENLIGHTENMENT"

According to Professor Lin Yun, one is "karmicly linked" to Dharma if one has opportunities to receive the teachings of Dharma and seize such opportunities. Therefore, one is not "karmicly linked" to Dharma if one does not have opportunities to receive Dharma or does not seize such opportunities when presented.

Professor Lin Yun composed this calligraphy in 2001 on the auspicious day of the Duan Wu Festival and offers his blessings to Suzan Hilton and her wonderful book, *The Feng Shui of Abundance*, and to the readers and editors of the book. The Professor chanted various mantras and visualized the blessings and powers of infinite numbers of mantras being incorporated in the calligraphy.

As a gesture of sincerity, Professor Lin Yun cleansed himself, offered incense, and meditated before he composed this calligraphy at Zi Hong Sun.

Translated by Jonathan Chau with input from Ms. Crystal Chu

Bibliography

Andrews, Ted. *Sacred Sounds: Transformation through Music & Word*. St. Paul, MN: Llewellyn Publications, 1999.

Brown, Simon. *Practical Feng Shui*. London: Ward Lock, 1997.

———. *Practical Feng Shui for Business*. London: Ward Lock, 1998.

Bryan, Mark, and Julia Cameron. *The Money Drunk*. New York: Ballantine Books, 1992.

Cameron, Julia, and Mark Bryan. *The Artist's Way*. New York: Jeremy P. Tarcher/Putnam Books, 1992.

Clason, George S. *The Richest Man in Babylon*. New York: Hawthorn/Dutton, 1955.

Collins, Terah Kathryn. *The Western Guide to Feng Shui*. Carlsbad, CA: Hay House, 1996.

Gawain, Shakti. *Creative Visualization.* New York: Bantam Books, 1978.

Govert, Johndennis. *Feng Shui: Art and Harmony of Place.* Phoenix, AZ: Daikakuji Publications, 1993.

Hendricks, Gay, Ph.D. *Conscious Breathing: Breathwork for Health, Stress Release, and Personal Mastery.* New York: Bantam Books, 1995.

————. *Learning to Love Yourself: A Guide to Becoming Centered.* New York: Fireside, 1982.

————. *The Ten-Second Miracle: Creating Relationship Breakthroughs.* San Francisco: HarperSanFrancisco, 1998.

————, and Kathlyn Hendricks, Ph.D. *At the Speed of Life: A New Approach to Personal Change Through Body-Centered Therapy.* New York: Bantam Books, 1993.

————, and Kathlyn Hendricks, Ph.D. *Centering and the Art of Intimacy.* New York: Fireside, 1985.

————, and Kathlyn Hendricks, Ph.D. *The Conscious Heart.* New York: Bantam Books, 1997.

————, and Kathlyn Hendricks, Ph.D. *Conscious Loving.* New York: Bantam Books, 1997.

————, and Kate Ludeman, Ph.D. *The Corporate Mystic.* New York: Bantam Books, 1996.

Hill, Napoleon. *Think and Grow Rich.* New York: Fawcett Crest, 1960.

Hopcke, Robert H. *There Are No Accidents: Synchronicity and the Stories of Our Lives.* New York: Riverhead Books, 1997.

Kingston, Karen. *Creating Sacred Space with Feng Shui.* New York: Broadway Books, 1997.

Linn, Denise. *Sacred Space.* New York: Ballantine Books, 1995.

Lip, Evelyn. *Feng Shui for Business.* Union City, CA: Heian International, 1990.

————. *Personalize Your Feng Shui.* Union City, CA: Heian International, 1997.

Peale, Norman Vincent. *Positive Imaging: The Powerful Way to Change Your Life.* New York: Fawcett Crest, 1982.

————. *The Power of Positive Thinking.* New York: Prentice-Hall, 1952.

Rossbach, Sarah, and Master Lin Yun. *Feng Shui Design: The Art of Creating*

Harmony for Interiors, Landscape, and Architecture. New York: Viking Penguin Group, 1998.

————, and Master Lin Yun. *Interior Design with Feng Shui.* New York: Arkana, 1987.

————, and Master Lin Yun, *Living Color.* New York: Kodansha International, 1994.

Shafarman, Steven. *Awareness Heals: The Fendenkrais Method for Dynamic Health.* New York: Addison-Wesley, 1997.

Simons, T. Ralph. *Feng Shui Step by Step.* New York: Crown Trade Paperbacks, 1996.

Sinetar, Marsha. *Do What You Love, the Money Will Follow: Discovering Your Right Livelihood.* New York: Dell Publishing, 1987.

Spangler, David. *Everyday Miracles: The Inner Art of Manifestation.* New York: Bantam, 1996.

Zukav, Gary. *The Dancing Wu Li Masters: An Overview of the New Physics.* New York: Bantam, 1980.

Resources

Please contact me at my website: *www.fengshuiofabundance.com*. I would be delighted to hear your success stories.

Contact His Holiness Grand Master Professor Thomas Lin Yun Rinpoche through his website: *www.yunlintemple.org.*, or at Yun Lin Temple, 2959 Russel St., Berkeley, CA, 94705, (510) 841-2347. This is an excellent source of feng shui cures that have been specially blessed by His Holiness Grand Master Lin Yun.

Contact my teacher, Ann-Marie Holmes, for her IN-Depth Feng Shui Study Group and consultations at Environmental Enhancement with Feng Shui, 80759 Lost Creek Road, Dexter, Oregon, 97431, or (541) 937-4237, or *AMFengshui@ aol.com*.

The Chinese watercolor landscapes may be obtained from Master I-Hong Chou at *www.artasiaart.com*.

Index

Illustrations are indicated in *italics*.

Stock market, 24, 29, 99–100, 111, 227
Stop signs, 33–34, 53
Streamlining
    clutter, 62, 225–26
    described, 61–62, 64
    money patterns, 264
    possessions, 46, 117, 124, 235
Stress, 91
Struggle, commitment to, 187–90
Stuck energy
    action steps for, 182–83, 225
    blaming and, 225
    clutter as, 62–63
    complaining as, 225
    of personas, 203–4, 206
    space clearing for, 65
    streamlining and, 61
    See also Doldrums; Sticky Triangle of Life
Swamps, 4, 218–19, 225, 265
    See also Sticky Triangle of Life
Symbols
    alignment of, 203
    Ba-gua, 34–36
    defined, 25
    for Helpful People Area, 76
    language of, 23, 24, 25
    octagon, 33–34
    red envelopes as, 287
    use of, 53, 69
    water as, 4, 24, 173–74
    wind as, 174
    words as, 147
    yin-yang, *26*, 35, *35*
    See also Ba-gua
Synchronicity, 256

Tai ch'i, 281, 282
Talisman, Black Sect Tantric Buddhist, *290*, 293–95
Tao, 283
Teachers, human and divine, 287–88
Thoughts
    affirmations for, 183
    breath's effect on, 91

contradicting, 146
Creative Current stopped with, 129
emotions behind, 146
hidden, 206
negative, 137, 153, 156, 179–81
quieting, 146–47
as Rational Energy current, 47, 144
stuck patterns of, 183
worrying and, 153
    See also Creative Current; Rational Current
Three Secret Reinforcements, 294, 295
Toilets, 70, 71
Tracing the Nine-Star Path, 294
Transcendental knowledge, xiii, 286
Travel Log, 15–16
Travel symbols, 203
Treasure Maps, 54, 77
    See also Collages
Truthfulness, 13, 149

Undertows and crosscurrents, 183–85
Underwater intentions, 14, 184, 185–87, 188
Unemployment, 233, 234
Unfinished projects, 187, 196, 198, 235
Ungrounded, 28, 29, 43
Uprising energy, 6–7, 196

Vacations, 268, 269
Values, finding, 232, 238–40, 275
Vibration
    of abundance, 89, 121, 260, 274, 275
    clutter's effect on, 62
    described, 19–20, 62
    of emotions, 36, 101
    enlivening, 65, 237
    love as, 101
    of thoughts, 36
    of words, 147
Victim-persecutor-rescuer triangle (V-P-R). *See* Sticky Triangle of Life
Victim role, 219, 220–21
Visualizations
    for business, 128

About the Author

Suzan Hilton has worked as a Certified Public Accountant and holds a Bachelor of Science in Business Administration with a Master of Taxation degree. She is now a Facilitator of Tranformation, and an Abundance and Feng Shui Consultant.

Hilton studied small- and large-group facilitation with Drs. Gay and Kathlyn Hendricks (authors of *The Conscious Heart, Conscious Loving,* and *At the Speed of Life*).

Her background also includes certification in Respiratory Therapy and Floral Technology and Design (Western-style floral arranging). She began her ikebana studies in 1989 and is a Certified Teacher in ikebana, the art of Japanese flower arranging, with the avant-garde Sogetsu School of Tokyo, Japan. She is second-degree Reiki with the Usui Shiki Ryoho lineage. Hilton lives outside Portland, Oregon.